Economic Report on
Africa
2004

UNLOCKING AFRICA'S
TRADE POTENTIAL

Economic Commission for Africa

Ordering information

To order copies of *Unlocking Africa's Trade Potential* by the Economic Commission for Africa, please contact:

Publications
Economic Commission for Africa
P.O. Box 3001
Addis Ababa
Ethiopia
Tel: +251-1-44 31 68
Fax: +251-1-51 03 65
E-mail: ecainfo@uneca.org
Web: www.uneca.org

ISBN 92-1-125094-3
Sales Number: E.04.II.K.12

Designed and produced by ECA Publication Cluster, Communication Team (CT).
Cover photographs provided by Photodisc.

Table of Contents

4 Poor Energy Infrastructure Hobbles Export Diversification   117

5 Trade Facilitation to Integrate Africa into the World Economy   155

6 Fiscal Implications of Trade Liberalization   191

Boxes

Figures

Tables

Note

Official ECA sources constitute the regular information and data received from Country Statistical Offices, country reports and surveys, Central Banks, Finance Ministries and other line Ministries, United Nations Specialized Agencies, IMF, World Bank, ADB and other international financial institutions.

We gratefully acknowledge the use of survey data and country data from the World Bank Africa Database and the World Bank's World Development Indicators, International Financial Statistics and World Economic Outlook as well as Country Reports from IMF, the Economist Intelligence Unit and the UNDP Human Development Report.

Foreword

The *Economic Report on Africa 2004* is the fifth in an annual series that reviews the continent's economic performance and near-term prospects. Targeted to African and global policymakers, the reports are meant to stimulate a process of discussion and change.

This year's report builds on the work of the previous reports by systematic benchmarking of economic performance. It finds that in 2003 Africa recovered from the economic downturn of the previous year with real GDP growth of 3.8%, compared to 3.2% in 2002. This encouraging increase reflects Africa's progress in a number of critical areas: the continent has continued to exhibit good macroeconomic fundamentals; fiscal deficits have been kept under control; inflation has largely stabilized; and the region's current account deficit fell. However, faster overall growth is needed if Africa is to make progress toward achieving the Millennium Development Goal of halving poverty by 2015. Indeed, it is sobering that in 2003 only five countries—Angola, Burkina Faso, Chad, Equatorial Guinea and Mozambique—achieved the necessary 7% growth to make this possible.

Trade is one of the main drivers of growth and development; yet Africa's trade performance is weak. The region's share in world merchandise exports fell from 6.3% in 1980 to 2.5% in 2000 in value terms. It recorded a meager 1.1% average annual growth over the 1980-2000 period, compared to 5.9% in Latin America and 7.1% in Asia. Further, while about 70% of developing countries' exports are manufactures, Africa has hardly benefited from the boom in these exports. Overall on the continent, and particularly in sub-Saharan Africa, progress on export diversification has been slow.

This year's report looks at what needs to be done to help the continent more expeditiously harness the benefits of globalization. The report identifies challenges that are both external and internal.

At the global level, priorities clearly lean away from Africa and developing regions: each year US$300 billion supports farmers in rich countries, while less than one-sixth of that amount flows to poorer countries in the form of aid. In order to create a fair global trading system, developed nations should show greater commitment to working with African countries on the development agenda of the Doha Round. Enhancing market access for African products is of particular importance.

The trade policies of rich countries are clearly only part of the problem. This report takes an introspective look at what reforms Africa needs to undertake in order to benefit from existing and future opportunities in the global trading system.

The report underscores that African countries need to make trade liberalization work for them within the context of broad development strategies. Trade liberalization can help boost trade performance and growth, and reduce poverty. But liberalization alone is not a silver bullet. The link between openness, growth and poverty reduction is complex and dependent on country specifics. Trade liberalization is most likely to bring benefits when accompanied by good macroeconomic policies, institutional reforms and good infrastructure facilities.

The continent must urgently improve its supply-side capacities. Only then will exporters be able to compete in global markets. The Economic Commission for Africa (ECA)-developed "Trade Competitiveness Index," which is introduced in this volume, combines the economic and political environment, availability of direct inputs to production and status of infrastructure as factors, to provide insight into why Africa is falling behind other developing regions. It clearly demonstrates that successful integration into the world economy will require better-educated and healthier workforces, improved economic and political governance, and better-quality infrastructure. Based on these findings, this year's report focuses on how to strengthen trade capacity, boost infrastructure facilities, particularly related to energy use, improve trade facilitation services and address the fiscal implications of trade liberalization. It provides a set of workable recommendations based on best-practice examples from Africa and elsewhere.

It is my sincere hope that this year's *Economic Report on Africa* will be of particular benefit to African policy makers and governments as they strive to build the long-term competitiveness of their economies and begin to reap more steadily the benefits of globalization, while minimizing the impact of its vagaries. In this way, more of the region's people will begin to feel and appreciate the tangible improvements in their daily lives brought about by enhanced trade.

K.Y. Amoako
Executive Secretary
August 2004
Addis Ababa

Acknowledgements

This report was carried out under the general direction of the Executive Secretary, K.Y. Amoako. A team under the overall guidance of Patrick Asea, Director of the Economic and Social Policy Division (ESPD), and Hakim Ben Hammouda, Director of the Trade and Regional Integration Division (TRID), of the Economic Commission for Africa (ECA) prepared this report. The team, led by Shamika Sirimanne, included Desta Asgedom, Mamadou Bal, Fabrizio Carmignani, Derrese Degefa, Mamadou Diagne, Niall Kishtainy, Tama R. Lisinge, Andrew Mold, Oliver Paddison, Vanessa Steinmayer and Charles Amo Yartey.

The team appreciates the secretarial support provided by Asnaketch Amde. Others in the division and in the ECA headquarters who contributed to the report include Kwabia Boateng, Chantal Dupasquier, Adrian Gauci, Marie-Therese Guiebo, Wilfred Lombe, Workie Mitiku, Pancrace Niyimbona, Abebe Shimeles, Karima Bounemra Ben Soltan and Elizabeth Woldemariam. The comments and contributions from colleagues in ECA's sub-regional offices, particularly Emile Ahohe, Aissatou Gueye, Sylvain Maliko, Guillermo Mangue, Andre Nikwigize and Abdelilah Ouaqouaq, are noted with appreciation. Augustin Fosu, Senior Policy Advisor to the Executive Secretary, worked closely with the team at various stages in the process.

The report benefited from the comments and suggestions of several peer reviews. Participating in the external peer review meeting held in Addis Ababa were a group of prominent African scholars: Ibi Ajayi, Michael Atingi-Ego, Mohamoud Ben-Romdhane, Haile Kibret, Teshome Mulat, Berhanu Nega, Charles Okeahalam and Terry Ryan. The report was enriched by comments received from Uri Dadush, Alan Gelb and Gobind Nankani of the World Bank. Chapter 1 on "Recent Economic Trends in Africa and Prospects for 2004" and Chapter 3 on "Measuring Africa's Trade Competitiveness" benefited from the comments of the participants of the Expert Group on World Economic Situation and Projects (Project LINK) in New York in November 2003 and April 2004 hosted by the Development Policy Analysis Division of the UN Department for Economic and Social Affairs (DESA). The team particularly appreciates support from Carl Gray, Pingfan Hong and Hung-Yi Li at DESA. Special thanks to Maaza Sisay and Yetinayet Mengistu who organized a wide range of consultations within and outside ECA.

The final report was edited by Richard Synge. Special thanks to Akwe Amosu, Seifu Dagnachew, Lorna Davidson, Carolyn Knapp, Teshome Yohannes, Bénédicte Walter and other members of ECA's Communication Team, who contributed to the copyediting, design and production of the report.

Overview

fter fifty years progress, the future of the multilateral system of trade negotiations is surrounded by uncertainty. The collapse of the Cancun World Trade Organization (WTO) Ministerial Meeting in 2003 has put pressure on the Organization of Economic Co-operation and Development (OECD) countries to reduce agricultural subsidies and other domestic support measures that distort global trade and contribute to the marginalization of Africa in the international trading system.

The *Economic Report on Africa (ERA) 2004* takes the view that OECD trade policies are a serious constraint to Africa's integration into the global economy. African exports have been handicapped by industrial country policies such as tariff escalation, tariff peaks and agricultural protectionism. The industrialized countries must commit themselves to the development principles of the WTO's Doha Round, by widening market access for developing country exports and providing more trade-related assistance to poor countries. Such assistance is necessary, both to bear the heavy costs associated with trade liberalization and to help countries exploit the opportunities arising from a more integrated global economy.

> *OECD trade policies are a serious constraint to Africa's integration into the global economy*

But the Report also argues that strengthening Africa's supply side capacity is essential to more successful integration into the global economy. Weak infrastructure, poor trade facilitation services, and inadequate physical and human capital are impediments to the development of Africa's export sectors. *ERA 2004* takes an introspective look at what Africa needs to do to put its house in order so as to benefit from existing and future opportunities in the global trading system.

Firstly, Africa needs to more quickly diversify its production structures. Secondly, countries must be more proactive in bringing about integration of their economies regionally and into the global economy. *ERA 2004* therefore makes specific recommendations to help African countries improve their compeititveness, including in the areas of energy policy for trade and trade facilitation.

Economic performance is improving, but not by enough to reduce poverty

Despite Africa's slow progress towards the Millennium Development Goals (MDGs), the overall message of the Report is optimistic. In recent years, the continent has begun to recover from the "lost decades" of the 1980s and 1990s. In 2003, Africa was the second fastest growing region in the developing world, behind Eastern and Southern Asia. Real Gross Development Product (GDP) grew by 3.8% in 2003 compared to 3.2% in 2002. This encouraging performance was driven by higher oil prices and production, rising commodity prices, increased foreign direct investment (FDI), better macroeconomic management, and good weather conditions. North Africa, with 4.8% growth was the continent's fastest growing subregion. West and Central Africa also achieved respectable growth rates of 4%. East and Southern Africa, in contrast, registered growth of only 2.5% (see figure 1).

Figure 1

North Africa tops subregional economic performance, 2003 (real GDP growth rates)

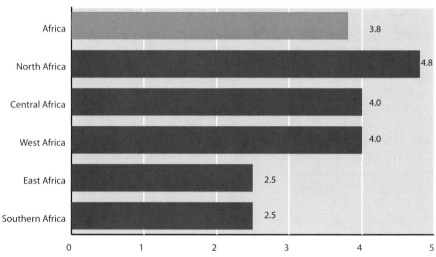

Source: ECA, from official sources

Apart from a few countries, the continent did well on other macroeconomic fundamentals. Fiscal deficits were largely kept under control despite the challenge faced by many countries of balancing increased spending for poverty reduction with the requirements of macroeconomic stability. Inflation rose slightly to 10.6% from 9.3% in 2002, reflecting higher food prices caused by poor weather conditions in some parts of the continent, increased oil-import prices, and currency depreciation in several countries. The regional current account deficit fell from 1.6% of GDP in 2002 to 0.7% of GDP in 2003 because of robust oil and commodity prices and high worker remittances.

On the downside, seven economies had negative growth rates, compared to one in 2000 and none in 1999. Compared to 2002, there was a slight deterioration in overall growth performance in sub-Saharan Africa (SSA), with a rate of expansion of 3.1% in 2003, down from 3.5% the previous year (see figure 2). Furthermore, rapid population increase meant that SSA's per capita growth was only 1.7% in 2003, much too low to achieve the MDG for poverty reduction.

Figure 2

Rates of economic growth – Africa, North Africa and sub-Saharan Africa, 2001-2003

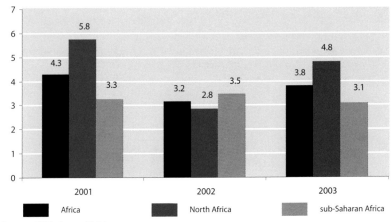

Source: *ECA, from official sources*

The recent establishment of a new Commission for Africa, launched by the British Prime Minister, Tony Blair, in March 2004, represents an important acknowledgement of the need to address Africa's underperformance. This should provide support for the principles and actions of the New Partnership for Africa's Development (NEPAD). The Executive Secretary of ECA, K.Y. Amoako, recently commented:

"The international community and Africa have agreed on the central importance of a partnership to achieve NEPAD's goals but we must now focus on implementation and action… We must agree on what we can really deliver for Africa's people."

The continent still awaits the "peace dividend"

One of the main reasons for Africa's poor economic performance has been the continuation of military conflicts. In the early 1990s, in the aftermath of the Cold War, there were expectations of a "peace dividend" through the resolution of long-running wars. But this never materialized: the 1990s was the most conflict-ridden decade since independence, and economic growth was sluggish. Without peace, there is little hope for social and economic progress in Africa.

In 2003, signs of a peace dividend finally appeared in some of Africa's most troubled countries. Peaceful political transitions in Angola and the Democratic Republic of Congo (DRC) began to produce economic benefits. Angola attracted substantial FDI during the year and GDP grew at over 7.5%. The DRC saw growth of over 5%. The country also made gains in macroeconomic stability, registering single-digit inflation in 2003 – remarkable progress given inflation of over 500% as recently as 2000. Since the departure from Liberia of ex-president, Charles Taylor, there is hope that civil wars in neighbouring countries will abate. In November 2003, the Government of Burundi signed a peace agreement with the main rebel group to end the country's civil war and took steps to integrate former rebels into the political process.

Continuing political instability in Côte d'Ivoire and Zimbabwe is cause for concern. In Zimbabwe, macroeconomic indicators deteriorated sharply in 2003: inflation rose to 420%, the fiscal deficit widened to 7.1% of GDP and the economy contracted for the fifth consecutive year. In other countries, such as Uganda, the persistence of low-intensity conflicts has hampered growth and poverty reduction.

> *Without peace, there is little hope for social and economic progress in Africa*

Insufficient and inconsistent external support hinders progress

Central to NEPAD is the idea that a future African renaissance requires substantial external support as well as internal reforms. It is estimated that there is an annual shortfall of $US 20-25 billion of resources needed for African countries to achieve the MDGs. Official development assistance (ODA) flows, at $19.4 billion in 2001, are well below their 1990 peak (ECA, 2003). At the International Conference on Financing Development held at Monterrey, Mexico in 2002, the industrialized countries made a pledge to increase the quantity and quality of ODA flows to Africa.

The Report highlights inconsistencies in donor approaches. For instance, despite donor acknowledgement of the importance of the role of women in development, gender-related projects for the whole of Africa receive a mere $81 million of ODA. Similarly, although there has been a welcome increase in ODA for tackling the HIV/AIDS epidemic, minimal support is given to the fight against malaria, one of the biggest killers in SSA.

Another concern is the continuation of tied aid linking ODA with the purchase of goods and services from the donor country. This reduces the value of aid to recipients by 25-40%[1], because countries are obliged to buy uncompetitively priced imports. Some donors have reduced tied aid: Denmark, the Netherlands, Norway, and the United Kingdom provided over 90% of aid untied in 2001. But many countries continue to tie aid flows to export purchases.

The challenges of trade liberalization for North and South

There have been various initiatives to improve market access for the poorest developing countries. The European Union (EU)'s "Everything but Arms" (EBA) agreement, and the United States' African Growth and Opportunity Act (AGOA) are two examples (see box 1). Preliminary evaluations of these initiatives show modest but important gains for some sub-Saharan countries (UNCTAD, 2003b). In this sense, the initiatives set encouraging precedents for future liberalization of industrial and agricultural markets in OECD countries. However, because neither initiative involves the reduction of agricultural subsidies in rich countries, they fall short of fulfilling Africa's needs for fully developing its export potential. For example, Mali lost $43 million in 2001 as a result of large subsidies to US and EU producers, which lowered the price of cotton, one of Mali's main exports.

Box 1

AGOA has had some encouraging results and should be extended

The United States' African Growth and Opportunity Act (AGOA) was signed into law on 18 May 2000. According to AGOA's webpage (www.agoa.gov), "the Act offers tangible incentives for African countries to continue their efforts to open their economies and build free markets". However, because most African countries already enjoyed preferential treatment due to their status as least developed countries, the preferences offered are not a major improvement over the existing general system of preference agreements. But for some products such as textiles and apparel, where tariffs and quotas are higher, there are significant advantages in belonging to the scheme.

Circumstantial evidence suggests that some African countries have benefited from the access agreement. For instance, South African exports to the USA under AGOA were 45% higher in 2002 than in the preceding year. Nigeria, too, has gained, and accounts for more than 60% of all AGOA exports to the US (although the bulk of this trade is related to the oil industry). Countries have also seen an increase in FDI as a result of AGOA. For example, companies from the Taiwan Province of China are the main investors in Lesotho's garment industry.

Nonetheless, this evidence has to be set against the backdrop of a 15% fall in total SSA exports to the US in 2002. The benefits from AGOA are limited because only "non-sensitive" products are included in the agreement. In addition, excessively tight rules of origin and the restricted list of countries admitted to benefits from the special textile preferences regime reduce the usefulness of the scheme for African textile producers. Moreover, the scheme expires in 2008, and this has dampened the reaction of potential investors. Finally, there is concern that AGOA's benefits will be diluted as the US Government seeks to negotiate free trade agreements with other regions such as the Middle East and Central America.

Africa would benefit if the US administration took on board some of the recommendations of the US Commission on Capital Flows, such as an extension of AGOA until 2018, and extended the preferences to include all products coming from Africa.

Sources: *Mattoo et al., 2003; UNCTAD, 2002 and 2003b; US Department of Commerce, 2003; US Commission on Capital Flows to Africa, 2003*

> *Initiatives such as AGOA and "Everything but arms" set encouraging precedents for future liberalization of industrial and agricultural markets in OECD countries*

The pros and cons of further liberalization for Africa...

A forthcoming study by ECA, "Trade Liberalization under the Doha Development Agenda: Options and Consequences for Africa", reveals the gains that might be realized by

African countries under liberalization of OECD agriculture. The study analyses three types of trade liberalization: "little", "modest" and "full"[2], using the Global Trade Analysis Project (GTAP) model, a multisector and multi-region framework. In the static version of the model, full liberalization of trade would increase global welfare (income) by 0.3%, and would add 0.7% to income in Africa. While the absolute gains for SSA are quite modest – some $704 million – when compared with the $15.9 billion gain for the EU15, the study shows larger gains from deeper liberalization. While North Africa benefits under all liberalization scenarios, SSA loses from partial liberalization. This is because of preference erosion as many African countries are beneficiaries of preferential trading arrangements. Partial market access (the "little" and "modest" scenarios) would thus increase the degree of competition they face in export markets.

Allowing for dynamic effects such as capital accumulation increases, the estimate of the gains to SSA from full liberalization rise to $4.3 billion, six times as large as in the simple static version. This underlines the importance of complementing trade liberalization with policies to enhance investment volumes.

There is, however, a potential downside from further agricultural liberalization. The findings of the simulation exercise suggest that liberalization may cause contraction of industrial activities and force further specialization in agricultural commodities in African countries. Although this is dictated by comparative advantage, it raises the risk of continued excessive dependence on commodities and vulnerability due to fluctuations in their prices. These findings drive home the urgency of adopting policies to promote export diversification towards higher value-added industrial and service sectors.

Africa must move beyond primary commodity production

Africa's high share of primary commodities in exports has been costly: terms-of-trade losses because of declining real commodity prices have had negative impacts on external indebtedness and investment, hampering income growth and poverty reduction (UNCTAD, 2003a). According to one study, non-oil-exporting African countries suffered cumulative terms of trade losses between 1970 and 1997 of almost 120% of GDP, offsetting the benefits of increased aid flows after 1973 (World Bank, 2000). Even oil producers such as Angola, Gabon and Nigeria have seen few developmental gains despite terms of trade increases; oil income has not brought economic diversification and these countries have therefore failed to achieve sustained growth.

There is an urgent need for a coherent strategy to promote diversification, particularly given the current deadlock in the WTO negotiations. Not only are OECD countries reluctant to reduce domestic export subsidies, the dismantling of domestic farm support measures (e.g. the EU's Common Agricultural Policy) is also politically unfeasible.

> *Africa's high share of primary commodities in exports has been costly*

Promoting domestic industries...

Over the last two decades African countries have reduced state support for domestic industries. But such support, aimed at bringing about diversification, need not be controversial:

- There is a strong theoretical and empirical case for selective interventions to overcome market and institutional failures in order to build the capabilities required for export sector development (Lall, 2003).

- Critics argue that the State is not capable of "picking winners". This has often been true in the past. But there could be a case for industrial policy targeted at general activities such as investment, research and development (R&D) and training instead of selective support to particular industries or firms. This has been the approach of many industrialized countries that have employed systems of incentives to encourage R&D and infrastructure development.

- Industrial policies have often failed because of poor coordination between different government bodies. Coherent interventions must be based on an integrated approach spanning key line ministries as well as trade and business organizations.

Such policies take time to implement. For this reason, the principle of "special and differential treatment" (SDT) continues to be of importance to African countries. Liberalization by African countries needs to be sequenced over time in order to strengthen supply-side capacities so that the continent can compete in global markets.

Selective interventions to overcome market and institutional failures inorder to build the capabilities required for export sector development

There are positive lessons from Asia...

High growth in many Asian economies was driven by dynamic trade policies that were based on a combination of liberalization and State control. Early explanations of the "Asian miracle" cited the apparent openness of the Asian economies to external markets. This contrasted with the failed import-substitution approach pursued in Africa. The root of Asia's success was thought to lie in State neutrality towards economic sectors, allowing existing comparative advantage to determine the composition of production and exports. State neutrality could take the form of equal exchange rates for exports and imports and equality between domestic and world market prices.

Later it began to be recognized that Asia's success did not lie in State neutrality and that the State played an important role in fostering export competitiveness by maintaining export-friendly effective exchange rates and granting large subsidies to exporters. Trade policies were part and parcel of broader national development strategies. There are important lessons to be learned here for Africa, although this goes against free trade arguments many of which focus on the need to remove import barriers without considering how to strengthen export capacity and promote diversification. The Mauritius experience suggests that *laissez faire* policy is not the route to export diversification (see box 2).

Box 2

The recipe for success in Mauritius

> *Asia's success did not lie in State neutrality*

The Mauritian economy has been a success story over the last two decades as indicated by its high ranking in ECA's Trade Competitiveness Index, Institutional Sustainability Index and the Economic Sustainability Index. Its economy is dominated by the sugar and tourism sectors and its export-processing zone (EPZ). Contrary to popular belief, the country has maintained a highly restrictive trade regime, with the market being relatively closed to imports. But its export sector has been kept open by segregating the sector from the import sector. Duty-free access was provided to all imported inputs, resulting in competitive exports. Tax incentives were given to firms operating in the EPZ, and the labour market for EPZ exporters has been made more flexibile in areas such as overtime payments and laying off workers. The country's ethnic diversity has attracted investment from Asia. In addition, political and macroeconomic stability has enhanced the trade environment.

Sources: ECA, 2003; Subramanian and Roy, 2003

In this vein, the report of the High-Level Panel on Financing for Development (the Zedillo Report) argued that WTO negotiations need to consider how to legitimize time-bound protection of certain industries, by country, in the early stages of industrialization:

"*However misguided the old model of blanket protection intended to nurture import substitute industries, it would be a mistake to go to the other extreme and deny developing countries the opportunity of actively nurturing the development of an industrial sector*" (UN, 2000).

Focusing on export diversification....

During the 1990s, it was often argued that trade drove economic growth and development.[3] Structural adjustment policies were aimed at increasing the "openness" of African economies to trade. African economies are now surprisingly open: SSA's share of trade in GDP is 62.2%, compared to a world average of 57% and 35.9% for Latin America and the Caribbean. Given Africa's falling terms of trade and the high level of unregistered informal trade, the continent's degree of integration into the world economy is higher than commonly thought.

Africa's performance in world trade reflects the continent's small GDP rather than a lack of openness per se. While the volume of trade is important, the share of manufactured goods in total exports is a more important determinant of economic success (Fosu, 2002a). Manufacturing is one of the main vehicles for technological development and innovation. Economies with higher shares of manufacturing in total value-added are less vulnerable to price and climatic shocks.

Over the last two decades Africa has made gradual but insufficient progress in export diversification (see Table 1). A few African countries, such as Kenya andUganda, have moved into non-traditional exports, typically, vegetables, fruits, and flowers. Even more encouraging are the few countries that have successfully promoted manufacturing exports, such as Mauritius and Tunisia. These experiences can provide lessons for other African countries.[4]

Table 1

Manufactures as % of export trade, selected African countries, 1980-2001

	1980	1990	2001
Algeria	0.3	2.6	2.3
Angola	12.9	0.1	..
Benin	3.4	..	6.2
Cameroon	3.8	8.5	4.7
Comoros	23.8	..	8.2[a]
Côte d'Ivoire	4.7	..	14.5[a]
Egypt	10.9	42.5	32.7
Ghana	0.9	..	15.8
Kenya	12.1	29.2	20.8[a]
Mauritius	27.4	65.8	74.2
Morocco	23.5	52.3	64.1[a]
Nigeria	0.3	..	0.2[a]
Senegal	15.1	22.5	28.8
South Africa	18.2	21.9	59.4
Togo	10.6	9.1	49.7
Tunisia	35.7	69.1	77.0[a]
Uganda	0.7	..	6.9
Zambia	16.0	..	12.7
Zimbabwe	35.8	30.9	28.1[a]

Note: [a] *Refers to data for 2000.*

Sources: *World Bank, 2003; UNCTAD 2003*

> *Trade liberalization alone is unlikely to lead to manufacturing export capacity*

Trade liberalization alone is unlikely to lead to manufacturing export capacity. A stronger supply-side is also required. Policies to improve infrastructure and the trading environment are critical. *ERA 2004* provides policy recommendations in these and other areas.

Policy actions needed to strengthen trade performance – lessons from ECA's Trade Competitiveness Index

This year's *ERA* presents a Trade Competitiveness Index (TCI). The TCI allows comparisons between African countries in different areas of trade competitiveness, and identifies bottlenecks to improved trade performance. It is calculated for a sample of 30 African countries. It also includes four Asian countries (India, Indonesia, Malaysia and Thailand) and four Latin American countries (Argentina, Bolivia, Brazil and Chile) – developing countries that had GDP per capita levels similar to today's African level in the 1960s, but have since followed a different development path.

The TCI is divided into three components, each capturing a different dimension of trade competitiveness: a *Trade-enabling Environment Index (TEI)*, reflecting the overall economic and political environment's conduciveness to trade; a *Productive Resource Index (PRI)*, capturing the availability of direct inputs to production, such as land and the labour force; and an *Infrastructure Index (II)*, measuring indirect inputs such as physical infrastructure and energy that enable the movement of goods and services. The results reveal a number of findings:

> **Competitive countries also have higher shares of manufactured exports**

- There is a positive relationship between the TCI and the degree of export diversification: competitive countries export a broader range of products. Competitive countries also have higher shares of manufactured exports. The challenge for African policy makers is to encourage competitiveness and diversification towards higher value-added goods and services with a greater technological content.

- Variations in competitiveness within Africa are driven by factors captured in the TEI including the macroeconomic and political environment as well as policies that affect the ease of trade. The top-scoring African countries in the TEI also do best in overall trade competitiveness. These countries have managed to diversify the most and have the highest exports of manufactured goods in GDP.

- The PRI reveals that labour-force indicators are key determinants of trade competitiveness on a global scale. Non-African countries dominate the overall TCI because of their high-quality labour forces. More successful integration by Africa into the world economy will require better educated and healthier workforces.

- Africa's trade with itself and with the rest of the world is hampered by inadequate infrastructure. These weaknesses lead to high transaction costs on the continent, a major cause of comparative disadvantage and limited diversification. Improved infrastructure is critical to better trade performance.

An active employment policy is vital...

Job creation is essential to Africa's future. Investments in human capital will have little return in the absence of job opportunities. In many African countries trade liberalization has been associated with a sharp fall in employment as consumers have switched from non-traded goods to imports. Policies are urgently needed to boost employment. One option, recently recommended by the US Commission on Capital Flows to Africa, is to provide more active support to small- and medium-sized enterprises (SMEs). Reflecting their importance as creators of employment and as seedbeds for technology acquisition and innovation, industrialized countries offer financial and technical support to their own SMEs. Africa needs to create similar small business institutions to coordinate comprehensive programmes of SME support. These institutions could strengthen technical and managerial capacities of SMEs; provide loan guarantees, and equipment and export financing; build links with multinational corporations; provide information on market and export opportunities; and facilitate "one-stop-shopping" on licensing, taxation, and other regulatory matters.

Box 3

Tackling unemployment in Tunisia

The Tunisian Government has taken measures to tackle unemployment, which stood at 15% of the economically active population in 2001. In January 2000, the National Employment Fund, popularly known as the "21-21 Fund", was launched. Its aim is to help find employment for job seekers, particularly the young.

The 21-21 Fund includes an internship programme for disadvantaged youths under 20. These individuals are placed in companies where they receive training to enhance their employability. University graduates can participate in advanced training programmes in computing and telecommunications. Those with liberal arts backgrounds are trained in fields such as pre-school teaching and participate in the national adult literacy programme. The 21-21 Fund provides financial assistance to 35 public and private training centres.

The most successful of the Fund's initiatives is an aid programme to help potential entrepreneurs establish small businesses, in collaboration with the Tunisian Solidarity Bank. Emphasis has been put on enterprise creation in poor areas. Approximately 204,000 people benefited from the Fund between January 2000 and November 2002. Most of the beneficiaries have since established their own businesses or have found stable employment. The Fund provides credit lines to guarantee commercial bank loans for those enlisted in its programmes who eventually start their own projects.

Source: ECA, from official sources

> *Africa needs to create small business institutions to coordinate comprehensive programmes of SME support*

To help the poorest segments of the population, State financing could be provided for public works projects such as road building and irrigation, especially during economic downturns (see box 3). In Ghana, for instance, youth are employed in forestry and urban sanitation programmes (Nwuke, 2002). Some countries such as Kenya and Ethiopia have tried "food for work" programmes; these have had varying degrees of success. Such schemes need to be improved upon and should be extended as far as financial resources allow.[5]

The key importance of energy

Firm-level surveys in countries such as Ghana, Kenya, Senegal and Uganda have identified infrastructure weaknesses as major constraints to export development and international competitiveness (Reinikka and Svensson, 1999).

In particular, Africa's poorly developed energy infrastructure hampers export diversification. Despite the continent's enormous potential for energy production, its energy-generating capacity is small relative to its geographic size and population. Electricity supply is prone to rationing, "brownouts" and blackouts. The sector is inefficient because of system losses in transmission and distribution, poor pricing policies, limited managerial capacities and ineffective government intervention. West African countries such as Mali and Senegal have energy unit costs as high as four times that of Tunisia, a country with an efficient state-owned energy sector and a well-diversified economy (see figure 3).

Figure 3

Cost of 1 kWh in Tunisia compared to selected ECOWAS countries (in CFA francs)

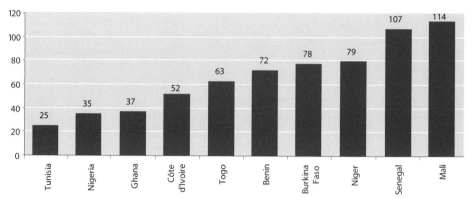

Source: *ECA, from official sources*

Africa has not attracted the levels of FDI needed to upgrade the continent's power network. FDI in the power sector in SSA between 1990 and 1998 represented only 6% of infrastructure-related FDI flows to the region. Energy schemes involving foreign private investors have sometimes had poor results, providing services at an excessively high cost, which hurts the poor.[6] On the other hand, privatized utilities have proved more efficient in extending service coverage (Ford, 2002).

But least developed countries (LDCs) may be less able to attract external flows to their power sectors. A recent UN report reminds us that "*the growing tendency to leave even LDCs to the mercies of the capital market to build power plants and upgrade their telecommunications facilities has led to growing under-provisioning of investments in this sector in the LDCs... Not all LDCs can access FDI in these areas or access it with sufficient urgency to meet their immediate demand for power or water*" (UN, 2000).

Reforming the electricity sector...

ERA 2004 makes a number of recommendations for power sector reform to help export diversification:

- Direct government control of the electric power sector has often had disappointing results, although this has not always been the case, as the case of Tunisia shows. However, a significant step is to transform power companies that are under government ownership into independent and self-reliant corporations, where feasible, operating on the basis of modern economic and business principles.

- African countries should promote energy efficiency. This reduces operating costs, enhances economic efficiency, and improves the productivity and international competitiveness of energy-consuming companies. An energy efficiency programme should include information dissemination activities to increase awareness of the issue, and incentives for energy conservation.

- Rural electrification programmes develop the energy sector and help export diversification by aiding structural transformation of the rural economy. African governments should promote rural electrification by facilitating the establishment of village-based energy systems.

- Increased private sector involvement in the energy sector brings the need for good regulation. Effective regulation prevents abuses of monopoly power and limits price increases to those compatible with appropriate profit margins. Regulatory bodies need to be independent, and distanced from political and corporate pressures.

- Regional integration in energy services could bring efficiency gains. A study by the Southern African Development Community (SADC) and the World Bank estimated a saving of $1.6 billion over ten years through the optimal use of regional electricity resources in Southern Africa.

> *Direct government control of the electric power sector has often had disappointing results*

Effective strategies for trade facilitation

Trade facilitation includes the ease of moving goods through ports and the speed of processing documents associated with cross-border trade. *ERA 2004* also considers broader aspects such as the transparency and professionalism of customs and regulatory institutions, and the harmonization of standards and regulations.

Greater efforts are needed to facilitate trade in the African continent. As well as strengthening Africa's infrastructure network, this requires harmonizing customs and administrative procedures.

African countries must remove their own trade impediments...

Trading more effectively requires a comprehensive approach by African countries. This should include improvements in infrastructure; the provision of good information and communications technology services; the removal of check points that constitute a *de facto* tax on trade; the simplification and harmonization of customs and border procedures; the promotion of new technology in customs agencies; and the strengthening of regional trade facilitation initiatives. Existing efforts through national, bilateral and subregional initiatives need to be better harmonized. Efficiency can be improved through the adoption of recognized trade facilitation mechanisms like the Automated System for Customs

Data (ASYCUDA) introduced by UNCTAD. A good example of a national-level facilitation initiative is the Tunisia TradeNet, an automated system designed to reduce shipment clearance delays.

At the multilateral level, trade facilitation is one of the four "Singapore Issues". This was introduced into trade negotiations at the First WTO Ministerial Conference held in Singapore in December 1996, despite strong opposition from developing countries, including those from Africa. Concerns surrounding the creation of a "multilateral framework" on trade facilitation centred on the limited human, financial and technical capacities to address the issue at the multilateral level.

African capital markets remain marginal in the global and emerging markets

Mobilizing domestic resources

African governments must promote domestic resource mobilization. The shares of savings and investment in GDP remained low during 2001 (the latest year for which data are available), and well under the levels needed to achieve the MDGs on growth and poverty reduction. In the region, 27 countries had savings below 10% of GDP in 2001, indicating a huge shortfall in resources needed to catalyze development. Rising private investment has been insufficient to offset the sharp drop in public investment seen during structural adjustment. Given complementarities between public and private investment, more public investment in infrastructure, health and education is required.

The Report also discusses the role of Africa's capital markets in resource mobilization. Amid the poor performance of developed country stocks over the last two years, many African stock markets have performed relatively well. This reflects Africa's partial insulation from global financial shocks due to the continent's low level of integration into the international financial system. Large increases in the value of stocks traded have occurred primarily in the regional powerhouses of Egypt, Morocco and South Africa. Overall, however, African capital markets remain marginal in the global and emerging markets: their share of world market capitalization fell from 1% in 1992 to 0.7% in 2001. External and institutional constraints limit the growth of African stock markets. Political instability and patchy macroeconomic performance hamper their performance, while settlement and trading mechanisms are often poorly developed.

Given the small size of African stock markets, the domestic banking system must play a central role in the provision of finance to businesses. Financial liberalization over the last two decades has not led to better banking sector performance: portfolios continue to be dominated by non-performing loans and excess liquidity. This contrasts with the relatively dynamic performance of the informal financial system. Africa has a "missing middle" in the provision of financial services: many potential borrowers are too large for the informal lenders but too small to access banks (Nissanke and Aryeetey, 1998). Reform of the banking system is critical in order to help firms break into the international market.

Challenges of fiscal reform in the face of trade liberalization

African governments' financial dependence on trade taxes raises the problem of how to maintain the fiscal base and preserve macroeconomic stability in the face of trade liberalization. In other regions, this issue is receiving increasing attention from policy makers. For example, all countries in Latin America, except for El Salvador, have either passed tax reforms or are in the process of so doing. In Africa, the domestic tax base is limited and tax administration inefficient. Taxes on international trade therefore make up a large share of fiscal revenue. In Africa as a whole, international trade taxes generated on average 28.2% of total current fiscal revenues over the last decade; for SSA the share rises to 30.5%. This contrasts with 0.8% for high-income OECD countries, 11.5% for upper-medium income countries, 18.42% for lower medium-income countries, and 22.5% for low-income countries. While the data shows a decreasing dependence on trade taxes worldwide, in Africa the share has fluctuated around a flat or slightly increasing trend.

Trade liberalization is therefore a potential source of fiscal instability for African economies. Revenue-related concerns are often mentioned as a reason for resistance to trade policy reform in low-income countries. In fact, some components of trade liberalization packages are likely to have a positive impact on revenues. These include the replacement of non-tariff barriers by lower tariff equivalents and the elimination of tariff exemptions and trade-related subsidies. Moreover, tariff cuts can increase total revenues if they generate a sufficiently large increase in trade flows. Trade liberalization measures can also be combined with tax and fiscal reforms to help buffer the revenue impact of trade liberalization.

The effects of trade liberalization on revenues and fiscal deficits depend on the existing level of trade restrictions. When trade restrictions are high, trade liberalization increases trade tax revenues and reduces the deficit. When, instead, trade restrictions are already low, further liberalization results in smaller revenues and a larger deficit unless appropriate policy responses are implemented. Liberalization is therefore more likely to lead to fiscal problems at later stages. Most African countries have already carried out trade liberalization over the 1990s. They are therefore likely to face revenue reductions as a result of further liberalization, such as that set out under the Economic Partnership Agreements (EPAs) between the EU and African subregions (see box 4).

Most of the African countries that made the fastest progress on trade liberalization over the last ten years saw a significant decrease in revenues from international trade taxes. But in some, such as Ghana, Morocco, Senegal, and Tunisia, this did not translate into higher deficits. Their experience suggests policy responses to buffer the negative fiscal impacts of trade policy reforms. Trade liberalization should be co-ordinated with measures on the revenue and spending side of the budget including raising domestic indirect and direct taxes, strengthening tax administration and collection and improving the effectiveness of public spending. In addition, a sound macroeconomic environment helps prevent fiscal distress during trade liberalization.

> *In Africa, the domestic tax base is limited and tax administration inefficient*

Box 4

EPAs and their fiscal implications

The Economic Partnership Agreements (EPAs) between the European Union and individual subregions in sub-Saharan Africa are an extension of the Cotonou Agreement with the African, Caribbean and Pacific (ACP) countries. Despite new initiatives on the part of the EU (such as the "Everything but Arms" agreement), the results from preferential agreements have been disappointing. For instance, over the first two decades of preferential access to the EU market under the Lomé accords, the exports of the ACP countries to the EU market fell from 6.7% of world exports in 1975 to 2.7% in 1995. This was partly due to ACP countries' dependence on primary commodities whose share in world trade had declined. Clearly, however, the concessions for the ACP countries did not offset this structural imbalance. The EPA initiative was a reaction to these poor results, and is part of a new approach by the EU on trade policy towards the poorest developing countries.

The planned establishment of free trade agreements with the EU under the EPAs represents an enormous challenge to African countries. They will have to completely liberalize their trade with the EU and carry out a range of institutional and regulatory reforms. One of the benefits of the EPAs is locking African countries into a reform programme, with the aim of making their economies more competitive internationally.

However, one concern is the impact of the EPAs on government revenues. Revenues from tariffs still amount to 2% of GDP in the median SSA country, reaching 4-6% of GDP in some cases (Hinkle et. al., 2003). For the countries most dependent on trade with the EU, such as the Central African Republic or Uganda, the loss of tariff revenue on imports could be a significant percentage of total government revenue, as high as 20%.

The EU has promised financial support for industrial restructuring and to compensate for lost tariff revenues. However, the EU may not be able to meet all its commitments in this area, given its overstretched budget as a result of EU enlargement. There are also concerns that financial help could come with new conditionalities.

Sources: Guggenbuhl and Theelen, 2001; Morrisey et al., 2003

Conclusions

Good progress, but continuing risks...

ERA 2004 stresses the progress that Africa has made in the last few years. After the disappointing economic performance of the 1980s and 1990s, there has been a return to positive rates of per capita economic growth across most of the continent. However, growth is still well below the annual average of 7% needed to attain the MDGs. Moreover, the economic recovery is fragile and in some parts of Africa has been overly dependent on favourable climate, something that cannot be counted on with certainty in the future. In addition, political instability and military conflict threaten the achievements of recent years.

Africa must focus on becoming more competitive...

In order to build on improved economic performance Africa must save and invest more, enhance its human capital, and achieve more dynamic export performance. *ERA 2004* tries to signpost the way towards a more competitive African economy. Greater efforts by African policy makers are needed to promote export capacity and diversification. This requires reconsideration of the way in which Africa has up until now attempted to achieve integration into the world economy. Although this is implicit in such initiatives as NEPAD, it is something that needs to be spelt out more explicitly in the future.

New initiatives are needed to help the continent diversify its exports...

Successful export diversification is dependent upon action by African governments themselves. But for most African countries the resource requirements for diversification are beyond what could possibly be mobilized at the domestic level. The United Nations Conference on Trade and Development (UNCTAD) has stressed the need to work out a financing mechanism at the international level to help these countries develop a system of supply rationalization and to diversify into other products. According to it, this may provide a rationale for a "diversification fund" for African countries (UNCTAD, 2003b).

And trade liberalization must be more equitable...

Helping African exporters through the removal of trade impediments by industrialized countries is essential. At the same time, the continent must focus on enhancing its ability to compete. African countries must be allowed to make use of special and differential treatments in order to build supply-side capacities. Over the long term, if the multilateral system does not produce the desired results, there is a possibility of a backlash against trade liberalization and the multilateral institutions. This should be avoided by ensuring now that the multilateral trading system is equitable.

Notes

[1] More than $12 billion of total aid (including most technical and emergency assistance) to developing countries is tied (or partially tied) to exports from the supplying country, which reduces its value to the recipient country by 25-40%. For a discussion on tied aid and its relationship with trade flows in an African context, see Lloyd et al., 2000. For a discussion on how tied food aid can negatively impact on aggregate welfare, see Osakwe, 1998.

[2] Policy changes envisaged in the "little" scenario are tariff reductions (agricultural goods by 36%, all other goods by 20%); reduction in export subsidies by 20%; reduction in domestic support by 20%; and trade facilitation by 1%. The "modest" scenario envisages tariff reduction of all goods by 50%; reduction of exports subsidies by 50%, and trade

facilitation by 1.5%. The "full" scenario encompasses 100% reduction in tariff, export subsidies, and domestic support, and trade facilitation by 3%.

[3] The classic reference to the importance of trade in development strategies has become Sachs and Warner, 1995.

[4] The case of Togo also stands out as a country which has apparently achieved a higher level of manufactured exports than the norm for Africa. However, this high figure is principally the result of transhipment, rather than the diversification of the economic structure towards manufacturing.

[5] See the recent study by Barrett et al., 2004. A good example of this kind of model is the Mahararastra Employment Guarantee Scheme, in India, which provides a minimum basic wage for rural workers during periods of economic hardship, and is financed by a consumption tax on urban areas.

[6] For a discussion on this, see Ford (2002) and Globalization Challenge Initiative (2002). On more than one occasion, the World Bank has questioned deals reached between multinationals and African governments. Such was the case of Enron's $800 million deal with the Nigerian Government. The World Bank and other foreign consultants were widely reported to have objected to the terms of the agreement, saying that in haste to solve the electricity supply problem the Nigerian Government had offered terms that were excessively favourable to Enron (Economist Intelligence Unit, 2000).

References

Barrett, C., Holden, S. and Clay, D. (2004), "Can Food-for-Work Programmes Reduce Vulnerability?," discussion paper #D-07/2004, Department of Economics and Resource Management, Agricultural University of Norway

Economic Commission for Africa (ECA) (2001), *Economic Report on Africa 2000: Transforming Africa's Economies*, Addis Ababa

————— (2002), *Economic Report on Africa 2002: Tracking Performance and Progress*, Addis Ababa

————— (2002), *Harnessing Technologies for Sustainable Development*, policy research report, August, Addis Ababa

————— (2004), "Trade Liberalization under the Doha Development Agenda: options and consequences for Africa," draft, March 2004

Economist Intelligence Unit (2000), "Nigeria Country Report," May, London

Ford, N. (2002), "Privatization in Africa: Panacea or Salvation?" *African Business*, May, pp16 -19

Fosu, A. K. (2002a), "The Global Setting and African Economic Growth," *Journal of African Economies*, 10 (3), pp282-310

—— (2002b), "Transforming Economic Growth to Human Development in Sub- Saharan Africa: the role of elite political instability," *Oxford Development Studies*, 30 (1), pp9-19

—— (2003), "Political Instability and Export Performance in Sub-Saharan Africa,", *Journal of Development Studies*, 39 (4), pp68-82

Globalization Challenge Initiative (2002), "Growing Dangers of Service Apartheid: how the World Bank Group's Private Sector (PSD) Strategy threatens infrastructure and basic service provision", *News and Notices for IMF and World Bank Watchers*, 2 (5), Takoma Park, MD

Guggenbuhl, A. and Theelen, M. (2003), "The Financial Assistance of the European Union to its Eastern and Southern Neighbours: a comparative analysis," in M. Maresceau and E. Lannon (eds), *The EU's Enlargement and Mediterranean Strategies: A Comparative Analysis*, Palgrave, Basingstoke

Hinkle, L.E, Herrou-Aragon, A. and Kubota, K. (2003), "How Far Did Africa's First Generation Trade Reforms Go? An intermediate methodology for comparative analysis of trade policies," Africa Region working paper no 58, World Bank, Washington DC

Lall, S. (2003), "Reinventing Industrial Strategy: the role of government policy in building industrial competitiveness," Queen Elizabeth House working paper series no 111, International Development Centre, University of Oxford

Lloyd, Tim, McGillivray, M., Morrissey, O. and Osei, R. (2000), "Does Aid Create Trade? An investigation for European donors and African recipients," *European Journal of Development Research*, 12 (1), pp107-23

Mattoo, Aaditya, Roy, D. and Subramanian, A. (2003), "The African Growth and Opportunity Act and its Rules of Origin: generosity undermined?" *The World Economy*, 26 (6), pp829-851

Morrissey O., Milner, C. and McKay, A. (2003), "A Critical Assessment of Proposed EU-ACP Economic Partnership Agreements," in A. Mold (ed), *EU Enlargement in a Changing World: Challenges for Development Cooperation in the 21st Century*, Taylor and Francis, London

Nissanke, Machiko and Aryeetey, E. (1998), "Financial Integration and Development: liberalization and reform in sub-Saharan Africa," Routledge Studies in Development Economics, London

Nwuke, Kasirim (2002), "Youth and Employment in Africa," paper prepared for the Youth Employment Summit, ECA, background paper no 1, September 2002, Addis Ababa

Osakwe, Patrick (1998), "Food Aid Delivery, Security and Aggregate Welfare in a Small Open Economy: theory and evidence," working paper 98/1, Bank of Canada, Ottawa

Reinikka, R., and Svensson, J. (1999), "Confronting Competition: firms' investment response and constraints in Uganda," in P. Collier and R. Reinikka (eds), *Assessing an African Success: Farms, Firms and Government in Uganda's Recovery*, forthcoming, World Bank

Sachs, J. and Warner, A. (1995). "Economic Reform and the Process of Global Integration," Brookings Papers on Economic Activity no 1, pp1-118, The Brookings Institution, Washington DC

Singh A. and Weisse, B. (1998), "Emerging Stock Markets, Portfolio Capital Flows and Long-term Economic Growth: micro and macroeconomic perspectives," *World Development*, 26 (4), pp607-622

Subramanian, A. and Roy, D. (2003), "Who Can Explain the Mauritian Miracle? Meade, Romer, Sachs or Rodrik?" in D. Rodrik (ed), *In Search of Prosperity: Analytical Narratives on Economic Growth*, Princeton University Press, Oxford

United Nations (UN) (2000), "Report of the High-level Panel on Financing for Development," (http://www.un.org/reports/financing/)

United Nations Conference on Trade and Development (UNCTAD) (2002), *World Investment Report 2002: Transnational Corporations and Export Competitiveness*, New York and Geneva

————— (2003a), *The Least Developed Countries Report 2002: Escaping the Poverty Trap*, New York and Geneva

————— (2003b), "Trade Preferences for LDCs: an early assessment of benefits and possible improvements," New York and Geneva

————— (2003c), *Handbook of Vital Statistics,* New York and Geneva

————— (2004), "Trade Performance and Commodity Dependence," New York and Geneva

US Commission on Capital Flows to Africa (2003), "A Ten-Year Strategy for Increasing Capital Flows to Africa," Washington DC (http://www.iie.com/publications/papers/africa-report.pdf)

US Department of Commerce (2003), "US-African Trade Profile," Washington DC

World Bank (2000), *Can Africa Claim the 21ˢᵗ Century?*, Washington DC

Recent Economic Trends in Africa and Prospects for 2004

Africa was the second fastest growing developing region in 2003 behind Eastern and Southern Asia. The continent's performance was underpinned by rising prices of oil and other commodities, an increase in foreign direct investment (FDI) and good macroeconomic fundamentals, backed up by improved weather conditions. As a result, real GDP grew at 3.8% in 2003 compared to 3.2% in 2002.

These signs of progress are encouraging, although they fall short of the continent's urgent need for much more rapid growth. Unfortunately, Africa is still a long way from achieving the 7% growth that is required to meet the principal Millennium Development Goal (MDG) of halving poverty by 2015. Only five countries – Angola, Burkina Faso, Chad, Equatorial Guinea and Mozambique – reached the 7% or higher growth rate in 2003. Out of 52 countries for which data are available, 16 registered growth of less than 4% while 7 recorded negative growth. The latter group consists of Zimbabwe (-11.2%), Ethiopia (-3.8%), Seychelles (-2.8%), Côte d'Ivoire (-2.3%), Guinea-Bissau (-1.8%), Central African Republic (-0.7%), and Burundi (-0.3%).

The largest economies in the continent did, however, greatly improve their 2003 performance over that of 2002, with the single exception of South Africa. North African countries recovered from their severe droughts in 2002 and achieved a record-level growth rate of 4.8% in 2003, on the back of a combination of good weather, high oil prices and production, increased worker remittances and a recovery in tourism. Nigeria registered real GDP growth of 4.5% compared to 2.6% in 2002; this resulted from the Government's expansionary fiscal stance, higher oil prices and production, bumper crops and the expanding benefits of the country's political transition. The South African economy's real GDP growth slowed to 2% in 2003 from 3% in 2002, reflecting the impact of a tight monetary policy and the currency's appreciation, which eroded the international competitiveness of some products.

It was highly reassuring that Africa, overall, continued to exhibit better macroeconomic fundamentals in 2003. Fiscal deficits were largely kept under control, despite the challenge faced by many countries of balancing increased spending for poverty reduction with the requirements of macroeconomic stability. Inflation rose slightly to 10.6% from 9.3% in 2002, reflecting higher food prices caused by poor weather conditions in some parts of Africa, increased oil-import prices and currency depreciation in several countries. The regional current account deficit fell from 1.6% of GDP in 2002 to 0.7% of GDP in 2003, thanks to robust oil and commodity prices, as well as high worker remittances. Out of the

Africa is far from the 7% growth needed to halve poverty by 2015

44 African countries for which data are available, 10 had current account surpluses while 34 registered deficits in 2003. Of the deficit countries, 21 had deficits of over just 5% of GDP, down from 23 in 2002.

2004 economic forecasts for Africa show a 4.4% growth

During 2003 there were significant improvements in several spots of political instability. Liberia pushed ex-President Charles Taylor into exile, raising hope that civil wars in neighbouring countries may now abate. In November, the Burundi Government signed a peace agreement with the main rebel group to end the country's civil war and took steps to integrate former rebels into the democratic political process. Uganda and Rwanda withdrew from the DRC, setting the stage for reconciliation. Peaceful political transitions in Angola and the DRC were beginning to pay off. Angola attracted substantial FDI during the year with more to come in 2004 and grew by over 12%. The DRC is on a steady path to macroeconomic stability, with single-digit inflation in 2003 (down from more than 500% as recently as 2000), economic growth at over 5% and the benefits of debt relief under the Highly Indebted Poor Countries (HIPC) initiative.

Continuing political instability in both Zimbabwe and Côte d'Ivoire is worrisome. In Zimbabwe, macroeconomic stability continued to deteriorate with inflation rising to 420% in 2003, the fiscal deficit reaching 7.1% of GDP and the economy contracting sharply for the fifth consecutive year.

The regional outlook for 2004 is again broadly positive and Africa's overall growth is forecast to accelerate to 4.4%. This should be helped by an expected increase in agricultural output and the likely rise in commodity prices, including metals and minerals, because of higher demand spurred by global recovery. FDI inflows to Africa are expected to continue their upward swing, although they will most likely be concentrated in South Africa and in the oil-producing countries of the region. Many poorer countries can, meanwhile, hope for a boost in their economic activities from innovative debt relief mechanisms and more expeditious delivery of donor financial commitments under HIPC initiative.

However, downside risks remain. The recovery in the global economy is marred by significant international imbalances, in terms of the large current account deficit of the United States and the matching surplus concentrated in very few countries. Adjustment through sharp depreciation in the US dollar could lead to a drastic decline in consumption, import demand and investment in the US, which could seriously damage the momentum of global economic recovery. Moreover, the large current account deficit has spurred protectionist sentiments in the US. Africa has already felt the repercussions of the large cotton subsidies granted by the US and other Organization of Economic Co-operation and Development (OECD) countries. These have damaged the economic prospects of cotton-producing West African countries – costing Mali 1.7% of its annual GDP, Benin 1.4%, and Burkina Faso 1%. The failure of the Cancun trade talks during 2003 thwarted Africa's hopes of better market access to industrial countries to help it trade its way out of poverty, and any further protectionist measures by developed countries could seriously harm Africa's medium-term prospects.

Strong global recovery in the second half of 2003

Despite fears of severe acute respiratory syndrome (SARS), uncertainties in Iraq, and worries of further terrorist attacks, the world economy grew more strongly at 2.6% in 2003, up from 1.7% in 2002. Global recovery was helped by robust growth in world trade, at 5% in 2003, up from 3% in 2002. Much of this growth has been driven by increased import demand by developing countries, particularly in Asia.

The recovery in the US in the second half of 2003 was the main driver of global growth. Rises in public spending, private consumption, and business investment in the US contributed to the country's robust 3.1% GDP growth in 2003. Strong growth in East and South Asia also helped the global recovery; the key factors were a stronger-than-expected performance in Japan, where GDP grew at 2.7% in 2003, combined with the sustained growth of the world's two most populous countries – China and India – at more than double the world growth rate.

Growth in the European Union (EU) area fell to 0.8% in 2003 from 0.9% in 2002. This poor performance reflects the stagnation of two major economies in the Euro Zone: Germany had zero growth and France grew by a mere 0.5%. Nonetheless, after the third quarter of 2003, the wider EU area showed good signs of recovery, mainly fuelled by strengthening world demand (see figure 1.1).

Figure 1.1

Annual real GDP growth of OECD, EU area and G-7 countries: 2001/Q3-2003/Q4 (percentage change over the same quarter of the previous year)

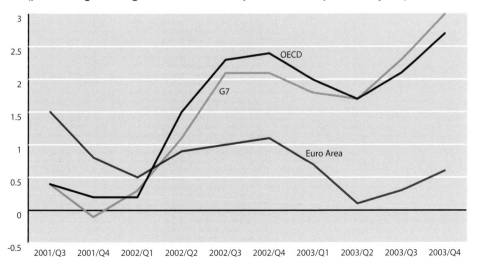

Figure 1.1 *(continued)*

Annual real GDP growth of OECD, EU area and G-7 countries: 2001/Q3-2003/Q4 (percentage change over the same quarter of the previous year)

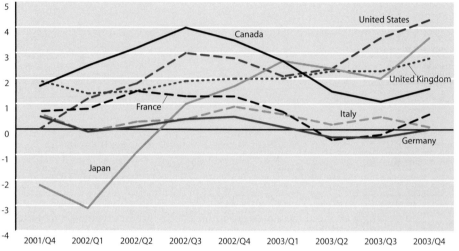

Source: OECD, 2003a

Table 1.1

Quarterly GDP growth rates of G-7 countries, 2001/Q1-2003/2004, (annualized growth over the previous quarter, %)

Group/Country	2001				2002				2003			
	Q1	Q2	Q3	Q4	Q1	Q2	Q3	Q4	Q1	Q2	Q3	Q4
Euro Zone	2.6	0.3	1.0	-0.6	1.5	1.8	0.9	0.2	0.1	-0.2	1.8	1.5
G7	1.0	-0.7	-1.1	0.3	2.8	2.4	2.7	0.7	1.3	2.0	5.1	3.6
Canada	1.3	1.1	-0.7	3.8	5.8	3.8	2.7	1.6	2.5	-1.0	1.3	3.8
France	2.1	-0.2	2.5	-2.5	3.5	2.0	0.7	-0.6	0.8	-1.5	2.8	2.7
Germany	3.5	-0.1	-0.6	-0.5	0.7	0.9	0.6	-0.2	-1.0	-0.6	0.8	0.9
Italy	3.0	0.0	0.0	-0.3	0.1	1.1	1.0	1.5	-1.0	-0.5	1.8	0.0
Japan	1.7	-4.2	-3.5	-3.0	-1.7	4.9	4.0	-0.2	2.2	3.5	2.5	6.4
United Kingdom	3.3	1.5	1.3	1.8	1.1	1.4	3.4	1.8	1.1	2.4	3.4	3.7
United States	-0.2	-0.6	-1.3	2.0	4.7	1.9	3.4	1.3	2.0	3.1	8.2	4.1

Source: UN Department of Economic and Social Affairs, 2004

The US twin deficit poses risks

The United States economy has staged an impressive recovery since the second half of 2003. In the third quarter of the year, the economy grew by 8.2%, the highest growth in over two decades (see figure 1.1 and table 1.1). For 2003 as a whole, growth was estimated at 3.1%. Private consumption recovered strongly as a result of tax cuts and other expansionary fiscal measures. Corporate profits rose and equity markets rallied strongly. In response, business spending strengthened, especially from the second quarter of 2003. The continuous growth of labour productivity since the beginning of 2003, buoyed by advances in the information technology sector, remains a key strength of the US economy.

Tax cuts and defence spending have supported this recovery. But the resulting US budget deficit of over $300 billion in 2003 now ranks among the highest in the industrial world. Public debt levels are also approaching those in other industrial economies. This deficit may not be sustainable and poses several downside risks to the world economy:

A $300 billion US trade deficit poses risks to the world economy

- Spurring economic recovery through a higher budget deficit may come at the cost of upward pressure on interest rates and a crowding out of private investment. This may put a stop to the fragile recovery in Europe and elsewhere.
- The sharp increase in the fiscal deficit has led to a large current account deficit of about 5% of GDP (see figure 1.2). Moreover, the current account deficit is increasingly financed by sales of government bonds rather than by equity inflows as in the past. This twin deficit and ballooning US external debt have weakened market confidence in the US dollar, triggering its depreciation (see figure 1.3).
- Even though the dollar depreciation is welcome, given the size of the current account deficit, concerns remain as to whether dollar adjustment will be orderly. Further deterioration of investor confidence as a result of the rising budget deficit could cause a rapid depreciation of the dollar and a sharp reversal of the current account deficit. If adjustment takes place through drastic declines in

Figure 1.2
Plunging US fiscal and current account deficits, 1990-2003 (% of GDP)

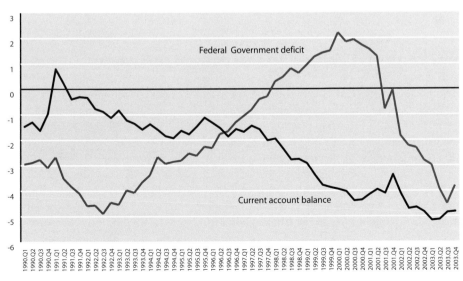

Source: *ECA, from official sources*

consumption, import demand and investment in the US, it may seriously damage the momentum of global recovery.

- The large current account deficit has already spurred protectionist sentiments in the US, which call for imposing trade barriers and demand that trading partners, China in particular, revalue their currencies.

Pursuing economic stimulus in the US through further widening of the budget deficit may not bode well for the global economy. It could thwart global recovery and seriously undermine Africa's growth potential in the near to medium term.

Figure 1.3

The falling dollar: US dollar versus euro and yen exchange rates, 1999-2003

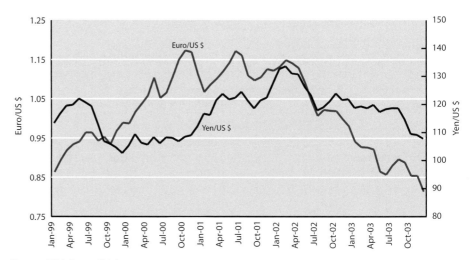

Source: *ECA, from official sources*

Euro Zone and Japan: on the path to recovery?

Economic activity in the EU area was sluggish in 2003 with a growth rate of 0.8%. However, there was a significant upturn by the G-7 economies in the third quarter of 2003, with all major economies recording positive growth (see figure 1.1 and table 1.1). Germany and Italy, which had been in recession, and France, which had experienced negative growth in the second quarter, all reported positive growth. There are some signs that these trends could be sustained, including rising global demand, which helped offset the negative impact of the appreciation of the euro on EU exports. Both consumer and investor confidence showed signs of recovery. Some countries, including France and Germany, exceeded the budget deficit limits set out in the EU's Stability and Growth Pact, and thus provided support to economic recovery. Throughout the euro area, there is little risk of inflation.

There are downside risks for the EU, however. First, further appreciation of the euro may harm the export competitiveness of the Euro Zone. The euro so far has taken the brunt of adjustment to the US dollar's depreciation; this raises serious concerns about export competitiveness, especially if the offsetting appreciation remains concentrated on the euro. Secondly, unemployment is still very high and persistent in France and Germany, at a rate of about 10%, and this could dampen consumer confidence.

The United Kingdom, the largest European economy outside the Euro Zone, fared better with a moderate growth rate of 2% in 2003, thanks to effective counter-cyclical policies. In 2003, the UK had a budget deficit of 2.7% of GDP, which is expected to rise to 3.1% in 2004. The UK does not suffer from the same labour market rigidities as Germany and France. This is reflected in the UK's lower unemployment rate, which stood at 5.1% in 2003.

After a decade of stagnation, 2003 marked a turning point for Japan with GDP growing at 2.7%, largely driven by strong demand from other East Asian countries. The recovery in equity prices that boosted corporate profits also contributed to recovery. This helped investor confidence, particularly in large manufacturing firms, leading to growth in business investment of around 5% over the year. Consumer confidence has improved, which should lead to an increase in household consumption. However, before getting onto a higher growth trajectory in the medium term, Japan must address several structural weaknesses, including a weak banking sector hobbled by non-performing loans, a large budget deficit and substantial public debt.

Growth momentum in other developing regions was led by China and India

Overall, developing countries grew by 4.3% in 2003 (see figure 1.4). Within this, there were strong regional variations ranging from growth of only 1.7% in Latin America and the Caribbean to a high 4.5% in Eastern and Southern Asia. While growth was sluggish in Latin America, mainly because of political and economic problems in Argentina, Brazil

Figure 1.4
Real GDP growth in developing countries and regions, 2002 and 2003 (%)

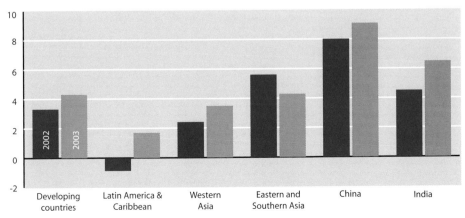

Source: *UN Department of Economic and Social Affairs, 2004*

and Venezuela, East and South-East Asia fared better than anticipated at the beginning of 2003 because SARS was less economically damaging than expected and trade boomed. China and India led the way, with growth of 9.1% and 6.5% respectively in 2003.

The emergence of China and India as global powerhouses has far-reaching implications for the world economy. China has become an important importer of raw materials; these include several important African exports, such as oil, iron, nickel, copper and aluminium. Africa's trade with China has increased by over 50% in the last three years (see box 1.1). At the same time, however, the competitive pressure from China, especially since its accession to the World Trade Organization (WTO), could pose difficulties for some African countries. In particular Madagascar, Mauritius and Tunisia may face stiff competition in apparel, leather goods, and other low-skills-intensive manufacturing industries.

> *Trade between China and Africa recently grew by over 50%*

Box 1.1
Sino-Africa trade links are growing fast

Trade and economic cooperation between China and Africa has gained momentum since 2000. Both sides have worked to establish a long-term, stable partnership symbolizing a new kind of South-South relationship. Trade between the two regions is increasing steadily, the more so in recent years because of China's growing demand for energy and raw materials. China's rapid economic upswing creates unprecedented opportunities for African exporters.

Trade between China and Africa reached over $12 billion in 2002. It hit a record of nearly $15 billion in the first ten months of 2003, a 54% increase over the same period the previous year. During this period African exports to China totaled $6.77 billion while imports from China reached $8.21 billion, leading to a decrease in Africa's trade deficit with China.

Rising exports from Africa to China are in primary commodities and oil, while imports are mainly manufactured goods such as electrical machinery, industrial products and textiles and clothing. Exports to China of wood-based products account for a large proportion of trade between the two regions. The Republic of Congo, Cameroon, Equatorial Guinea, Gabon and Liberia are among the largest exporters of timber products to China. China also imports a substantial amount of crude oil from Libya, Nigeria and Sudan, cotton from Benin, Cameroon and Egypt as well as manganese, wood and oil from Gabon. South Africa is China's largest trading partner in Africa accounting for 27% of total trade between the continent and China. South Africa's exports to China include iron ore, diamonds, crude oil, copper, aluminum, paper pulp, paper and paperboard, and coal.

Growing trade with China will help African countries to diversify their export destinations away from the traditional markets of the US and Europe. Trade has also brought stronger economic ties between the two partners more broadly. China has expanded technical assistance to African countries and encouraged its enterprises to invest in Africa. Chinese investors have established 602 businesses in 49 African countries in the last few years. Similarly, African enterprises, including some from South Africa and Uganda, have invested in China.

Source: ECA, from official sources

FDI to Africa was on the rise in 2003

Foreign direct investment inflows to Africa increased from $11 billion in 2002 to $14 billion in 2003. The region's share in global FDI inflows remained at around 2%. The outlook for FDI flows to Africa in 2004 is equally positive. New opportunities in the oil sector, the continuation of privatization programmes and the implementation of regional and interregional free-trade initiatives should allow for a moderate increase in FDI.

FDI to Africa has mainly been concentrated in natural resource sectors. Oil-producing countries, particularly Algeria, Angola, Chad and Nigeria have been the main beneficiaries, but not the only ones. The major FDI inflows in 2003 included Mozambique's aluminium plant, owned by BHP Billiton, which extended operations with new investment of $1 billion. Ghana's gold sector is set to receive $1.4 billion as a result of the acquisition of Ashanti Goldfields by Anglogold of South Africa. The garment sector, particularly in Botswana, Kenya, Lesotho and Mauritius, also continued to attract investment. FDI flows into services in 2003 targeted tourism, telecommunications, banking and finance, transport, wholesale and retail trade, and business and legal services.

> *Oil-producing economies benefited more from FDI*

Figure 1.5

Economic activities in Africa with the largest FDI potential as perceived by transnational companies (TNCs), 2000-2003 (share in overall responses, %)

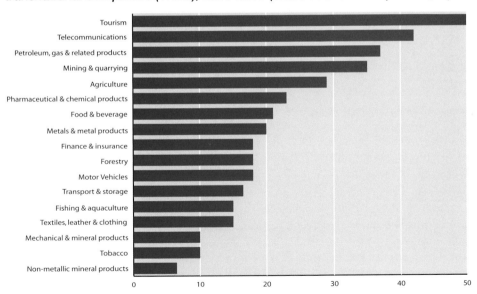

Source: *ECA, from official sources*

Although resource-seeking FDI dominates in Africa, in recent years, there has been a shift towards market-seeking investments as a result of privatization (i.e. transportation) and efficiency-seeking investments (i.e. textiles and clothing) as well as services (i.e. telecommunications) (see figure 1.5).

Table 1.2

Obstacles to FDI in Africa as perceived by TNCs, 2000-2003 (%)

Determinants with negative influence on FDI decisions	
Determinants	**Share in overall responses (%)**
Level of extortion & bribery	49
Access to global markets	38
Political & economic outlook	27
Access to finance	27
Administrative costs of doing business	27
State of physical infrastructure	25
Tax regime	24
Access to low-cost unskilled labour	24
Regulations and legal framework governing FDI	22
Access to natural resources	21
Access to skilled labour	21
Investment incentives	21
Size of local market	17
Profitability of investment	16
Trade policy	14
Access to regional markets	13
Growth of local market	11

Source: *ECA, from official sources.*

The obstacles to FDI in Africa are still numerous and formidable. According to a survey of transnational companies, the biggest impediment is extortion and bribery, with almost 50% of companies citing this as a major deterrent (see table 1.2). Poor links with global markets, an uncertain political outlook and the lack of access to finance have been identified as other serious impediments to investment, particularly outside the natural resources sector.

The most attractive countries for FDI are those with large markets such as South Africa, Egypt, Morocco and Nigeria, and those that have addressed impediments to investment by improving the business environment such as Ghana, Ethiopia, Mauritius, Mozambique, Tanzania and Uganda (see figure 1.6).

Higher commodity prices, especially for minerals

The prices of most commodities rose in 2003. The depreciation of the dollar throughout the year has largely contributed to increases (see figure 1.7).

Figure 1.6

Most attractive African countries for FDI as perceived by TNCs, 2000-2003 (% share in overall responses)

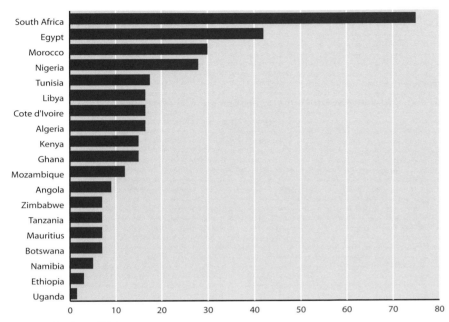

Source: *ECA, from official sources*

Coffee: Although coffee prices increased in 2003, they remain at near-historical lows with average prices of $0.82 per kg and $1.42 per kg for coffee robusta and coffee arabica, respectively. This is a reflection of high supply and weak demand.

Cocoa: Cocoa prices fell only slightly from $1.78 per kg in 2002 to $1.75 per kg in 2003. In the last two years, prices have been extremely volatile as a result of the political instability in Côte d'Ivoire, the world's largest cocoa producer. Volatility will remain high if the country's political crisis drags on.

Tea: Prices of tea have been low in recent years. This is expected to continue because of oversupply and slow consumption growth. With an average price of $1.52 per kg, 2003 prices were largely unchanged from 2002.

Cotton: Cotton prices increased by 37% in 2003 to $1.40 per kg. However, this is just a slight recovery after declines in the two previous years that took prices to 30-year lows. The upturn in 2003 was mainly due to a reduction in supply from China from the previous marketing season. The recovery is likely to be short-lived with prices expected to decline in 2004, particularly given the large subsidies provided by the US to its cotton farmers.

Copper: Prices went up by 14% in 2003. This was mainly the result of production cutbacks that began in 2001.

Gold: The 2003 higher–than–average price of $363.5 per troy ounce (toz) was over 17% as registered the previous year, the result of buybacks of hedged positions by gold producers. The price rose to $408.4 per toz in the first quarter of 2004.

Crude Oil: Crude oil prices rose to $32.88 per barrel in February 2003 just before the start of the war in Iraq, because of expectations of supply disruption. Prices then slightly declined, averaging $28.91 per barrel over the year. Since January 2004, they have increased, reaching $37.63 per barrel in May as a result of strong oil demand.

Figure 1.7
Prices of Africa's key commodities, January 2002-May 2004

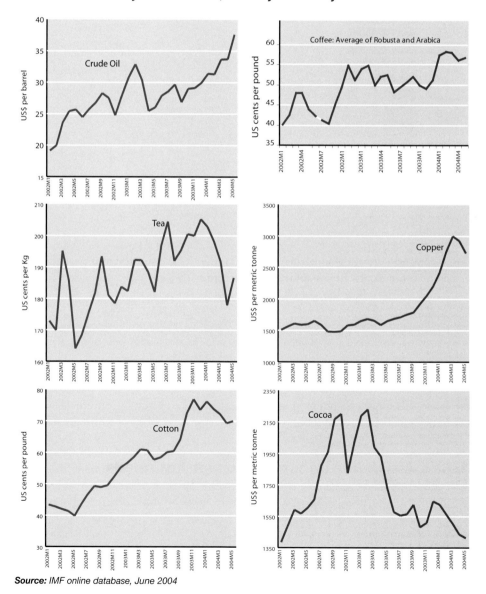

Source: IMF online database, June 2004

Where is the development round after Cancun?

The purpose of WTO's Cancun meeting in September 2003 was to take stock of issues that were agreed upon in the Doha Development Agenda (DDA) and those that emerged following the November 2001, Qatar, Doha meeting. Especially important to Africa were the following:

- On agriculture, improving market access to industrialized countries through substantial reductions in tariffs, tariff peaks and tariff escalation; and reductions in domestic support and export subsidies by industrial countries;
- On cotton, a reduction in subsidies by industrialized countries with a commitment to phase out by a specified time and the provision of financial compensation to developing countries in the transition period (see box 1.2);
- On non-agricultural products, improving market access to industrialized countries through reductions in tariff, tariff peaks and tariff escalation; and
- On public health, interpreting the Agreement on Trade Related Intellectual Property Rights (TRIPs) so as to ensure that African countries have the right to protect public health and promote access to medicines for all.

> *Breakthrough Geneva trade talks in July 2004 mended multilateral negotiations*

While the Cancun agenda was ambitious and WTO members did not have an agreed position on the DDA issues, the collapse of the talks reflected a lack of political will by the developed countries to make concessions on Doha promises, especially on market access in agriculture. It was a missed opportunity for all as well as a major setback for the WTO. On the positive side, there is a consensus that talks should be revived and that the promise made in Doha to focus on a Development Round should be fulfilled. However, progress is possible only with sufficient will from the industrialized countries. In this regard, it is noteworthy that trade talks were successfully concluded in Geneva at the end of July 2004, which may signal the much-needed breakthrough for resumption of the post-Doha development round of multilateral trade negotiations.

In the meantime, Africa needs to engage more effectively in trade negotiations. African countries need to build their capacities to understand complex agreements, and to develop appropriate negotiation strategies. Clear African positions on major issues such as trade in agriculture, Trade-related Aspects of Intellectual Property Rights (TRIPS) and public health are needed to strengthen Africa's position at future negotiations. Even if market access issues are resolved, Africa may not be in a position to exploit the opportunities fully, because of serious supply-side constraints. Weak infrastructure, poor trade facilitation services, and inadequate physical and human capital limit the continent's export sector development.

ODA to Africa has begun to recover but needs to be more effective

After ODA flows to Africa in 2000 fell to $18.8 billion, they increased to $19.4 billion in 2001, ending a long period of decline that commenced in the early 1990s (see figure 1.8). Africa is, however, designated to receive up to half of the additional funds that were pledged at the Monterrey Conference in 2002. Donors and recipients are also undertaking new measures designed to improve the effectiveness of aid.

Box 1.2

US subsidies destroy African cotton farming

Cotton farmers in the United States, about 25,000 in total, benefit from a wide range of government-authorized subsidies that support production and export levels. These farmers received $2.1 billion in domestic support in 2001 and $3.4 billion in 2002, much more than the size of the US aid budget for Africa and considerably higher than the GDP of poor cotton-producing countries such as Mali and Burkina Faso. Farmers also benefit from a generous crop revenue and insurance programme. The US also provides assistance to cotton millers and exporters to help stabilize the difference between domestic and international prices. This amounted to $197 million in 2001. Export credit guarantee programmes provide further support to exporters.

Thanks to the subsidies they receive, US cotton farmers are a major force in the world market, contributing 30% of world exports. Subsidies have been blamed for the fall in cotton prices over the past decade. This decline has made millions of small farmers in West and Central Africa unable to cover production costs. African farmers continue to see their earnings decline, even when they boost output: between 1999 and 2002, African cotton farmers managed to increase output by 14% but saw the value of their countries' exports decline by 31%. In 2001/2002 falling prices led to GDP and export earnings losses of 1% and 12% in Burkina Faso, 1.4% and 9% in Benin, and 1.7% and 8% in Mali. Had it not been for the high demand for cotton from China in 2003, which pushed prices up again, the effects of subsidies on African producers would have been disastrous.

Critics maintain that US subsidies on cotton do not conform to the Uruguay Round Agreement on Agriculture, which only allows domestic support measures under its "green box" measures on products with minimal trade-distorting effects. Most US cotton farmers benefit from direct payments, and the withdrawal of subsidies from other crops generates incentives for farmers to switch to cotton. The Agreement specified that payments triggered by low prices, which enhance production when it would otherwise decline, fall into the "amber box" category; these products are not exempted from subsidy reduction measures.

It has been estimated that a complete elimination of US cotton subsidies would lead to an increase in world prices of 25-30%, boosting the export earnings of West and Central African countries by $250 million (Badiane et al., 2002). Some 11 million people in eight countries depend on cotton production for their livelihoods.

Source: Oxfam, 2003; ECA, from official sources

In 2001, multilateral donor contributions to Africa picked up with an increase of 32.7% over the previous year. The World Bank's International Development Association (IDA) is the biggest donor to Africa and has increased its contributions since 1999. In 2001, IDA flows totalled $2.3 billion, with most going to sub-Saharan Africa (SSA). On the bilateral side, the UK almost doubled its aid flows to Africa between 1995 and 2001; about 96% of its ODA to Africa was targeted to SSA in 2001. The US has also increased aid flows to SSA since 1996, although 32% of all net flows to Africa go to Egypt, on account of its important geo-strategic position.

Figure 1.8

Recovering ODA flows: total flows to Africa, 1960-2001 ($US billions)

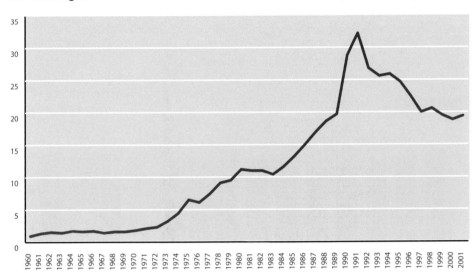

Source: *OECD, 2003b*

> *Only around half of aid is spent in recipient countries*

Making aid more effective. A total $52 billion of aid (net of debt service) is disbursed to developing countries each year. Of this, only half, or $26 billion, is spent in recipient countries. The rest is spent as follows: $3 billion on bilateral aid administration; $13.6 billion on technical assistance, little of which actually enters the recipient economy; $2.3 billion on debt relief, actually paid to other creditor agencies; and $3.2 billion on emergency assistance (DAC, 2003).

Despite the consensus about the need for country-owned policies, programme aid (including budget and sectoral support) makes up less than 20% of total aid, even on average in the best-performing countries. Large amounts of aid go to projects that do not reduce poverty and to middle-income countries, including some which could easily reach the MDGs without external support. Aid would better support the MDGs if it was better targeted to the poorest countries and to MDG-oriented projects.

The impact of aid on progress towards the MDGs would be increased by:

- Donors setting clear targets to reduce administrative costs, moving to capacity-building, untying aid, increasing budget support, focusing aid on low-income countries and on poverty reduction efforts; and
- Donors making multi-year and rising commitments to countries where budget transparency and anti-poverty efforts are high.

More than $12 billion of aid to developing countries is tied (or partially tied) to export purchases from donor countries. This includes most technical and emergency assistance. For example, in 2001, only 30% of Canada's ODA was untied. Between 1995 and 1999 the US on average gave less than 25% untied aid annually. Tying conditions reduce the value of aid to recipient countries by 25-40% through purchases of uncompetitively priced exports. No recent aid pledges go further in untying aid, apart from those of additional funds from countries that have already committed to 100% untying and those for multilateral facilities. Over 90% of aid from Denmark, the Netherlands, Norway and UK was untied in 2001 (see figure 1.9). Other donors should rapidly reach agreements to untie aid, especially technical assistance and emergency aid.

Figure 1.9
Tied versus untied aid, by donor, 2001 (%)

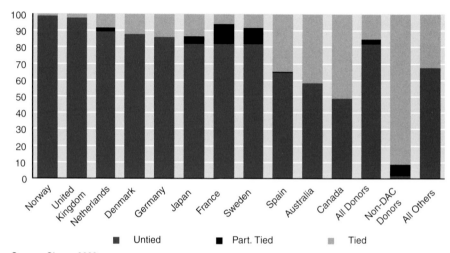

Source: Simon, 2003

Most bilateral ODA flows to Africa in 2001 went to social sectors, with $1.3 billion going to education and $1.2 billion to the health and population sector (see figure 1.10). Production sectors including agriculture, forestry and fishing; industry, mining and construction; and trade and tourism received ODA flows of only $1 billion in 2001. ODA flows to transport and communications and energy have decreased by 48% since 1998. This trend is worrying given the crucial role of infrastructure in economic growth and poverty reduction. While Canada, France, Germany, the Netherlands, UK and US invest a large proportion of their ODA budget in health and education, Japan is the only donor that prioritizes the productive sectors and supports infrastructure.

Aid to MDGs. In 2001, about half of ODA to Africa was aimed at addressing the MDGs on poverty, primary education, gender equality, child mortality, maternal health, HIV/AIDS and other infectious diseases, and environmental sustainability. But it is estimated that an additional $50 billion of ODA per year is necessary to reach MDGs in developing countries (UNECA, 2003). ODA flows for two MDGs (3 and 6) are as follows:

Figure 1.10
Bilateral ODA flows to Africa, by sector, 2001 ($US millions)

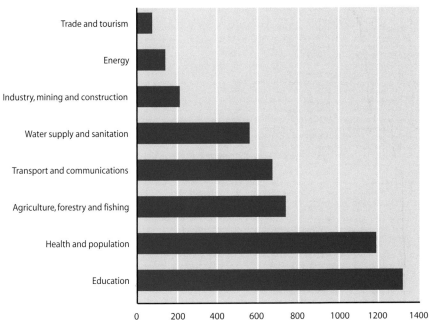

Source: OECD 2003b

Figure 1.11
ODA specific to MDG 3 by recipient region, 2001 ($US millions)

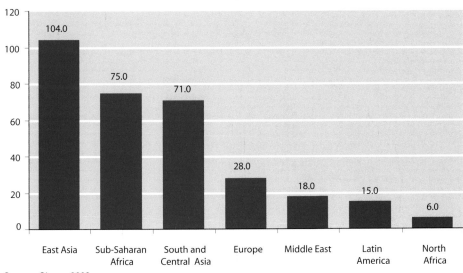

Source: Simon, 2003

- **MDG 3: Promoting gender equality and empowering women.** This area receives relatively little ODA (see figure 1.11). In 2001, $75 million of ODA was targeted to gender projects in SSA, and $6 million in North Africa. This was equivalent to only 11 US cents per capita in SSA and 4 cents per capita in North Africa compared to 27 cents per capita on projects in the developing and transition countries of Europe.

- **MDG 6: Combating HIV/AIDS, malaria and other diseases.** Almost half of worldwide ODA related to this MDG is allocated to SSA (see figure 1.12). But in per capita terms Africa receives under $2. Almost half the funds for MDG 6 are targeted to HIV/AIDS programmes. However, malaria is a big killer and the 25 US cents allocated to combating it in SSA is too low.

Figure 1.12
ODA specific to MDG 6 by recipient region, 2001 ($US millions)

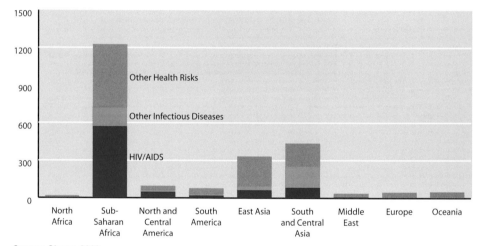

Source: Simon, 2003

Africa's improving economic performance in 2003

Africa's economic performance improved in 2003 with real GDP growth reaching 3.8% compared to 3.2% in 2002. The continent benefited from the recovery of the world economy in the second half of 2003, rising commodity prices and favourable weather conditions in many parts of the region. Sixteen out of 53 countries registered low growth of under 4% while seven contracted. Only five countries achieved the 7% or higher growth needed to meet the MDGs (see table 1.3).

Stronger economic performance in the continent was led by recovery in the North Africa subregion, which grew by 4.8% because of favourable weather (see figure 1.13). Growth in Algeria shot up to 6.9%, from 4.1% in 2002 as a result of a construction boom, fiscal expansion and increased oil production. In Tunisia, growth rose from 1.9%

in 2002 to 4.2% in 2003 because of a pickup in tourism and high agricultural growth. Morocco registered increased growth of 5%, up from 4.3% in 2002, driven by good agricultural performance, high growth in remittances and a rise in domestic investment.

Figure 1.13
North Africa leads Africa's subregional growth, 2003 (%)

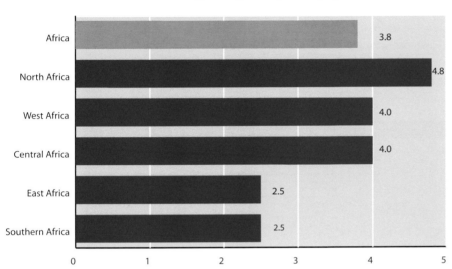

Source: ECA, from official sources

Sixteen out of 53 African countries registered growth of under 4%

Sub-Saharan Africa grew at 3.1% in 2003 compared to 3.5% in 2002, with slowdowns in Southern and Eastern Africa. In West Africa, growth picked up to 4% in 2003 compared to 3.1% in 2002. This was partly the result of increased growth in Nigeria, the subregion's largest economy, which grew by 4.5%, compared to 2.6% in 2002. The country's rise was because of an expansionary fiscal stance, higher oil prices and production, a good harvest, and relatively peaceful political conditions. However, the economy remains vulnerable to oil price movements and internal political tensions. Growth in Ghana also increased because of high cocoa and gold prices. Burkina Faso achieved a 7% growth rate, up from 5.1% in 2002, mainly because of a bumper harvest of cereals and cotton. Senegal recorded a 6.3% growth rate in 2003, compared to 4.9% in 2002. On the downside, there were sharp slowdowns in the economies of Côte d'Ivoire and Guinea-Bissau (see figure 1.14).

In Central Africa, growth remained unchanged from the 4% achieved in 2002. The subregion's largest economy, Cameroon, slowed to 4.2% growth from 4.9% the previous year. In Equatorial Guinea, growth remained high in 2003 at over 10%, nevertheless a considerable decline from the previous year's rate of over 24%, which had been driven by rising oil production. Because of the expanding oil sector, Chad was the fastest growing economy in Africa with a growth rate of over 14%. Having passed a law stipulating that 80% of oil revenues be invested in health, education, transportation and other development infrastructure, with 10% set aside for future investment, Chad is taking steps to ensure that benefits from the petroleum sector are spread widely (see box 1.3).

In East Africa, growth fell from 3.6% to 2.5%. Growth in Burundi stagnated while in Ethiopia economic activity contracted as a result of unfavourable climatic conditions. Growth also slowed in Rwanda and Uganda. In Southern Africa, growth slowed to 2.5% from 3.3% the previous year. This was largely driven by worsening economic conditions in Zimbabwe and by the downturns in Angola and South Africa, in the latter case because of tight monetary policy in response to rising inflation.

Food security prospects in Africa in 2004 are mixed. In 23 countries, it is seriously affected by weather, conflict and instability and forced movements of refugees and internally displaced peoples (IDPs), see box 1.4.

Table 1.3
Growth performance distribution in Africa, 1999-2003 (number of countries)

	1999	2000	2001	2002	2003
Negative growth	0	1	5	5	7
Zero & positive growth	53	52	48	48	45
Low (0-3.9%)	26	37	19	27	16
Medium (4%-7%)	23	14	24	16	25
High (> 7%)	4	1	5	5	4

Source: *ECA, from official sources*

Savings and investment levels far too low

Investment to GDP ratios remained low during 2001 (the latest year for which data are available) and below the 25% level needed to speed up growth. For the continent as a whole, the investment and savings ratios averaged around 20% in 2001. Only 14 countries had investment ratios above 25%. The largest category of 20 countries had investment ratios between 10% and 20% (see table 1.4). Only eight countries had savings ratios of above 25%. Twenty-seven had savings ratios of less than 10% of GDP, indicating a huge shortfall in the resources needed to catalyze development.

In recent years, the continent has seen rising private investment and falling public investment as a percentage of GDP (see figure 1.15). Private investment rose from 13.1% of GDP in 2000 to 15.3% of GDP in 2001 while public investment fell from 6.4% of GDP to 5% of GDP, in a continuation of trends seen through the 1980s and 1990s. The higher share of private investment in GDP shows that gradual progress is being made in the development of the private sector. The declining share of public investment since the mid-1980s has resulted from efforts to contain the fiscal deficit. The waning trend in public investment is a cause for concern, especially now that it is more widely recognized that the public and private sectors need to play complementary roles in the development process.

Figure 1.14
Highest and lowest real GDP growth rates in Africa, 2003 (%)

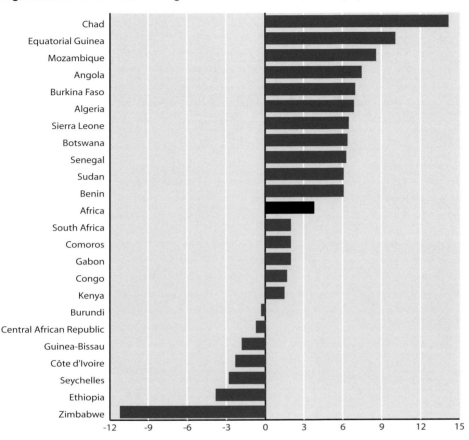

Source: *ECA, from official sources*

Capital markets are growing but suffer constraints

Amid the poor performance of developed countries' stocks over the last two years, many African stock markets have performed relatively well, reflecting Africa's partial insulation from global financial shocks and the continent's low level of integration into the world economy. Africa's capital markets show strong potential for increasing the pace of private investment. These markets have also become an important part of institutional reform processes such as privatization and broad liberalization. For the 17 out of 18 African stock markets for which data are available, market capitalization as a percentage of GDP has risen significantly in all countries between 1990 and 2002, except for South Africa (see figure 1.16). In terms of listed firms, 15 out of 17 countries showed increases in the number of listings over the same period.

Despite these encouraging trends, many markets have remained fairly inactive with the actual value of shares traded as a percentage of GDP stagnating over a 12-year period

Box 1.3
Who will benefit from Chad's oil bonanza?

Some African countries are enjoying an unprecedented oil bonanza, although the benefit from it has not thus far reached the poor. Chad — Africa's newest oil producer and one of its poorest — hopes to change the trend. As oil is capital-intensive, only a few of Chad's people — in addition to those who were paid compensation for land acquisition — can benefit directly. At most 3,500 were employed in building the pipeline that runs through this giant but largely empty Saharan State and the other facilities. Some complain that they had to bribe employment agents to be hired. With the oil now flowing, the project workforce is down to just over 1,000. However, car dealers and private security firms have profited from the arrival of well-paid expatriates.

For the long journey ahead, Chad is undertaking a bold experiment to avert a disaster from its unprecedented oil boom. Over the next 25 years, the country is expected to make $80 million a year from oil. With a 50% boost to its tiny budget, Chad is to set up an independent Revenue Oversight Committee that will inspect how the Government spends its oil revenue. The Committee so far has rejected more than half of the Government contracts it has screened, and is insisting on open bidding. However, the Committee is understaffed and its scrutiny slows an already laborious and mostly manual process for disbursing funds.

The objective of these measures is to ensure that Chad's oil money is used for the well-being of all Chadians, particularly the poor, by helping define and implement a comprehensive oil-management programme. It is deliberately trying to avoid the pattern of foreigners coming in, taking the money and telling Chad how to use it. Rather, it is about setting up a structure in which the Chadians put in place their own system of checks and balances.

The most important impact of this project should be in the use of oil revenues to improve education and health services, to improve infrastructure (roads, power, water) and to improve rural development, through small-scale community development projects, agricultural projects, etc. In short, it promises faster progress towards fulfilling the MDGs.

Source: ECA, from official sources

Table 1.4
Gross savings and investment in Africa, 2000 and 2001 (number of countries)

	2000	2001
Investment ratio (% GDP)		
< 10	3	5
10-20	25	20
> 20 but less than or equal to 25	10	10
> 25	12	14
Total number of countries	50	49
Savings ratio (% GDP)		
< 10	28	27
10-20	11	11
> 20 but less than or equal to 25	2	3
> 25	9	8
Total number of countries	50	49

Source: ECA, from official sources

Figure 1.15

Trends in private and public investment in Africa, 1985-2001 (% of GDP)

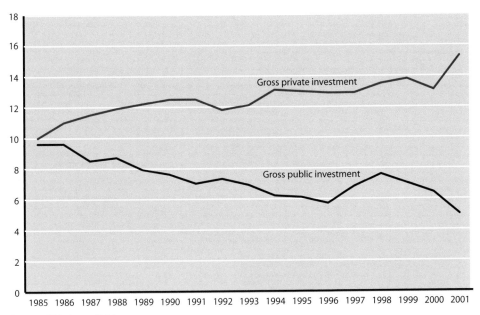

Source: *ECA, from official sources*

(see figure 1.17). Large increases in value traded occurred primarily in the regional power-houses of Egypt, Morocco and South Africa. Amid an economic crisis, Zimbabwe's markets showed large increases in traded values and market capitalization; as property rights came under threat in the real economy, investors increasingly turned to the stock market to protect their capital base. In many other markets, such as those of Côte d'Ivoire and Kenya, the value traded remained a very small percentage of GDP. Nonetheless, 15 out of 16 markets for which data exist showed increases in the ratio.

Overall, African capital markets remain marginal in the global and emerging economies. Their share of emerging market stock capitalization fell from 11.6% in 1992 to 7.6% in 2001. Africa's share of world market capitalization also fell from 1% in 1992 to 0.7% in 2001. However, over the same period, the continent increased its share in emerging markets, in terms of traded values, from 1.3% to 3.2%. This mixed performance is the result of external and institutional constraints that hamper the growth of African stock markets. Political instability and patchy macroeconomic performance block the development of vibrant capital markets. Stock market infrastructure such as settlement and trading mechanisms are often poorly developed; markets frequently suffer from severe informational deficiencies; and regulatory regimes need to be strengthened.

Box 1.4

Food insecurity in Africa caused by conflicts

Twenty-three countries face food shortages while others expect good harvests. Apart from weather-related factors, which affect 14 countries, food security is also seriously hampered by the effects of conflict and forced population movements (see table below). However, in ten countries civil strife has been an important factor; 11 countries face problems because of internally displaced persons (IDPs); three because of refugees and two because of returning populations. These problems are due to conflicts and political instability.

In Uganda, for example, intensified fighting in the north and east of the country has increased the number of displaced people, increasing humanitarian assistance needs. In Côte d'Ivoire, food insecurity has been driven by fighting, with food supply problems being especially apparent in the west and rebel-controlled north. Similarly in Burundi and the Democratic Republic of Congo, food production continues to be hampered by insecurity. In Angola, despite good harvests in 2003, food assistance is needed for 1.4 million returnees and other vulnerable groups.

Reasons for food emergencies (number of countries)

Civil strife	10
IDPs	11
Refugees	3
Returnees	2
Economic disruption	1
Drought	13
Adverse weather	1

Source: FAO, 2003

Countries still face severe fiscal challenges

African governments continue to be challenged by the tension between the need to increase spending on poverty-reducing areas, as set out under their Poverty Reduction Strategy Papers (PRSPs), and to preserve macroeconomic stability within the context of their limited domestic resources. Even amid such difficulties, however, fiscal deficits have largely been kept in check. In 2003, six countries showed fiscal surpluses and 36 had fiscal deficits, the same as in 2002, of which 26 had large deficits equivalent to over 3% of GDP (see table 1.5).

Some countries' deficits fell in 2003 thanks to improved economic conditions and better fiscal policies. Tunisia saw a reduction in its deficit to less than 3% of GDP as a result of increasing tax revenue as the economy picked up. In Ghana, the deficit fell markedly as a result of improved budgetary management. Several of the countries with fiscal surpluses were oil producers that benefited from the high oil prices and increasing production levels of 2003. These included Algeria, Equatorial Guinea, Gabon and Libya.

Fiscal laxity remains a problem in some economies. In Egypt, the fiscal deficit rose to over 6% of GDP in 2003, driven by the high civil service wage bill, social spending and consumer subsidies. In Nigeria, the deficit remained at nearly 6% of GDP, because of upward

Figure 1.16

African stock market capitalization, 1990 and 2002 (% of GDP)

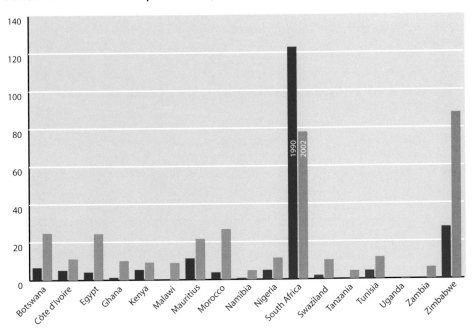

Source: ECA, from official sources

Figure 1.17

African stock markets, values traded, 1990 and 2001 (% of GDP)

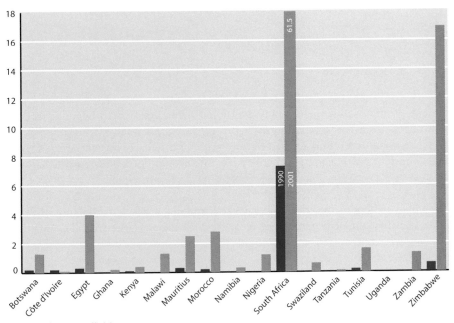

Source: ECA, from official sources

pressure on state expenditure. In Southern Africa, all countries showed deficits, with nine out of 11 countries having deficits of over 3% of GDP and six countries showing rising deficits over the year. Of these countries, Malawi recorded a deficit of more than 7% of GDP in 2003, reflecting poor expenditure management. Angola suffered problems tracking and managing its public expenditure and recorded a deficit of nearly 9% of GDP in 2003.

Inflation and exchange rates largely stable in 2003

Inflation remained largely unchanged in 2003 with the regional rate rising slightly to 10.6% from 9.3% in 2002, reflecting lax fiscal policy in some countries and low agriculture production in others. The number of countries with single-digit inflation rose from 33 to 38 (see table 1.6). Some countries in East Africa switched from deflation to price growth mainly as a result of poor agriculture performance. These included Ethiopia, which saw inflation of 14.6% up from a 7.2% decline the previous year because of the effects of the poor harvest in 2002, which pushed up grain prices. Faster price growth was also seen in Kenya and Uganda as a result of higher food prices. Burundi registered inflation of 11% in 2003 compared to deflation of 1.3% in 2002. In West Africa, Sierra Leone also returned to price growth after falling prices in 2002.

Table 1.5

Distribution of fiscal deficits in Africa, 2002 and 2003 (number of countries)

	2002	2003
Deficit countries	36	36
Deficit < 3% of GDP	9	10
Deficit > 3% of GDP	27	26
Surplus countries	6	6
Total countries	42	42

Source: ECA, from official sources

In Zimbabwe, macroeconomic stability continues to deteriorate with inflation rising to 420% in 2003 from 140% in 2002, the result of shortages caused by the country's ongoing political and economic crisis. High inflation also remains of concern in Eritrea, Ghana, Mozambique, Nigeria and Zambia. In Angola, although price growth has been reduced, the inflation rate remained very high, at over 90% in 2003.

On the other hand, some countries made gains in restraining prices. In particular, DRC, now emerging from a long and disruptive war, achieved single-digit inflation in 2003, remarkable progress considering that inflation was above 500% as recently as 2000. In the CFA zone, despite political instability in Côte d'Ivoire, inflation has remained manageable, partly the result of a sound monetary policy because of the the currency's link with the euro. Twelve out of 14 countries registered inflation of under 4% in 2003 (see figure 1.18). Only Equatorial Guinea showed a significantly higher level of inflation than the average, 10% in 2003, as a result of growing demand arising from the oil boom.

Figure 1.18

Inflation in CFA countries, 2002 and 2003 (%, year on year)

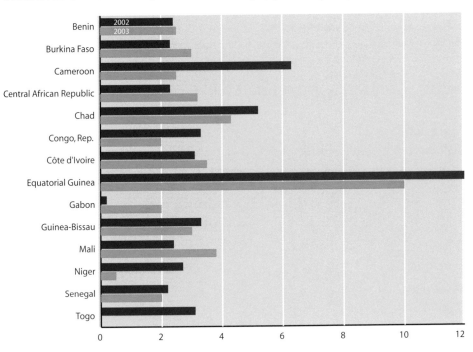

Source: *ECA, from official sources*

In North Africa, inflation remained modest, with four out of the seven countries registering inflation of under 3% in 2003. In Egypt, however, upward price pressures are increasing following the depreciation of the Egyptian pound. Libya returned to price growth of 1.8% in 2003 following deflation the previous year, as the result of its currency devaluation. In Morocco, despite higher GDP growth in 2003, inflation fell to 0.9% from 2.8% in 2002, because of the effects of improved agricultural performance on food prices.

Fifteen countries saw appreciations of their currencies against the US dollar over 2003, with 21 weakening and one country showing no change. Ten countries had very high levels of exchange rate volatility, up from six the previous year. The currencies of Angola, Gambia, Malawi and Zimbabwe showed sharp depreciations against the dollar. The Egyptian pound also continued its depreciation over 2003 following floatation of the currency in January (see figure 1.19). However, the authorities have continued to intervene to stem the decline and the black market remains active. The Libyan Government unified the exchange rate in June, leading to devaluation of the currency. The South African rand appreciated against the weak dollar in 2003, as a result of relatively high domestic interest rates. The CFA franc also continued to appreciate over 2003 because of its linkage to the euro.

Current account developments were mixed, but helped by remittances

The regional current account deficit fell from 1.6% of GDP in 2002 to 0.7% of GDP in 2003, driven partly by the effect of robust oil prices in the oil-producing economies. Of the 44 African countries for which data are available, ten had current account surpluses while 34 registered deficits in 2003. Of the deficit countries, 21 had deficits of over 5% of GDP, down from 23 in 2002 (see table 1.7 and fig. 1.20).

Table 1.6

Distribution of inflation rates, 2000-2003 (number of countries)

Rate	2000	2001	2002	2003
<0	6	4	5	1
0-4.9	19	24	25	23
5-9.9	14	14	8	15
10.0-19.9	5	3	9	9
20.0-50.0	4	3	2	1
>50.0	3	3	2	2

Source: *ECA, from official sources*

Of the surplus countries, six showed reductions in the size of their surpluses. In Mauritius and Namibia this was due to higher imports as these economies picked up. In Côte d'Ivoire the smaller surplus resulted from the fall in world cocoa prices; Morocco saw a reduction in its surplus as a result of depressed exports. The surpluses of Algeria and Libya rose as their external accounts benefited from high domestic oil production and robust international oil prices.

Of the deficit countries, 13 registered increases in the size of their deficit or a shift from surplus to deficit. Higher deficits were driven by a variety of external and internal factors. The Central African Republic, Mali and Niger all saw increased deficits partly caused by trade disruptions as a result of conflict, in the latter two cases flowing from the ongoing instability in Côte d'Ivoire. South Africa's current account balance slipped into a small deficit in 2003 because of depressed export markets and the strong rand.

Countries showing decreases in their current account deficits were mainly represented by oil-producing countries that benefited from higher international oil prices and robust production levels. These were Angola, Congo, Equatorial Guinea, Gabon and Sudan. Burkina Faso's and Togo's external positions were helped by higher cotton prices over 2003. Swaziland reduced its current account deficit thanks to higher international sugar prices and increased production volumes.

Remittance inflows are a major source of external finance for African countries and they have helped to moderate some countries' current account deficits. They became more significant as ODA flows declined over the 1990s. Between 1970 and 2001, remittances into Africa showed less volatility than net FDI flows and were considerably more stable

Figure 1.19

Exchange rate trends for major currencies, 1993-2003 (CFA franc, South African rand and Egyptian pound)

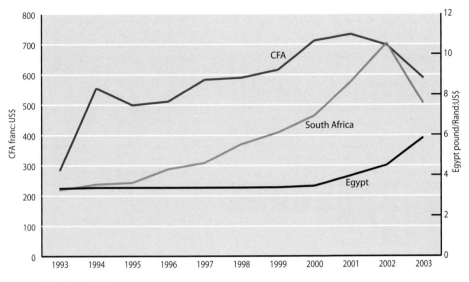

Source: *ECA, from official sources*

than net ODA (see figure 1.21). Remittances to low-income countries tend to be higher as a percentage of GDP and imports than to middle-income countries. The countries with the highest volumes of remittances on the continent in 2001 were the middle-income countries of Morocco and Egypt, which received $3.3 billion and $2.9 billion respectively. But as a percentage of GDP, the top country was low-income Lesotho, followed by Cape Verde; they received inflows equivalent to 26.5% and 13.6% of GDP respectively. Next were Morocco and Uganda whose inflows amounted to 9.7% and 8.5% of GDP. Remittances can usefully contribute to development of the economy when they are invested for productive purposes, as has been the case in Egypt.

Table 1.7

Distribution of current account positions in Africa, 2002 and 2003 (number of countries)

	2002	2003
Deficit countries	32	34
Deficit < 5% of GDP	9	13
Deficit > 5% of GDP	23	21
Surplus countries	11	10
Total countries	43	44

Source: *ECA, from official sources*

Figure 1.20

Current account positions of Africa's ten largest surplus and deficit countries, 2003 (% of GDP)

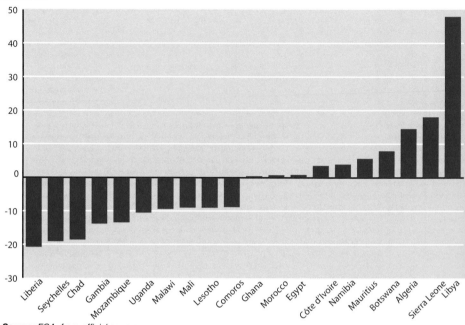

Source: *ECA, from official sources*

Broadly positive medium-term outlook

Real GDP growth in Africa is expected to increase to 4.4% in 2004, up from 3.8% in 2003, driven by increased agricultural output as weather conditions improve, and a rise in metals and minerals prices because of higher demand generated by global economic recovery. Although the prices of most agricultural commodities are expected to decline in 2004, export values will be supported by global recovery and rising exports to Europe because of the appreciation of the euro. FDI inflows to Africa are expected to rise in 2004, although they will be overwhelmingly concentrated in South Africa and in oil-producing countries. Efforts to improve debt relief mechanisms and to quicken the delivery of HIPC financial commitments by donors should also support growth.

Thirty-five African countries are expected to grow faster in 2004. Twenty-one are forecast to expand by at least 5% compared to only 18 in 2003. However, only Angola, Burkina Faso, Chad, DRC, Equatorial Guinea, Liberia and Mozambique are expected to see 7% or higher growth. As new oil producers, Chad and Equatorial Guinea will benefit from expected increases in oil prices and output, while growth in Angola will be pushed along by substantial investment to expand oil production capacity. The Democratic Republic of Congo is expected to grow fast thanks to aid inflows and a strong commitment to policy reforms. The end of the political crisis in Liberia will

Figure 1.21

Flows of remittances, FDI and ODA to Africa, 1970-2001 ($US billions)

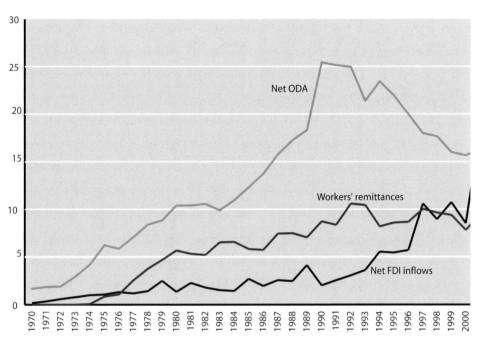

Source: *ECA, from official sources*

allow donor-supported rehabilitation projects, which will contribute to high growth. Mozambique will continue to benefit from sound economic reforms in addition to substantial investments by South Africa in infrastructure and industrial sectors.

Economic growth is projected to increase in all subregions except North Africa. In North Africa growth is expected to fall from 4.8% in 2003, to 4.1% in 2004. This will result from a decline in private consumption in Egypt in response to high inflation following depreciation of the Egyptian pound, an anticipated fall in agricultural output in Morocco, and a slowdown in government consumption in Libya. The three countries in the subregion that are expected to fare the best are Sudan (projected to grow at 6.4%), Tunisia (5.7%), and Mauritania (projected to grow at 5.6%).

Central Africa's growth is expected to increase from 4% in 2003 to 9% in 2004, mainly the result of high oil-driven growth in Chad (58%) and Equatorial Guinea (23%). Growth in Cameroon, the subregion's largest economy, is expected to slow because of a decline in industrial production and a shortage of electricity.

Economic growth will increase in all countries of West Africa except Burkina Faso, Nigeria and Senegal. Overall, growth will be 4.5% in 2004. Of the 15 countries in the subregion, nine are expected to grow by 5% or more; eight of these are least developed countries. Thirteen countries are expected to register growth of at least 3.7%.

The exceptions are Cote d'Ivoire, which has been hit by the effects of political turmoil, and Guinea-Bissau whose performance is hampered by economic mismanagement; these will grow by under 3%. Ghana, the third largest economy in the subregion, is projected to grow by 5%, helped by strong gold prices.

East Africa, the most agricultural-dependent subregion in the continent, should see faster growth of 5.2% provided favourable weather conditions continue. Kenya, the subregion's biggest economy, will benefit from substantial aid inflows as the new government rebuilds relations with donors. As a result, the country is expected to post real GDP growth of 3% in 2004, the highest for the last five years. Ethiopia is likely to recover strongly from drought, while Uganda should benefit from continued economic reforms. The political situation in Rwanda and Burundi is expected to improve, helping to increase aid inflows. The DRC will show the fastest growth in the subregion at 7%, up from 5.5% in 2003, the highest rate of expansion in a decade.

Growth in South Africa, the largest economy in the continent, is expected to pick up from 2% in 2003 to 3.1% in 2004 because of the recovery in the global economy, the continued growth in tourism, and a rebound in domestic demand. Despite the projected increase in growth in Angola (8.9%), Mozambique (8%), Botswana (5.5%) and Mauritius (5.4%), Southern Africa is expected to lag behind the other subregions with real GDP growth of 3.6% in 2004, held back by contraction in Zimbabwe (-5.5%).

Africa's near-term prospects are promising in view of both internal and external factors. Internally, many countries are expected to benefit from continued progress in political and economic reforms, from better macroeconomic stability and from good weather conditions. Countries that move from conflict to peace may enjoy quick gains in terms of higher growth, aid and investment.

On the external front, global economic recovery ensures strong demand for African exports especially metals and minerals. Fast-growing developing countries, particularly China, will boost demand for African exports of oil, metals, minerals and some commodities. Though oil exporters in the region will benefit from the anticipated increase in oil prices this will push up the import bill for other countries. The region will gain from the preferential market-access provisions of AGOA and Europe's "Everything but Arms" initiative. Although skewed towards oil-producing countries, FDI inflows should continue to rise. ODA and debt relief are also likely to increase.

Nonetheless, downside risks remain. Any halt to global recovery caused by a sharp decline in the US dollar and a consequent contraction in US demand, would hurt Africa's prospects. The protectionist sentiment building up in the US and other developed countries could dampen recovery in Africa given its dependence on agriculture. If political turmoil in Zimbabwe and Côte d'Ivoire persist, the resulting contagion effects could hit their respective subregions.

References

Badiane, O., Ghura, D., Goreux, L. and Masson, P. (2002), "Cotton Strategies in West and Central Africa," World Bank Policy Research working paper no 2867, World Bank, Washington DC

Development Assistance Committee (DAC) (2003), Development Cooperation Report, DAC, OECD, Paris

Economic Commission for Africa (ECA) (2003), "Financing Debt Relief and Genuine Development: Time to Get Serious?" issue paper presented at Expert Group Meeting on External Debt, Dakar, 17-18 November 2003, Addis Ababa

Organization for Economic Co-operation and Development (OECD) (2003a), OECD Quarterly National Accounts, 15 December 2003, Paris

———— (2003b), International Development Statistics, CD ROM, Paris

Oxfam (2003), "Cultivating Poverty: the impact of US cotton subsidies on Africa," briefing paper, Oxfam, Oxford

Simon, David (2003), "Official Development Assistance and the Millenium Development Goals," draft baseline report prepared for the Millennium Project Secretariat and the Task Force on Poverty, 29 October 2003

United Nations (UN) (2004), World Economic Situation and Prospects, Department of Economics and Social Affairs, January 2004, New York

Trade Liberalization—Panacea or Mirage?

In the search for broad-based human development in Africa, is trade liberalization likely to bring real long-term benefits? Considering how meagre the benefits from Africa's trade reforms have been up to now, what is the correct trade policy for African countries? These are the questions at the heart of this chapter, which looks at three areas of central concern to African policy makers: (a) the reasons for Africa's continuing marginalization in world trade, by contrast with the success of some Asian economies; (b) the potential impact of multilateral trade liberalization on Africa's agricultural sector; and (c) the effects of trade reform on the reduction of poverty and income inequalities in Africa. The chapter concludes that liberalization in itself is not a miracle cure and that trade must be liberalized cautiously. Trade has rescued millions from deprivation and poverty, but successful development requires more than the pursuit of free trade alone.

Africa has not yet achieved much from trade liberalization – very little in terms of economic growth and certainly no better integration into the global economy. The continent has simply not been growing fast enough for long enough to break out of poverty and, to make matters worse, it has become increasingly marginalized in international trade. Africa's share of global exports saw a sharp fall from 4.1% to 1.6% between 1980 and 2000, and its share of imports fell from 3.2% to 1.3% over the same period. Even in raw materials, its share in world trade dropped from 8% in 1980 to 4.4% in 2000 (Submaramanian and Tamirisia, 2003).

The chapter compares the performance of African economies since the 1950s to that of the most successful economies of East and South East Asia. Whereas trade policies in Africa have tended to be static and applied with little reference to overall development objectives, those used in key East Asian countries have been both proactive and strategically focused, at different times employing new combinations of selective openness and restriction. A lesson that Africa can draw from the Asian experience is that trade strategy can seek to apply a well-sequenced and optimal combination of openness and control within the context of overall development strategies, while avoiding the kinds of protectionist policies of the 1960s and 1970s that seriously constrained competitiveness.

A major challenge to Africa's agricultural sector is posed by the continuation of developed country protectionism. Despite the commitments entered into during multilateral trade negotiations, rich countries continue to subsidize their agricultural sectors while African countries, under successive structural adjustment programmes (SAPs), have made large cuts in all forms of support to their farmers. Agreement has not yet been reached on the modalities of trade liberalization in agriculture, but there are growing indications of

> *A major challenge to Africa's agricultural sector is posed by the continuation of developed country protectionism*

the need for much more substantial cutting of tariffs by developed countries and of the potential benefits that would accrue to developing countries, especially if their own trade liberalization measures were complemented by investment-enhancing policies.

An overriding issue is the need for African countries' trade policies to be harmonized with their national development policies. Although the evidence concerning the effects of trade liberalization on poverty and inequality tends to be ambiguous, we attempt to identify some broad policy issues that policy makers should consider when drawing up trade liberalization packages. It is noted that trade reform may need to be accompanied by asset redistribution, new skills formation and other kinds of deliberate intervention designed to mitigate income inequalities. In addition, macroeconomic stability helps ensure the effectiveness of trade liberalization itself and maintains the impact of various poverty-reducing initiatives.

> *African countries' trade policies need to be harmonized with their national development policies*

Trade liberalization packages and Asia's success

When growth in Africa faltered in the 1980s and the continent became increasingly marginalized in the world economy, countries of East Asia and South East Asia were achieving record growth rates and becoming more integrated into global markets, many of them as dynamic exporters of technology-intensive products. Africa has not been as successful as East and South East Asia in growth performance, agricultural and industrial development and in the assimilation of new technology, four areas of comparison that we examine in more detail below. In spite of the Asian economic crises of the late 1990s, there are still important best practices applicable to Africa from the Asian development experience, especially on the complementary role of trade and industrial policies in the construction of competitive national economies.

Growth performance

Many East and South East Asian economies sustained high growth and investment rates over long periods, linked to large productivity gains. By contrast, African economies have failed to maintain high growth and investment rates. Between 1965 and 1990, Hong Kong, Indonesia, Japan, Malaysia, Singapore, South Korea, Taiwan and Thailand had the world's highest growth rates (World Bank, 1993). Even when the world economy was in deep recession in the 1980s the Asian countries continued their rapid expansion: between 1979 and 1992 annual growth was 8.1% in South Korea, 7.6% in Taiwan, 7.5% in Thailand, 7.3% in Singapore, 6.7% in Hong Kong and 6.6% in Malaysia. In Africa, although growth was strong in the 1970s, fell sharply in the early 1980s and fluctuated before improving towards the late 1980s, only to plunge again in the early 1990s (see figure 2.1).

Strong growth was underpinned by high investment rates in most of the Asian countries: the annual average was more than 20% of GDP between 1960 and 1990 (Page, 1994; see figure 2.2). This went hand in hand with a large push in education and research. Even when African investment rates were high in the 1970s, they never equalled those of the Asian countries. In the 1980s, overall growth and investment in Africa fell sharply as public investment declined.

Figure 2.1

Africa and South East/East Asian economies: comparative growth performance (real annual GDP growth)

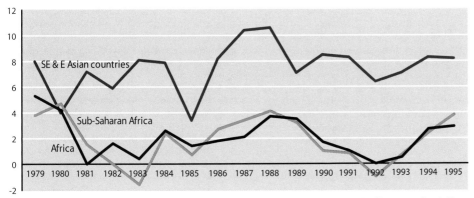

Note: *The countries referred to here as "South East & East Asia" are: Hong Kong, Malaysia, Singapore, South Korea and Thailand*

Source: *ECA, from official sources*

Figure 2.2

Africa and South Eastern/East Asian economies: gross fixed capital formation (% of GDP)

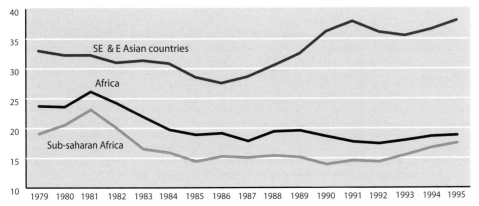

Note: *The countries referred to here as "South East & East Asia" are: Hong Kong, Malaysia, Singapore, South Korea and Thailand*

Source: *ECA, from official sources*

Agricultural modernization

Agricultural modernization played a critical role in the development of several Asian countries. Following the Second World War, Japan, South Korea and Taiwan implemented radical agrarian reforms, which led to strong growth in agricultural production. In South Korea, agricultural value – added grew by 10.3% annually between 1968 and 1979, higher than Brazil, Argentina and the United States (Kim, Hajiwara and Watanabe, 1984). Agricultural yields also increased during this period. This enabled a large part of the rural population to work in industry, and there was a steep fall in agricultural employment as a proportion of overall employment. Growth in rural incomes generated demand for products from the emerging industrial sector.

In Africa, however, a long-running agricultural crisis contributed to the development malaise of many countries. Various modernization strategies, based initially on heavy state intervention and subsequently on free market policies, failed to boost African agriculture. Archaic agrarian structures led to heavy external food dependency in many countries. In turn, low agricultural incomes constrained the success of the import-substitution strategies that most African countries adopted in the 1960s and 1970s. High levels of poverty among the rural population generated waves of migration to urban areas despite already high unemployment in cities.

> *Industrial development and local mastery of new technologies played a major part in the growth of the most successful Asian economies*

Industrial expansion

Industrial development played a major part in the growth of the most successful Asian economies. Between 1950 and 1990, manufacturing sector employment increased from 7% to 26.9% in South Korea, from 12% to 32% in Taiwan, from 15.4% to 24.1% in Japan and from 19% to 29.5% in Singapore (World Bank, 1993). Growth in industrial output brought about a rapid transformation in the composition of exports, with a shift towards manufactured products. Between 1967 and 1993, the proportion of industrial exports in total exports rose from 3.7% to 50.5% in Indonesia, from 12.6% to 65.5% in Thailand, from 21% to 78% in Singapore, from 24.9% to 68.4% in Malaysia, from 67.3% to 93.7% in South Korea and from 93.4% to 96.8% in Japan (UNCTAD, 1996). In Africa, industrial development faced considerable problems. Although industrial growth was strong in the 1970s, the economic crisis of the 1980s stymied this progress; industrial development strategies failed to bring about the emergence of competitive industries.

New technology

African and Asian countries also differed in their approach to technology. African countries initially chose strategies based on turnkey technology transfers in order to reduce risks, but this led to greater external dependency particularly through technical-maintenance contracts. The Asian countries developed strategies based on local mastery of new technologies. In both Africa and Asia, access to new technology came through imports rather than local invention and innovation (Bhagwati, 1978). But in Asia this was accompanied by a considerable local effort towards learning, adaptation and imitation of the imported technologies (Amsden, 1990).

The role of the State

Early explanations of the Asian "miracle" focused on the apparent openness of the most successful Asian economies to external markets, by contrast with the import-substitution approach pursued in Africa. The root of Asia's success was thought to lie in state neutrality towards economic sectors, allowing existing comparative advantage to determine the composition of production and exports. State neutrality could take the form of equal exchange rates for exports and imports and equality between domestic and world market prices (Krueger, 1983).

Later it began to be recognized that many Asian States were not at all neutral in their promotion of individual sectors and did much to foster export competitiveness, using mechanisms such as the maintenance of export-friendly effective exchange rates and the granting of large subsidies to exporters (Johnson, 1984). Trade policies were therefore part and parcel of broader national development strategies.

In addition, it is recognized that today's most advanced economies used a range of industrial and trade policy tools during early stages of their development to support emerging industries. British industrial capacity was built up by early protection; external openness only came once the country had emerged in the mid-19th century as the world's most developed nation. It was only after the Second World War that the United States opened its economy after a century of restrictive trade policies. France, Germany and Japan also pursued industrial development in a highly controlled context, and were able to take advantage of high levels of protection to achieve strong growth rates (Clemens and Williamson, 2001; O'Rourke, 2000). Recent research has cast further doubt on studies claiming a clear link between openness and growth (see boxes 2.1 and 2.2).

World Bank research has shown how the Asian countries began import-substitution strategies, later shifting to export promotion, has shown in the late 1950s for Japan, in the late 1960s for the first generation and in the early 1980s for the second-generation industrializers (World Bank, 1993). Large investments in human resources and new technologies brought about significant gains in productivity. States also intervened to build economic competitiveness by maintaining low interest rates, protecting selected infant industries, providing export subsidies and credit and establishing export-support institutions.

This new thinking stressed the complementary roles being played by the State and by the market. Pervasive market failures made state intervention necessary and governments built a complex network of institutions to help market actors overcome problems of informational imperfection. This interlocking set of institutions included an organized and qualified civil service, organized forums for negotiation and dialogue between government and business circles, as well as sector institutions which supported the development of new industrial activities (Stiglitz, 1996). In South East Asia, the State organized competition and built institutions to support export activities. Governments strictly regulated financial institutions, channelling loans and subsidies into favoured sectors (Stiglitz and Uy, 1996). State control of markets has thus been critical to the success of these late-developing economies, particularly in bringing about the assimilation of new technology and techniques through imitation and adaptation by producers (Amsden, 1989). In addition, governments promoted education, infrastructure development, and satisfied basic needs such as health (Stiglitz, 1997).

> *Today's most advanced economies used a range of industrial and trade policy tools during early stages of their development to support emerging industries*

Box 2.1

Measuring economic openness

Assessing the openness of economies is difficult. Measures can be based on the extent of use of certain policy levers such as tariffs or be constructed from outcome variables such as the composition of trade flows. Some popular indicators are listed below:

"Policy" variables

- **Non-tariff barrier frequency:** Fraction of imports subject to non-tariff barriers

- **Average tariffs:** Average tariff rates (with import categories weighted by their share in total trade)

"Outcome" variables:

- **Structure adjusted trade intensity**: Deviation of trade share of GDP from its expected value based on structural characteristics

- **Leamer's openness index:** Ranking of deviation of trade volumes from values predicted by neoclassical trade theory

- **Price distortion:** Deviation of price levels from value expected by purchasing power parity, adjusted for income level

- **Leamer's trade distortion index:** Deviation of trade pattern from values predicted by theory

- **Dollar's real exchange rate distortion and variability indices:** The extent to which the real exchange rate deviates from its free trade level and the actual variability in the real exchange rate

- **Black market premium:** Currency black market premia

Each of these variables captures different features of a country's trade stance, although it has been argued that some of these may be driven by factors unconnected to the trade regime. In addition, statistical analysis has shown that these different indicators are uncorrelated, highlighting the difficulty of unambiguously capturing the nature of countries' trade regimes in indices.

Sources: *Pritchett, 1996; Rodriguez and Rodrik, 1999*

Trade policy needs to be aligned with development strategy

The East and South East Asian experience shows that trade policies cannot be pursued in isolation from broader development strategies (see box 2.3). Trade policies were integrated into the construction by the State of a dense and multi-layered network of institutions that spearheaded structural transformation and growth (Rodrik, 2002). State support of industry – including tariff and non-tariff barriers, export subsidies and credits and favourable exchange-rate policies – was not directed passively at all economic sectors but was highly selective (World Bank, 1993; Amsden, 1989). State support gradually shifted from final consumer goods sectors towards labour-intensive sectors and later into technology-intensive manufactures. In East Asia not all interventions were positive, while some were aimed at emulating a free trade regime. But in Africa most State interventions were applied haphazardly to economic sectors without any attempt at targeting or sequencing. This tended to generate speculative and rent-seeking behaviour rather than sustained structural transformation and growth.

Box 2.2

Openness and growth: new controversies

New growth theories have stressed the importance of human capital, learning processes, technical change and spill-overs rather than the factors concerned with increasing production alone. These theories have begun to influence thinking on international trade, and they raise questions about the ability of free trade alone to guarantee optimum resource allocation and promote high growth.

Increasing returns may lead to cumulative effects on growth and competitiveness, favouring those countries that can most quickly mobilize human capital, knowledge and the results of research and development. National policies on human capital formation and their support for certain export activities may be of critical importance in fostering international competitiveness. In addition, recent research by Rodrik and Rodriguez (1999) has cast doubt on influential earlier studies purporting to show a relationship between trade openness and growth. The studies critiqued are outlined below:

Dollar (1992): Dollar assesses the degree of openness of economies using indices of real exchange-rate distortion and exchange-rate variability. The first captures the extent of openness to intermediate goods resulting in real exchange rates favourable to exporters and the second captures uncertainties in investment decisions. Using cross-country regressions, Dollar finds that high levels of distortion and exchange-rate variability are correlated with low per capita income growth, a result that leads to the conclusion that openness has a positive effect on growth and development.

Rodrik and Rodriguez argue that Dollar's distortion index does not accurately capture the extent of trade restrictions: in many cases such distortions are the result of monetary or exchange rate policies. Finally, Dollar's regression results are not satisfactory under alternative specifications.

Sachs and Warner (1995): This study measures openness using an index constructed from average tariff levels, non-tariff barriers, the nature of the economic system, the existence of a state monopoly over key exports and the presence of a black market in foreign currency. This openness index is found to be positively correlated with the per capita income growth rate.

Rodrik and Rodriguez find that just two components of the index drive the econometric results: these are the existence of a state monopoly over exports and the presence of a black market in foreign currency. Neither of these accurately captures trade restrictions. Black markets in foreign currencies are caused by various political and economic factors, not just by lack of external openness. Export monopolies were found only in the 29 African countries that had embarked upon SAPs between the late 1980s and early 1990s, and cannot therefore be generalized to conclude a relationship between openness and growth.

Other studies: Rodrik and Rodriquez also cast doubt on the findings of other studies. Edwards (1998) found a positive relationship between productivity growth and nine different

> *National policies on human capital formation may be of critical importance in fostering international competitiveness*

Box 2.2 *(continued)*

Openness and growth: new controversies

> *In Africa, the debt crisis of the early 1980s marked the failure of import-substitution strategies*

indicators of openness. Rodrik and Rodriguez argue that the indicators that drive the results raise methodological problems in terms of capturing the degree of trade restriction and therefore in showing a link between openness and growth. Similar criticisms relating to the use of openness indicators apply to the study by Ben-David (1993).

The relationship between trade openness and growth is therefore hard to prove. It is difficult to condense the various aspects of trade policy into single indicators. But in addition the strong linkage between trade policy and broader economic policies makes it difficult to isolate the impact of trade policy on growth. For policy purposes it is therefore more useful to focus on more concrete features of the complex linkages between trade policies and growth. For this, the comparative perspective used in this chapter is useful.

Source: ECA, from official sources

Box 2.3

Assessing economic openness: example from Mozambique

Mozambique liberalized its cashew sector and banned restrictions on exports of raw cashews in the early 1990s. In 1980, Mozambique had 14 processing factories and was the first African country to process cashews on a large scale. The ban on exporting raw cashews was lifted in 1991/92 and replaced with an export quota and export tax. The quota was subsequently removed, and the export tax on raw nuts came down from 60% in 1991/92 to 14% in 1998/99. Following these measures, farm-gate prices rose, raw cashew exports increased, and resources were pulled out of cashew processing. However, even under the most favourable assumptions, the magnitude of the benefits generated by these effects were quite small—both in economic terms and in relation to the amount of time and energy that Mozambique's Government spent on this issue over the years. The standard gains from the liberalization have to be set against the efficiency losses that have resulted from the idling of processing plants.

In theory, the workers employed in these plants should have found alternative sources of employment after a reasonable time, perhaps suffering some wage losses in the process. In reality, a large number seem to have remained unemployed. One account claims that 90% of the sector's 11,000 workers were unemployed in 2001. Even if one takes a fraction of this number, the loss in real output is roughly equivalent to the direct efficiency gains generated by the liberalization. Disappointing outcomes were also partly due to complications arising from imperfect market structures in the cashew sector. This means that increases in export prices are not passed on one-for-one to farmers. In other words, traders rather than the poor captured much of the benefits from the liberalization. Externally, the world market for raw cashews is significantly less competitive than that for processed cashews. In effect, India is the dominant buyer of raw cashews from Mozambique. Mozambique's transformation from an exporter of processed cashews to an exporter of raw cashews can be expected therefore to produce a terms-of-trade loss for the country, which limits any gains from liberalization.

Source: McMillan et al., 2002

In Africa, the debt crisis of the early 1980s marked the failure of import-substitution strategies (see box 2.4). A new consensus then emerged, emphasizing the role of trade liberalization in growth and development. Openness and export promotion would ensure greater efficiency of resource allocation and bring easier access to new technologies and capital goods. Under SAPs, African countries liberalized trade through the reduction of tariff and non-tariff barriers (although the latter remain a major constraint on intra-African trade). Currencies were devalued to help exporters. The aim was to boost exports and growth, fostering the integration of Africa into the global economy.

Box 2.4

Import substitution in Africa: poor outcomes

The import-substitution strategies adopted by developing countries from the 1950s onwards were meant to produce locally the consumer goods which had previously been imported from developed nations, so as to help bring about the diversification of economies. These strategies, which aimed to begin with the production of final goods and move gradually towards intermediate goods and capital goods, were accompanied by restrictive external trade policies and considerable protection for emerging industries. Complex systems of tariff and non-tariff protection, exchange control and import licensing were set up to defend local production. Protection was designed to help emerging industrialists move up the learning curve during a transitional period when the domestic price of production exceeded international prices.

Import substitution was at the heart of African development strategies during the 1960s and 1970s. African countries established industries to produce consumer goods, mostly intended for the new urban middle classes. Import-substitution strategies enabled African countries to begin modernizing production structures inherited from the colonial period and the results were seen in an average annual industrial growth rate during the 1970s of 5.5% (followed by a 2.5% contraction between 1980 and 1984 and 0.4% growth from 1984 to 1987). Manufacturing as a proportion of GDP increased rapidly and there was a rise in industrial employment and in its share of overall employment.

These strategies soon ran into problems (Bruton, 1998). The development of final goods production led to a rapid increase in imports of intermediate and capital goods, leading to worsening trade imbalances and balance-of-payments deficits. Small domestic markets did not generate sufficient demand for the products of emerging industries, preventing industries from taking advantage of economies of scale. Import substitution was biased towards elite urban consumers to maintain political support, focusing on consumer goods for the middle class.

The disappointing outcome of import-substitution strategies in Africa was seen most starkly in the poor productivity performance of the new enterprises. The purpose of protection was to help emerging firms close the gap in productivity with their developing country counterparts; enterprises were supposed to use the protection period to invest and learn so as to increase their productivity. But protection in Africa failed to make enterprises more competitive. Instead it generated rent-seeking behaviour by firms, as they took advantage of insulation from international competition. Import substitution delivered very poor results in terms of productivity improvement, structural transformation of the economy and export diversification.

Source: ECA, from official sources

> *The disappointing outcome of import-substitution strategies in Africa was seen most starkly in the poor productivity performance of new enterprises*

The results were disappointing. African growth recovered in the 1990s, with average annual rates of 4% in 1996, 2.9% in 1997 and 3.3% in 1998. There were increases in per capita income, but growth remained unstable and too low to significantly reduce poverty. The share of industry in GDP fell from 39% to 32% between 1980 and 1997. Productivity growth decreased from 3.8% in 1997 to 3.2% in 1998. Africa's share in world merchandise exports fell from 6.3% in 1980 to 2.5% in 2000 in value terms. Exports recorded a mere 1.1% average annual growth over the 1980-2000 period, compared to 5.9% in Latin America and 7.1% in Asia (UNCTAD, 2003).

About 70% of developing countries' exports are manufactures but Africa has hardly participated in the recent boom in manufactured exports. Seventeen of Africa's 20 most important non-fuel export items are primary commodities and resource-based semi-manufactures. The region's share of manufactured exports in total merchandise exports increased only by 10 percentage points in two decades—from 20% in 1980 to 30% in 2000. This figure includes South Africa: for Sub-Saharan Africa (SSA) excluding South Africa the share would be significantly lower. The value of manufactures grew at an average annual rate of 6.3% per annum in the 1980-2000 period. This is only about half the growth rates recorded by Latin America (11.5%) and Asia (13.6%) over the same period.

The share of Africa's manufactures in world manufactured exports remained unchanged at 0.8% over the two decades. Latin America's share of global manufactures exports rose from 1.9% in 1980 to 4.6% in 2000. Asia's performance was even more significant, with its share in global manufactures trade reaching 21.5% in 2000, up from only 7.1% in 1980 (UNCTAD, 2003).

Africa's opening up to external markets did not bring about a strong recovery in growth or integration into the international economy. In an environment marked by weak infrastructure in a number of African countries, trade liberalization efforts in themselves could not easily yield results. High transport costs, the inefficiency of logistical services to international trade and weaknesses in support services certainly affected the export performances of the African economies.

Planning for the longer term

The critical difference between the African and Asian experiences lies not so much in the extent to which these regions opened up, but in the extent to which policies and services supported and implemented a long-term strategic plan, correctly sequenced over time. Industrial development in East and South East Asia was driven by a combination of import substitution and export promotion. Most African countries have so far proved unable to develop their industrial export capacities. In many countries, the bulk of production and investment remains tied to import-substitution strategies that relate to the production of final consumer goods. In Asia, ever since the late 1960s export promotion has been designed to meet the dual purpose of importing capital goods (and new technologies) and of exporting goods to boost growth and maintain long-term equilibrium in the balance of payments, while in Africa, the majority of countries have remained focused solely on supplying their domestic markets. When these countries were forced to open up in the 1980s, the expected gains could not then be realized because of the weakness of their production capacity.

> *The critical difference between the African and Asian experiences lies in their capacity to formulate and implement effective long-term development strategies*

Effective trade policy is therefore not a simple, static choice between openness and control but a matter of correctly sequencing these over time. In Korea, the import substitution pursued in the 1960s took the form of a restrictive trade policy to defend domestic producers against imports. From the late 1960s, certain sectors were opened up (Amsden, 1989; Wade, 1990). The development of infant industries was helped along by restrictive trade policies that enabled them to build their competitive edge. At the same time, the country was wide open to the import of capital, intermediate and high-technology goods needed for the development of new industrial activities. Later on, trade liberalization was pursued for those products that had reached maturity. Openness then both generated export revenue and provided firms with the incentive to expand, so reducing speculative behaviour.

The ordering and sequencing of openness and control across different sectors over time will certainly pose great challenges for African governments, for reasons of both capacity and political economy. Given the negative outcomes of import substitution and the ambiguous results of liberalization, African countries now need to identify the correct mix of state and market actions and avoid the kinds of policies that may generate rent-seeking behaviour by firms.

> " *By restricting the use of trade policy instruments, WTO rules leave today's developing countries less room for manoeuvre than many of the East Asian countries had in the past* "

The challenge of multilateral liberalization

Trade policies can support growth and development. However, an important question is whether this potentially diverse set of tools can still be used within the context of the increasing liberalization of the world economy and, moreover, can be compatible with World Trade Organization (WTO) regulations. By restricting the use of trade policy instruments, WTO rules leave today's developing countries less room for manoeuvre than many of the East Asian countries had in the past. Together with lower customs duties, less progressive tariffs and the reduction of tariff peaks, the Uruguay Round negotiations brought about the transformation of non-tariff barriers into tariffs. The Uruguay Round also required countries to reduce export subsidies apart from those on agricultural products. The WTO, which arose out of the Uruguay Round, aimed to further reduce trade barriers.

Has the birth of the WTO heralded the end of national trade policies? Certainly not: despite the WTO rules' overarching aim of deepening trade liberalization, the rules are in fact flexible enough to allow individual countries to pursue national trade policies. The rules do allow differential treatment, especially for the least developed countries, exempting them from certain provisions and giving them longer transitional periods. For example, developing countries can raise duties when imports pose problems for their balance of payments position or threaten their local industries. These provisions were used by Mexico in 1995 when it raised customs duties on textiles and clothing from 20% to 35% in order to cope with a rapid increase in imports.

The rules also allow some support for export industries. Although certain kinds of subsidies are prohibited, they can be used to promote research activities and to support vulnerable regions or pre-competition product development (Amsden, 2003).

Effects of liberalizing agricultural trade

A critical area of concern for African countries is agricultural trade liberalization. This sector is the most vital component of African economies. It makes up the bulk of national income and provides livelihoods for 80-90% of the population. At the same time, about 20% of Africa's merchandise exports come from agriculture. Some countries receive well over half of their export revenues from the sector.

In terms of world trade, however, the agricultural sector has become the most distorted market of all. Agriculture and food would account for 64.8% of the total global welfare gains if all trade barriers were removed by 2005. But the distribution of these gains differ from country to country and also from region to region with the largest share going to developed countries (Anderson, 2003).

Agreements under the Uruguay Round of trade negotiations were intended to reduce the effect of distortion in the agricultural trade market. It is clear that the commitments made during the Uruguay Round were not enough. Envisaging the negative effects of distortions on agriculture, at the conclusion of the Uruguay Round Agreement, agriculture and the service sectors were the only mandated sectors for further trade liberalization negotiations. On this basis, since the year 2000, negotiations on the modalities of liberalization of trade in agriculture continued. Countries submitted their proposals as the Doha Declaration set a deadline of 31 March 2003 for producing formulae and numerical targets for countries' commitments.

Three proposals were put forward for further liberalization of trade in agriculture. These refer to cuts in tariffs, quotas and domestic support (see table 2.1).

> *Agriculture makes up the bulk of national income and provides livelihoods for 80-90% of the population*

Table 2.1

Proposals to reduce agricultural trade barriers

	Out of quota tariff[1] (% cut)	Export subsidy (% cut)	Domestic support (% cut)	Import quota (% cut)	Swiss coefficient[2]
European ("conservative")					
Developed countries	36	45	55	-	-
Developing countries	24	30	37	-	-
Swiss ("ambitious")					
All countries	-	100	100	-	25
Harbinson					
Developed countries	-	80	60	20	2
Developing countries	-	70	20	20	1

Notes:
1. "Out of quota tariff" refers to tariffs applying above the import quota under the Uruguay Round's two-tier tariffication system;
2. The Swiss cuts higher tariffs by a higher percentage, so tending towards harmonization. The "coefficient" refers to the maximum final tariff rate.
Source: ECA, from official sources

Although agreement has not been reached on the different proposals it is useful to identify the effect of each of them on Africa. Using the United Nations Conference on Trade and Development (UNCTAD)'s Agricultural Trade Policy Simulation Model (ATPSM) the impact of changes in the agricultural trade policy regime on welfare can be estimated (see Annex A2.1 for description of the main features of the model). Table 2.2 shows the net effect on welfare of each of the proposals at a global and African level. Figure 2.3 shows the results for Africa. This impact is the sum of changes in consumer surplus, producer surplus and government revenue as a result of changes in trade volumes and prices.

Under the European proposal, all subregions in Africa - apart from North Africa - suffer from welfare losses under liberalization. SSA as a whole loses some $280 million while North Africa gains $50 million. North Africa gains because of benefits to its consumers through cheaper meat, fruit, cotton and tobacco products, although producers and governments would lose. In other regions of SSA, consumers would be hurt by higher prices. Benefits to producers because of easier access to developed country markets would not be large enough to offset this. Developed countries would benefit from this proposal, leading to welfare gains for the world as a whole: gains to consumers as a result of reduced prices, and gains to government because of reduced provision of subsidies, outweighing the losses to producers flowing from less domestic support. For developing regions and SSA, however, the gains to producers, as a result of better market access from this kind of liberalization, would be insufficient to outweigh welfare losses as a result of higher consumer prices and lower government revenues.

Table 2.2

Annual net welfare change from liberalization ($US billions)

	European	Swiss	Harbinson
West Africa	-0.09	0.03	-0.20
Central Africa	-0.01	-0.02	-0.02
East Africa	-0.05	0.59	-0.08
Southern Africa	-0.12	0.07	-0.24
North Africa	0.05	-0.03	-0.16
Sub-Saharan Africa	-0.28	0.66	-0.55
Least Developed Countries	-0.26	0.86	-0.74
Developing Countries	-0.04	5.07	5.02
Developed Countries	11.63	18.77	15.99
World	11.32	24.7	20.28

Source: *ECA, from official sources*

Under the Swiss proposal, there would be overall welfare gains to all regions except North and Central Africa. SSA as a whole would accrue overall welfare gains of $660 million. Central Africa would lose through the negative impact on consumers of higher prices for dairy products, meat and fruits, although consumers would gain on vegetables. In SSA as a whole, consumers would gain through lower prices for vegetables, meat, tobacco, cotton and oilseeds. This outweighs government revenue and producer losses. North and Central Africa lose under this proposal as a result of subsidy cuts because these such regions are net importers of subsidized agricultural products from developed nations. North Africa loses because of falls in government revenue and losses to producers, which outweigh consumer gains. Declines in government revenues are driven by sharply reduced tariffs on tobacco and cotton, which are important sources of revenue in this region. Although SSA as a whole also sees losses in government revenue and producer welfare, the gains to consumers outweigh these.

In the Harbinson proposal, all of Africa's subregions suffer welfare losses. This overall loss is caused by reductions in government revenues, because of lower tariffs, and losses to consumers, because of higher agricultural prices. Globally there are welfare improvements driven by large gains in developed countries.

This analysis shows that the Swiss proposal brings the greatest benefits to Africa, particularly SSA. Developed countries also gain, with the largest share of the gains going to them. So, agricultural liberalization based on deeper cuts to higher tariffs will be more beneficial to Africa than linear tariff reduction formulae.

> *This analysis shows that the Swiss proposal brings the greatest benefits to Africa, particularly sub-Saharan Africa*

Figure 2.3

Impact of agricultural trade liberalization on welfare in Africa

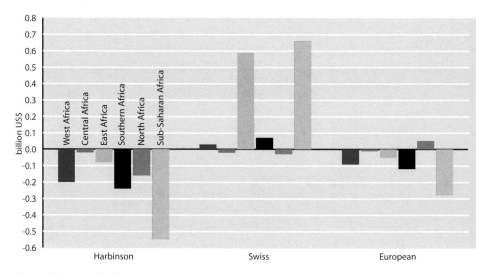

Source: *ECA, from official sources*

Africa has to diversify its exports — as an ECA study underlines

A forthcoming study by ECA, using a general equilibrium model, reveals the extent of the gains that might be realized by African countries if full liberalization of Organization for Economic Cooperation and Development (OECD) agriculture is to be achieved. Using the Global Trade Analysis Project (GTAP) model, which is a multisector and multiregion model widely used by trade analysts to examine the impact of trade policies, the study analyses three different trade reform scenarios, capturing different degrees of trade liberalization: "little", "modest" and "full"[1]. In the static version of the model, the study finds that full liberalization of trade would increase global welfare (income) by 0.3%, but would add 0.7% to income in the African region. But the absolute gains for SSA are quite modest – some $704 million – when compared, for example, with the $15.9 billion gains for the EU15[2]. The study also suggests that the gains from liberalization grow with the depth of reforms. While North Africa benefits from all liberalization scenarios, SSA incurs losses when partial liberalization is carried out. This is largely due to the impact of preference erosion, with many African countries being major beneficiaries of existing preferential trading arrangements. Partial market access (the "little" and "modest" scenarios) reforms would thus increase the degree of competition they face in export markets.

However, when the model is modified to allow for dynamic effects, the study finds that there is a substantial increase in the benefits of trade reforms to all regions of the world. For the SSA region, the welfare gains from full liberalization increase from $704 million in the static model to $4.3 billion in the dynamic model. That is, the gain to SSA in the dynamic model is about six times as large as in the static model. The huge welfare gain from the dynamic model is associated with the impact of capital accumulation. The results therefore emphasize the importance of complementing trade liberalization with investment enhancing policies.

There is a potential downside from further agricultural liberalization – the findings of the simulation exercise suggest that the reforms may force countries to specialize more in the production of agricultural commodities. In particular, they result in the contraction of industrial activities in the region and the shift of resources into the production of commodities such as grains, sugar and cotton. Although this change in the pattern of specialization is dictated by comparative advantage, there is cause for concern because excessive dependence on commodities increases the degree of vulnerability faced by the region. These findings drive home the urgency of adopting policies to promote export diversification out of primary commodities and into industrial and service industries with a higher value-added.

> *These findings drive home the urgency of adopting policies to promote export diversification out of primary commodities and into industrial and service industries with a higher value-added*

How trade liberalization affects human welfare

In considering the impact of trade liberalization on human well-being, it is vital to consider its effects on poverty and inequality. Some of the key questions are: What risks to vulnerable groups arise as a result of trade reforms? What are the transmission channels in the short and long term?

The linkages between trade policies, income distribution and poverty in Africa are growing areas of research. Although little is known about how trade liberalization affects income distribution and poverty, it is possible to draw some general preliminary policy lessons. Trade policies affect household welfare through the following mechanisms (Winters, 2000):

- Prices of consumption goods;
- Factor prices, income and employment;
- Government revenue;
- The incentives for investment and innovation, which affect long-run economic growth; and
- Short-run risk and adjustment costs.

The effects of trade policies on prices of consumption goods and factors of production are the most documented linkage: these channels have a direct bearing on the state of income growth, wealth creation and income distribution. Some studies, particularly those based on economy-wide models, address the fiscal impact of trade policies and analyse the effects on household welfare through changes in public expenditure patterns. The effects of trade policies on incentives for investment and on short-run adjustment costs are less well known because of limited data.

Poverty and inequality

Empirical evidence on the effects of trade policies on income distribution and poverty are mixed because of diverse country experiences and methodologies. Most approaches start from standard trade theory which says that trade liberalization will benefit a country's relatively abundant factor of production. In Africa, unskilled labour is a relatively abundant factor and trade liberalization should therefore reduce income inequality, but this is not borne out by the evidence. Many of the underlying assumptions of standard trade theory such as factor mobility and perfect competition are unlikely to hold in developing countries.

Other approaches suggest that countries abundant in natural resources such as land can experience a rise in income inequality following trade liberalization (e.g. Bourguignon and Morrison, 1990; Fischer, 2000). Countries that are abundant in land are relatively poor in capital and labour, and hence the return to their ownership is raised. Since both capital and labour are owned inequitably in Africa, inequality tends to rise (see figure 2.4). (A lower population density represents higher land abundance; for these countries, inequality is higher).

Cross-country evidence has shown that openness is positively correlated with income inequality (Spilimbergo et al. 1999; Fischer, 2000; Easterly, 2002; see figure 2.5) although other studies have found a weak or neutral effect (Dollar and Kraay, 2001). Political economy explanations have focused on the fact that resource-rich countries, which mainly depend on a few export products, tend to have institutions that favour the persistence of income inequality (Easterly, 2002).

Economy-wide models identify the effects of trade liberalization on household welfare, government revenues and inequality, through three main channels (Bourguignon et al., 1991):

- Changes in factor incomes following trade liberalization affect income distribution. This occurs through the labour market, where changes in the prices of tradable goods (exportables and importables) cause changes in labour demand;

> *Empirical evidence on the effects of trade policies on income distribution and poverty are mixed because of diverse country experiences and methodologies*

Figure 2.4

Endowment of land and income inequality

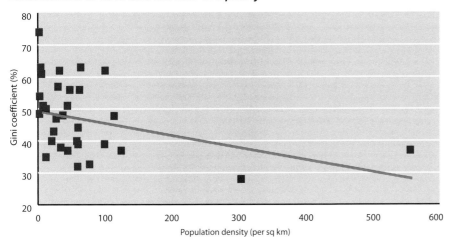

Source: *ECA, from official sources*

Note: *The Gini coefficient is a measure of inequality with values between 0 and 1; values closer to 1 indicate greater inequality*

Figure 2.5

Openness and income inequality in Africa in the 1990s

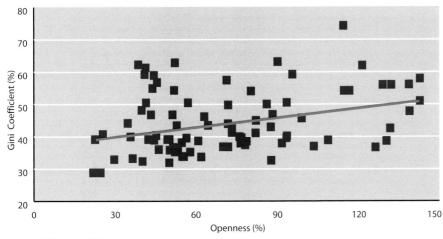

Source: *ECA, from official sources*

Note: *Openness is measured as the share of exports and imports in GDP*

- Changes in relative prices affect consumption expenditure. Depending on the pattern of consumption of households belonging to different groups, changes in the prices of tradables and non-tradables cause changes in welfare; and
- Changes to the return to capital affect the distribution of household wealth creation.

Box 2.5 illustrates the effects of some measures of trade liberalization on growth, household incomes and poverty for a fairly typical African economy, based on an economy-wide model. The analysis shows that tariff reform could be beneficial to the poor, while removal of export subsidies could increase the incidence of poverty. In both cases, GDP falls due to declines in all factor incomes. The reason that tariff reduction led to a decline in poverty is mainly explained through the possibility of achieving basic needs at a lower cost than before the reform.

> " *In some cases, trade liberalization could worsen income distribution by reducing the demand for unskilled labour* "

Box 2.5

Trade reform in a typical African economy

Using a stylized model of a small open African economy, the welfare effects of trade reforms across sectors can be simulated. Households can be divided into six types: rural, small landowner, large landowner, urban low-income, urban high-income and capitalist. Factors of production are skilled and unskilled labour, land and agricultural capital. The sectors in the economy are agriculture, producing traditional and export crops, services (private and public), industry and mining. The base-level income distribution is approximated on the basis of actual data sets and the poverty line is allowed to vary with relative prices and is determined by the model.

Variables	Percentage change following a reduction of the price of exports by 30%	Percentage change following a reduction of tariffs by 50%
GDP (factor cost)	-5.88	-1.56
Wage of unqualified labour	-6.56	-1.31
Wage of qualified labour	-3.83	-1.69
Small land/owner	-6.93	-1.46
Large land/owner	-6.91	-1.69
Mean household income	-4.1	-1.7
Headcount ratio	7.2	-3.4
Poverty gap	11.4	-13.2
Square poverty gap	13.8	-3.1

Both a 30% reduction in the price of exports (caused say by a removal of export subsidies), and a 50% reduction in tariffs on imports will have an effect of reducing GDP and household income. Rates of return to all factors of production also decline, leading to an increase in the incidence of poverty.

Although the tariff cuts lead to lower GDP, poverty falls. This is because of a fall in the domestic price for imports that compete with traditional agriculture and the industrial sector. With a reduction in import prices, agents substitute their consumption of domestic products for imported goods. This, in turn, favours a decline in the consumption price of locally-produced goods. Although exports increase, this will not be enough to absorb the overall decline in demand for domestically produced goods. As a result, factor prices fall and thus GDP declines. Poverty decreases mainly because of the adjustment of the poverty line to changes in relative prices.

Source: Declauwe et al., 1999

Country experiences as to the effect of trade liberalization on poverty vary considerably, depending on consumption patterns and economic structure. If resources cannot move quickly in response to new price conditions, tariff reductions may not stimulate exports enough to bring about reductions in poverty. If domestic firms cannot compete with producers of imported products, and the labour market is rigid, employment may fall and poverty increase in the short term. In some cases, trade liberalization could worsen income distribution by reducing the demand for unskilled labour.

A study of South Africa showed that trade liberalization has the potential to benefit poorer people. A complete removal of tariffs would boost the welfare of black South Africans who depend heavily on the export sector, but would cut that of white South Africans (Devarajan and Mensbrugghe, 2000). Similar analysis of Tanzania demonstrated that a 50% reduction in import duties would improve household welfare in a revenue-neutral setting for the government budget. Smallholder farmers would be the primary beneficiaries of export expansion. This may apply to other countries where the export sector is made up of poor and smallholder farm households. In economies where large-scale farmers dominate the export sector, and smallholders dominate the non-tradable sector, trade liberalization may not lead to such a reduction in poverty.

The welfare impacts of trade reform in Africa are complex, depending on the initial income distribution, the structure of the economy, levels of market integration and export diversification, as well as on a country's overall trade orientation. Trade reform has different welfare effects on different social groups. For some, the effect is transitory, while for others it could

> *A study of South Africa showed that trade liberalization has the potential to benefit poorer people*

Figure 2.6

Illustration of impact of trade reform on household welfare

Source: ECA, from official sources

be of a long-term nature. Trade reform can have effects on intra-household inequality and gender disparity. There may be changes in job opportunities and in the composition of workforces with the evolution of female-intensive or male-intensive employment groups.

The welfare of households can be evaluated in light of partial equilibrium analysis, which considers labour income, capital income, transfers and other exogenous income now affected by liberalization (see figure 2.6). In a small open economy, the price of traded goods is determined by the international market and by the tariff level. Tariff reductions affect wages in the traded goods sector and prices of non-traded goods, leading to changes in income and expenditure of the household.

The net effect on household welfare depends on the budget shares spent on traded versus non-traded goods by households, the extent to which prices of non-tradable goods respond to changes in the prices of tradables, and by the degree to which earnings are affected by a change in the price of tradable goods.

Detailed household survey data can be used to analyse the net impact of several types of trade reforms on overall income distribution. It is also possible to look at the "pro-poorness" of a trade policy using this approach. Tariff reductions on commodities consumed by the poor (such as food) can have substantial welfare gains and improve income distribution. Case (1998) found that in South Africa the consumption effect alone of trade reform could improve the welfare of both black and white households, with the effect for black households being larger.

In a typical agrarian economy, the removal of tariffs, export subsidies, or export taxes affects household welfare in more than one way since households are both producers and consumers (Winters, 2002). Gains on the consumption side could easily be offset by losses in production if the household is a net producer of non-tradables.

In most African countries, the market structure of agricultural exports is oligopolistic, principally dominated by middlemen with substantial power in the determination of prices. As a result, they are the primary beneficiaries of any increase in the price of exports. The pro-poorness of trade liberalization therefore also depends on market structure, and the role of poor farmers in price determination. In primary products, supply responses can be weak and price gains to producers small, and this suggests a small welfare gain to the poor.

Employment and wages

Some trade models predict the short-run and long-run effects of trade liberalization reforms (changes in import tariffs) on employment and wages for a small, open developing economy without wage rigidities. In the short run, employment in the exportable sector increases, while it declines in the importable sectors. The employment effects in the non-tradable sector are ambiguous (see tables 2.3 and 2.4). This situation also remains unchanged in the long run. Thus, the effect of trade liberalization on employment both in the short run and in the long run is the same in all sectors. But, the effect on wages is different. In the short run, wages tend to decline in all sectors and then rise in the long run. In the short run, in the exportable sector, the wage rate falls because of an increase in the supply of labour. Wages fall in the importable sector because of lower demand for its products. In the long run, wages in the exportable sector rise as labour demand increases in the sector. In the importable sector, wages also rise as labour shifts to the exportable sector. Wages in the non-tradable sector increase as labour shifts to other sectors.

Table 2.3

Short-run employment and wage adjustments following trade liberalization in traditional trade models

Sectors	Employment	Wages
Exportable	Increasing	Decreasing
Importable	Decreasing	Decreasing
Non-tradable	Ambiguous	Decreasing

Source: *Fosu, 2002, adapted from Edwards, 1988*

Table 2.4

Long-run employment and wage adjustments following trade liberalization in traditional trade models

Sectors	Employment	Wages
Exportable	Increasing	Increasing
Importable	Decreasing	Increasing
Non-tradable	Ambiguous	Increasing

Source: *Fosu, 2002, adapted from Edwards, 1988*

> *Positive welfare effects can be enhanced if liberalization is well timed and carried out under conditions of macroeconomic stability*

In Africa, under import liberalization, large numbers of enterprises have simply been unable to compete, and this has led to employment contraction. In Ghana, Malawi, Mali, Senegal and Tanzania, firms that adapted by upgrading workers' skills with training were net beneficiaries of import liberalization, while those that were less prepared faced stiff competition and eventually lost out. In Zambia, a reduction in protection led to a significant contraction of output; the laid-off workers are now working in the informal sector, where incomes are much lower.

The case of Tunisia's manufacturing industry shows the effects of import liberalization accompanied by access to external markets (mainly in Europe) on employment and wages. Tunisia's case illustrates the preparedness of industry to benefit from import liberalization as well as the ready market for its exports in Europe. It contrasts sharply with the case of Zambia, where there was no export sector that could absorb the employment that was lost in the importable sector. In the case of Mauritius, unskilled and female labour benefited from trade through increases in wages and employment, particularly in the export sector. In both Tunisia and Madagascar, investors have responded positively to changes in market conditions and incentives, in terms of change of product lines, introducing new machinery and seeking export markets (and availability of finance).

Trade liberalization may lead to a decrease in wage levels in the short run but these can increase in the long run, with the acquisition of experience and skills (i.e. the lowering of costs of production and subsequent increases in efficiency). Trade liberalization accompanied by adequate and appropriate responsiveness, as well as by supportive policies, can increase employment, which in turn can improve the welfare of society. Meanwhile, the effect that trade reforms may have on the informal sector should be of interest to policy makers, as this is a source of livelihood to a significant majority of self-employed people, especially women and the younger members of society.

In summary, some of the lessons from looking at the link between trade liberalization and human welfare are as follows:

- The effect of trade liberalization on household welfare and poverty varies across countries. Outcomes will depend on the consumption patterns of the poor, the state of domestic industries, the degree of labour mobility and the market structure of the tradable and non-tradable sectors.

- The welfare effects of trade liberalization depend on the state of income distribution. With income inequality already quite high in most African countries, the distributional consequences of trade reform are of critical importance. Trade liberalization needs complementary measures, such as asset redistribution, skills formation and other interventions to mitigate possible rises in income inequality.

- Positive welfare effects can be enhanced if liberalization is well timed and carried out under conditions of macroeconomic stability (Winters, 2002; Bhagwati and Srinivasan, 2002). Some components of trade liberalization packages can be inflationary and thus damaging to the interests of the poor, unless they are accompanied by appropriate macroeconomic policies.

- Integrating poverty diagnostics with trade policies can minimize adverse effects on the poor. Poverty mapping, which identifies where the poor live, how they are affected by agro-climatic conditions and their demographic characteristics, and earning attributes (wages, subsistence production, etc.) could assist in devising pro-poor trade policies. Poverty studies along sector lines could also identify winners and losers, and help to minimize adverse poverty effects (Kanbur, 1988).

Conclusions

This chapter has drawn attention to the role of trade policies in any country's development strategy. In order to contribute effectively to national development efforts, trade policies must be dynamic and thus avoid giving constant and linear support to the economy as a whole or to certain sectors above all others. On the contrary, they must be adaptable, and differentiated between sectors and between the various segments of a given sector. Consideration of this issue, therefore, must not be restricted to the sterile debate between openness and control.

> Trade liberalization may lead to a decrease in wage levels in the long run run, but these can increase with the acquisition of experience and skills

The key priority is to focus on: seeking the optimal combination of the different instruments of trade policy; and building the necessary institutions to support the economic development process, by improving the competitiveness of the economy as a whole. At the same time, African countries must avoid the kinds of damaging protectionism that have already hampered the integration of their economies into global markets.

While the recent reforms of the rules of international trade in the WTO framework have left the developing countries with less room for manoeuvre, they also offer them a degree of flexibility to use trade policy in their development efforts. It is this flexibility which the developing countries are seeking to strengthen in the context of international negotiations and the Doha Round. For Africa in particular, cuts in agricultural tariffs, particularly high tariffs, are critical to enhancing overall welfare.

Finally, trade policies must be framed with reference to impacts on vulnerable groups. These effects will depend on an economy's consumption patterns across groups as well as market structures and the functioning of labour markets. Trade liberalization may need to be accompanied by measures to mitigate possible negative distributional impacts. Adverse social effects of trade liberalization may be contained by macroeconomic stability. Finally, trade policies need to be more closely aligned to national approaches to poverty alleviation.

> *In order to contribute effectively to national development efforts, trade policies must be dynamic*

Annex

A2.1: Agricultural Trade Policy Simulation Model (ATPSM)

ATPSM was developed by UNCTAD in 1990 and significantly enhanced in the late 1990s to address issues arising from the outcome of the Uruguay Round. The principle of ATPSM is that trade policy modifications induce price changes that alter supply, demand, exports and imports. The model calculates a market clearing world price where the global sum of net import changes equals zero. It is a deterministic and static model covering 176 countries. It is also a partial equilibrium model, dealing only with the agricultural sector. These characteristics make it different from the Global Trade Analysis Project (GTAP) model, which is a general equilibrium model.

The model consists of a system of equations representing supply, demand and trade flows for different agricultural goods for each country in the model. One of ATPSM's main advantages is that it covers 36 agricultural commodity groups and detailed policy changes can be simulated so as to trace the welfare effects of different kinds of agricultural trade liberalization. The model can capture changes to agricultural tariffs, subsidies (domestic support and export subsidies) and quotas.

Unlike other models such as GTAP, which require information on elasticities to determine domestic demand, ATPSM estimates domestic consumption and production prices using composite tariffs.

Notes

[1] Policy changes envisaged in the "little" scenario are tariff reductions (agricultural goods by 36%, all other goods by 20%); reduction in export subsidies by 20%; reduction in domestic support by 20%; and trade facilitation by 1%. The "modest" scenario envisages tariff reduction of all goods by 50%; reduction of exports subsidies by 50%, and trade facilitation by 1.5%. The "full" scenario encompasses 100% reduction in tariff, export subsidies, and domestic support, and trade facilitation by 3%.

[2] The EU15 countries are Austria, Belgium, Denmark, Finland, France, Germany, Greece, Ireland, Italy, Luxembourg, the Netherlands, Portugal, Spain, Sweden and the United Kingdom.

References

Amsden, A. (1989), *Asia's Next Giant: South Korea and Late Industrialization*, Oxford University Press, Oxford

———— (1990), "Third World Industrialization: 'global fordism' or a new model?" *New Left Review*, no 182

———— (2003), "Industrialization under New WTO Law," in John Toye (ed), *Trade and Development: Directions for the 21st Century*, Edward Elgar, Cheltenham

Anderson, K. (2003), "Trade Liberalization, Agriculture and Poverty in Low-income Countries," *World Institute for Development Economics Research (WIDER) Discussion Paper* no 2003/25, Helsinki

Ben-David, D. (1993), "Equalizing Exchange: trade liberalization and income convergence," *Quarterly Journal of Economics*, 108 (3)

Bhagwati, J. (1978) "Foreign trade and economic development: anatomy and consequences of exchange control regimes," National Bureau of Economic Research (NBER), New York

Bhagwati, J. and Srinivasan, T.N. (2002), "Trade and Poverty in the Poor Countries," *American Economic Review*, papers and proceedings, May

Bourguignon, F. and Morrison, C. (1990), "Income Distribution, Development and Foreign Trade," *European Economic Review*, pp1113-32

Bourguignon, F., de Melo, J. and Suwa, A. (1991), "Distributional Effects of Adjustment Policies: simulations for two archetype economies," World Bank Trade Policy working paper, WPS 215, World Bank, Washington DC

Bruton, H. (1998), "A Reconsideration of Import Substitution," *Journal of Economic Literature*, 37 (2)

Case, A. (1998), "Income Distribution and Expenditure Patterns in South Africa," paper prepared for Conference on Poverty and the International Economy, Stockholm, October 20-21, 2000

Clemens, M. and Williamson, J. (2001), "A tariff growth paradox? Protection's impact around the world 1875-1997," working paper no 8459, September, National Bureau of Economic Research (NBER), New York

Declauwe, B., Patry, A., Savard, L. and Thorbecke, E., (1999), "Income Distribution, Poverty Measures and Trade Shocks: a computable general equilibrium model of an archetype developing country," working paper, pp 99-14, Department of Economics, University of Laval, Quebec

Devarajan, S. and Mensbrugghe, D. (2000), "Trade Reform in South Africa: impacts on households," paper prepared for Conference on Poverty and the International Economy, Stockholm, October 20-21, 2000

Dollar, D. (1992), "Outward-oriented Developing Economies Really Do Grow More Rapidly: evidence from 95 LDCs, 1976-1985," *Economic Development and Cultural Change*, 40 (3)

Dollar, D. and Kraay, A. (2001), "Trade, Growth and Poverty," mimeo, World Bank, Washington DC

Easterly, W. (2002), "Inequality Does Cause Underdevelopment," Center for Global Development, Institute of International Economics, Washington DC

Edwards, S. (1988), "Terms of Trade, Tariffs, and Labour Market Adjustment in Developing Countries," *World Bank Economic Review*, 2 (2)

———— (1998), "Openness, Productivity and Growth: what do we really know?" *Economic Journal*, 35 (1), March

Fischer, R.D. (2000), "The Evolution of Inequality after Trade Liberalization," mimeo, Faculty of Economic Sciences and Administration (CEA-DII), Universidad de Chile, Santiago

Fosu, A. (2002), "International Trade and Labour Market Adjustment in Developing Countries" in Greenaway, D., Upward, R. and Wakelin, K. (eds) *Trade, Investment, Migration and Labour Market Adjustment,* Palgrave Macmillan, London

Johnson, C. (1984), "The Industrial Policy Debate Re-examined," *California Management Review*, 27 (1)

Kanbur, R. (1988), "Structural Adjustment, Macroeconomic Adjustment and Poverty: a methodology for analysis," *World Development,* 15, pp1515-1526

Kim, C., Hajiwara, H., and Watanabe, T. (1984), "A Consideration on the Compressed Process of Agricultural Development in the Republic of Korea," *The Developing Economies*, June

Krueger, A. (1983), "Trade and Employment in Developing Countries: synthesis and conclusions," vol 3, National Bureau of Economic Research (NBER), New York

McMillan, M., Rodrik, D. and Welch, K. (2002), "When Economic Reform Goes Wrong cashews in Mozambique," Faculty Research working papers series, John F. Kennedy School of Government, Harvard University, Boston

O'Rourke, K. (2000), "Tariffs and Growth in the Late 19th Century," *Economic Journal*, 110

Page, J. (1994), "The East Asian Miracle: an introduction," *World Development*, 22 (4)

Pritchett, L. (1996), "Measuring Outward Orientation in LDCs: can it be done?" *Journal of Development Economics*, 49 (2)

Rodrik, D. (2002), "Trade Policy Reform as Institutional Reform," in Bernard Hoekman Aaditya Mattoo and Philip English (eds), *Development, Trade and the WTO: A Handbook*, World Bank, Washington DC

Rodriguez, D. and Rodrik, F. (1999), "Trade Policy and Economic Growth: a skeptic's guide to the cross national evidence," working paper 7081, National Bureau of Economic Research (NBER), New York

Sachs, J., and Warner, A. (1995), "Economic reform and the process of global integration," Brookings Papers on Economic Activity, 1, The Brookings Institution, Washington DC

Spilimbergo, A., Londono, L. and Skezely, M. (1999), "Income Distribution, Factor Endowments, and Trade Openness," *Journal of Development Economics*, 59, pp77-101

Stiglitz, J. (1996), "Some Lessons from the East Asian Miracle," *The World Bank Research Observer*, 11 (2), August

———— (1997), "The Role of Government in Development Economics," in M. Bruno and B. Pleskovic (eds), *Annual World Bank Conference on Development Economics 1996*, World Bank, Washington DC

Stiglitz, J. and Uy, M. (1996), "Financial Markets, Public Policy and the East Asian Miracle," *The World Bank Research Observer*, 11 (2), August

Submaramanian, A. and Tamirisia, N. (2003), "Is Africa Integrated in the Global Economy?," IMF Staff Papers, 50 (3), Washington DC

United Nations Conference on Trade and Development (UNCTAD) (1996), *Trade and Development Report 1996*, Geneva

———— (2003), *Economic Development in Africa: Trade Performance and Commodity Dependence*, Geneva

Wade, R. (1990), *Governing the Market: Economic Theory and the Role of Government in East Asian Industrialization*, Princeton University Press, Oxford

Winters, A. (2000), "Trade, Trade Policy & Poverty: what are the links?" paper prepared for the World Bank's *World Development Report 2000/01*

———— (2002), "Trade Policies for Poverty Alleviation," in Bernard Hoekman, Aaditya Matoo, and Philip English (eds), *Trade, Development and the WTO: A Handbook*, World Bank, Washington DC

World Bank (1993), The East Asian Miracle: Economic Growth and Public Policy, Oxford University Press, Oxford

Measuring Africa's Trade Competitiveness

Despite the uncertainties surrounding the future of the multilateral system of trade negotiations, it was concluded in the previous chapter that African nations still have the opportunity to develop trade policies that are both dynamic and adaptable to evolving circumstances. The chapter examined how countries' trade policies can have direct effects on the economic welfare of their populations, on government revenues and on the prevailing investment climate, and it argued that African countries should maintain a clear focus on enhancing their trade potential.

Chapter 3 considers the vital determinants of a country's trade competitiveness, which can be defined as its intrinsic ability to compete successfully in the global economy and to sustain improvements in real output and wealth. The Trade Competitiveness Index (TCI) presented here is intended as a tool for policy makers in Africa who seek to lay the foundations for future growth in their nations' trade. The TCI can be used not only for comparison of the competitiveness performances of countries but also to indicate some specific areas where new policy measures and/or institutional changes may be necessary.

The TCI is computed for a sample of 30 African countries. Because of the unavailability of data in several countries, 23 were excluded from the sampl. Those surveyed are highly representative, accounting for approximately 95% of African GDP, 82% of its population and 65% of its landmass. Of those excluded, only Angola and Tanzania contribute more than 1% to African GDP.

To provide an intercontinental comparison, the sample also includes eight non-African "comparator" countries: four from Asia (India, Indonesia, Malaysia, and Thailand) as well as four from Latin America (Argentina, Bolivia, Brazil, and Chile). These are all developing countries that had GDP per capita levels similar to African levels in the 1960s, but have since followed wide variations in their development paths.

The TCI consists of three components, each capturing a different dimension of trade competitiveness: a Trade-enabling Environment Index (TEI), a Productive Resource Index (PRI) and an Infrastructure Index (II) (see fig 3.1 and box 3.1). A total of 31 indicators are used to construct the three sub-indices. These three sub-indices receive equal weighting to constitute the overall TCI, which allows identification of the most competitive countries on the continent in terms of trade as well as identification of bottlenecks to improved trade performance. In summary, the results show that Mauritius, South Africa, Namibia, Tunisia and Gabon are the most competitive African countries, while the Democratic Republic of Congo, Mali, Nigeria, Burkina Faso and Sierra Leone are the least competitive.

> *The TCI can be used to indicate specific areas where new policy measures and/or institutional changes may be necessary*

A close look at the results of the TCI shows that the key drivers for competitiveness within Africa are the trade-enabling environment in general and institutional quality in particular. The top-scoring African countries in terms of the trade-enabling environment – which captures the macroeconomic and political environment as well as policies conducive to trade – are also the top-scoring countries in terms of overall trade competitiveness. These countries have managed to diversify the most and have the highest export shares of manufactured goods. Low scoring African countries tend to be hampered by a combination of political and institutional weaknesses.

The comparison with selected non-African countries reveals that, on a global scale, labour force competitiveness is one of the key determinants of overall trade competitiveness. Non-African countries dominate the TCI largely as a consequence of their better-educated and healthier labour forces. Among other things, this suggests that a greater integration into the world economy will require increased efforts in educating the African people, fully utilizing and retaining their expertise in the region, and improving their health.

Infrastructure is another vital factor. The poor condition of much vital infrastructure – despite the progress accomplished in the last decades – is a hindrance both to intra-African trade and to African trade with other regions of the world. Africa faces unusually high transaction costs, which are often related to infrastructure. This is a major source of both comparative and competitive disadvantage in manufactured exports, which are more "transactions-intensive" than primary products. Poor infrastructure tends to inhibit a country's efforts to achieve greater vertical diversification. It has long been apparent that African countries need to reduce their reliance on exports of raw materials to move up the value chain by producing manufactured goods or processed raw materials. If Africa is to follow a development path geared toward greater global integration, the critical steps include addressing inadequate infrastructure, including energy (a topic dealt with in Chapter 4) and enhancing trade facilitation (discussed in chapter 5). Any moves in this direction would help to ease the flow of goods and services across the continent.

Measuring trade competitiveness

Competitiveness is a dynamic concept related to the economic policies and institutions that countries use to facilitate their trade and growth. While firms, for obvious reasons, need an educated labour force to produce, their requirements also span dimensions relating to the institutions, economic policies and business environment prevailing in a country. These are aspects which do not flow into the concept of "comparative advantage", which is itself a static notion, relating primarily to the resource endowments of economies.

Competitiveness is relevant for policy makers as it is based on variables that they can act upon to create the conditions conducive to economic activities and prosperity. Environments that involve significant bureaucratic procedures will not allow for flexible production processes; corrupt institutions will extract rents from firms, increasing their costs and rendering them less competitive; and environments with a poor economic infrastructure deter productive investment.

The three TCI components are detailed below:

- a *Trade-enabling Environment Index (TEI),* reflecting the overall economic and political environment's conduciveness to trade;
- a *Productive Resource Index (PRI),* measuring the availability of direct inputs to production, such as land and labour – countries are compared in terms of the resources required to produce goods and services; and
- an *Infrastructure Index (II),* measuring the availability of indirect inputs that enable the movement of goods and services – transport networks, energy infrastructure and communication networks all help to determine the competitiveness of the economic infrastructure.

The three sub-indices capture these and other core components of trade, in comparing African economies. The components of each sub-index are presented in box 3.1. In addition, a composite index, comprising all three core components is used to measure overall trade competitiveness. (For more on hte medthodology see annex A3.1 and A3.2)

> *Competitiveness is relevant for policy makers as it is based on variables that they can act upon to create the conditions conducive to economic activities and prosperity*

Trade-enabling Environment Index

The TEI is twofold: the quality of institutions, and the overall macroeconomic environment and policies pertaining to trade.

Figure 3.1

Elements of the Trade Competitiveness Index

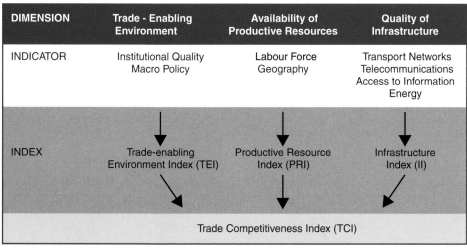

DIMENSION	Trade - Enabling Environment	Availability of Productive Resources	Quality of Infrastructure
INDICATOR	Institutional Quality Macro Policy	Labour Force Geography	Transport Networks Telecommunications Access to Information Energy
INDEX	Trade-enabling Environment Index (TEI)	Productive Resource Index (PRI)	Infrastructure Index (II)
		Trade Competitiveness Index (TCI)	

Source: *ECA, from official sources*

Several authors have shown the significance of institutions in explaining a country's trade performance (e.g. Gyimah-Brempong, 2003). Economies that have weak institutions (such as weak judicial systems or corrupt administrations) will find it difficult to attract capital required for production and export. In addition, countries with a complex bureaucracy and stringent licensing requirements may discourage investors from tapping available economic resources and potential. These issues are captured by the political indicators that flow into the TEI.

Another dimension is the macroeconomic environment prevailing in a country. It is widely accepted that adverse macroeconomic conditions are unconducive to trade in general and growth in particular (Savvides, 1995; Pourgerami and Djeto, 1989). Hence, the TEI captures, for example, whether the country has a stable exchange rate, whether it suffers from high inflation, how competitive its interest rates and real effective exchange rate are, and whether its trade policy is geared to export promotion with a rational tariff regime.

Productive Resource Index

PRI measures the availability of resources in a country to produce goods and services ultimately meant for export. The quality of the labour force and the geographical indicators of the country are generally referred to as human capital and land.[1] The index explicitly ignores wealth in non-renewable resources (minerals, oil etc.), which are considered to be high in Africa.

In today's increasingly global environment, African countries need to diversify their export base in general and decrease their reliance on unprocessed raw materials in particular. An intermediary step is to increase the proportion of semi-processed raw materials, but ultimately the goal should be to reduce vulnerability to volatile commodity prices by creating more value-added in their economies and thus produce and export manufactured goods. The PRI attempts to capture a country's potential to move up the "quality ladder" in terms of its products. Competitiveness is a dynamic concept, in which the relevant indicators consist of variables that ultimately can be changed by policy and/or economic decisions of agents in the economy. Thus, the inclusion of non-productive natural resources or minerals would distort the index by giving resource-rich countries, such as Botswana, the Democratic Republic of Congo or Nigeria, a higher competitiveness score. In fact, numerous authors have argued that non-renewable resource wealth in Africa may be harmful to growth (Asea and Lahiri, 1999; Sachs and Warner, 1999).

Infrastructure Index

II captures the physical investments necessary to carry out trade effectively. To be able to produce and export goods, a minimum physical infrastructure is needed. Reliable energy sources should be available and roads are needed to link production facilities with points of exit for goods. In addition, today's global environment has created the need for good communications. Producers need to be able to communicate quickly and effectively with their trade partners to maintain a country's competitiveness.

> Economies with weak institutions will find it difficult to attract capital required for production and export

In this regard, it is commonly accepted that for most of Africa unusually high transaction costs are a major source of comparative disadvantage in manufactured exports, which constitute a more "transactions-intensive" sector than primary production (Collier, 1997). The II assesses infrastructure bottlenecks and progress in infrastructure investment and policy reform to reduce these costs, which are vital for trade competitiveness. As such, it consists of four sub-indices, measuring respectively telecommunications, energy, transport and access to information infrastructures available in a country.

Box 3.1

Indicators used in the TCI sub-indices

TRADE-ENABLING ENVIRONMENT INDEX

Macroeconomic Environment Index

- Average tariff rate
- Real GDP per capita growth
- Inflation, consumer prices (annual %)
- Lending interest rate
- Real effective exchange rate (base 1995)
- Domestic credit to private sector (% of GDP)

Institutional Quality Index

- Corruption
- Rule of law
- Government stability
- Bureaucratic quality
- Democratic accountability

PRODUCTIVE RESOURCE INDEX

Labour Force Index

- Labour force (% total population)
- Illiteracy rate, adult total (% of people ages 15 and above)
- School enrolment, gross primary rate
- School enrolment, gross secondary rate
- School enrolment, gross tertiary rate
- Urban population (% of total)
- Life expectancy at birth, total (years)

Geography Index

- Landlocked
- Land use, arable land (% of land area)
- Actual renewable water resources (cubic kilometres per 1,000 workers)

INFRASTRUCTURE INDEX

Telecommunications Index

- Fixed line and mobile phone subscribers per 1,000 people
- Telephone mainlines per 1,000 people
- Telephone average cost of local call (★US per three minutes)

> *In today's increasingly global environment, African countries need to diversify their export base*

Box 3.1 *(continued)*

Indicators used in the TCI sub-indices

> *The five most competitive countries are Mauritius, South Africa, Namibia, Tunisia and Gabon*

Energy Index
- Electricity production (kWh per capita)
- Electricity consumption (kWh per capita)

Transport Networks Index
- Roads, total network (km per 1,000 people)
- Roads, paved (km per 1,000 people)

Access to Information Index
- Personal computers (per 1,000 people)
- Radios (per 1,000 people)
- Television sets (per 1,000 people)

Source: ECA, from official sources

Africa's overall competitiveness is improving

A country's overall trade competitiveness has to be assessed from its performance in all three indices, the TEI, PRI and II. Countries with a consistently poor performance in all three will perform poorly in terms of their overall trade competitiveness, while good performance in one index may, to some extent, counterbalance the negative impact of a low ranking in the other indices.

In terms of trends in Africa's overall trade competitiveness, a cluster analysis of the TCI's results shows that trade competitiveness has been improving in Africa over the last two decades, and half of the sample countries now lie in the moderate cluster (see table 3.1). The most highly competitive economies have been Mauritius and South Africa, and they were joined by Namibia and Tunisia in the 1990s. Mauritius and South Africa also hold the first two places for the TEI and the II, while Mauritius is the second most competitive African country in terms of the PRI, with the third most competitive labour force.

Currently, 11 of the 30 sample African countries are considered to exhibit low levels of competitiveness. While the number of moderately competitive countries fluctuated over the last two decades, it increased slightly over the 1997-2001 period. Compared to the situation at the beginning of the 1980s, all countries saw an increase in their competitiveness (see annex A3.3 for ranks across periods). However, Zimbabwe has witnessed a deterioration of its competitiveness score by 9% in the 1990s to exhibit a low level of trade competitiveness in the period, 1997-2001. Côte d'Ivoire also experienced a marginal decline in competitiveness in the 1990s (see box 3.2).[2]

Table 3.1

TCI clusters for 30 African countries, 1980-2001

Period	High cluster		Moderate cluster		Low cluster	
	Number of countries	GDP share (%)	Number of countries	GDP share (%)	Number of countries	GDP share (%)
1980-1984	0	0	2	39	28	57
1985-1989	2	39	4	5	24	53
1990-1994	2	33	11	39	17	21
1995-1999	4	37	15	42	11	14
1997-2001	4	37	15	42	11	14

Source: *Calculations by Economic Commission for Africa*

> *The least competitive countries are the Democratic Republic of Congo, Mali, Nigeria, Burkina Faso and Sierra Leone*

The five most competitive countries

The overall TCI for the period 1997-2001 is depicted in figure 3.2. The five most competitive countries, in terms of trade competitiveness, of the 30 sample African countries are Mauritius, South Africa, Namibia, Tunisia and Gabon. Mauritius has been one of the fastest growing countries on the continent over the last decades, has the most competitive trade-enabling environment and infrastructure, and is third in productive resource competitiveness. South Africa is the fifth most competitive country in the whole sample of 38 countries, both in terms of the TEI and II. Namibia is in third place, despite a moderate PRI score, because it is third in both the TEI and II. Tunisia's fourth place results from its high performance in all three dimensions of competitiveness – it is in the top five in the TEI and PRI and is sixth in the II. Gabon's first place in the PRI and moderate score in the II, confer it the fifth place in overall trade competitiveness in Africa.

The five least competitive countries

The least competitive of the sample countries are the Democratic Republic of Congo, Mali, Nigeria, Burkina Faso and Sierra Leone. Sierra Leone and the Democratic Republic of Congo are slowly recovering from years of violent conflicts and political instability. Sierra Leone has the third lowest score in the TEI, ranking only above the Democratic Republic of Congo in macroeconomic policy and outperforming only the Democratic Republic of Congo and Guinea-Bissau for institutional quality scores. Sierra Leone has also a weak performance in terms of the PRI because of low human resources competitiveness (the third lowest among the 30 African countries). While Mali and Burkina Faso are the least competitive in the PRI, as measured here, Burkina Faso performs better than Mali in terms of the II and the TEI. Nigeria's PRI score is low despite a moderate score for its labour force, while its TEI score is among the bottom five of all sample countries because of a combination of high inflation and low governance scores. Its II score is weak as a result of, *inter alia*, poor telecommunications and energy infrastructure relative to the size of its population.

Box 3.2

Institutional decline in Côte d'Ivoire and in Zimbabwe

Côte d'Ivoire and Zimbabwe were considered success stories or promising countries in the continent in the first decade following their independence. In fact, "Côte d'Ivoire, a booming country" was the magazine *Jeune Afrique's* description in 1967. However, the picture is different more than four decades after Côte d'Ivoire's independence and 24 years since that of Zimbabwe.

Institutional quality has eroded in **Côte d'Ivoire** since the beginning of the 1990s: corruption, bureaucratic quality, and democratic accountability scores fell. The poor institutional quality coupled with high tariff rates and economic recession over the period 1999-2001 has resulted in creating an uncompetitive trade-enabling environment. In 1999, real GDP growth slowed to 1.5% and the government finances dried up again, as a result of a fall of 18% in world cocoa prices, a 32% fall in world coffee prices and strained relations with external donors, notably the EU and the IMF. The social and political situation was volatile because of the controversy on the concept of nationality ("*Ivoirité*"), and deteriorated further in 2000, when all external assistance was frozen following a military coup. Real GDP growth turned negative. The year 2001 appeared to mark the beginning of the period of political normalization with the resumption of relations with donors, but the situation worsened following the September 2002 rebellion. Analyzing the factors that generated Côte d'Ivoire's celebrated development miracle of the 1960s and 1970s and that led to cycles of crisis and modest recovery throughout the last two decades, it emerges that the interplay between external shocks, ethnic diversity and weak conflict management institutions – proxied by the five indicators of institutional quality (see box 3.1) – are some of the root causes of the current crisis (Rodrik, 1998).

The nature, causes, and effects of this crisis in **Zimbabwe** are as varied as they are controversial. It is however clear that growing corruption and weak governance have undermined confidence in the economy. Corruption is rampant, with the lowest score in the sample. Democratic accountability has deteriorated compared to the early 1990s and is essentially non-existent. The bureaucratic quality rating is consistently low and the rule of law sharply declined in 2000 and 2001. Politically-motivated intimidation and violence have led to mutual suspicion between the independent media and the public media and between the media and civil society. The government's strategy for reversing the economic decline centres on the Millennium Economic Recovery Programme (MERP) introduced in 2000, but this has failed to turn the tide, in large part because of difficulties with policy implementation, policy inconsistencies, and racial integration.

Source: ECA, from official sources

How Africa compares with others

The most competitive African countries outperform some of the comparator countries, as figure 3.2 shows. Mauritius is more competitive in the TCI than seven comparator countries (Argentina, Bolivia, Brazil, India, Indonesia, Malaysia, and Thailand) because it has a high II ranking. It outperforms seven comparator countries in the II, five in the TEI and four in the PRI. However, the comparator countries are more competitive than 20 out of

30 African countries in the sample. They score higher in terms of productive resources, as their educational enrolment rates are significantly higher than those in Africa and their populations are healthier and live longer. In fact, their higher score in terms of productive resources gives them a competitive edge in terms of overall trade competitiveness.

Figure 3.2

Overall Trade Competitiveness Index (TCI), 1997-2001

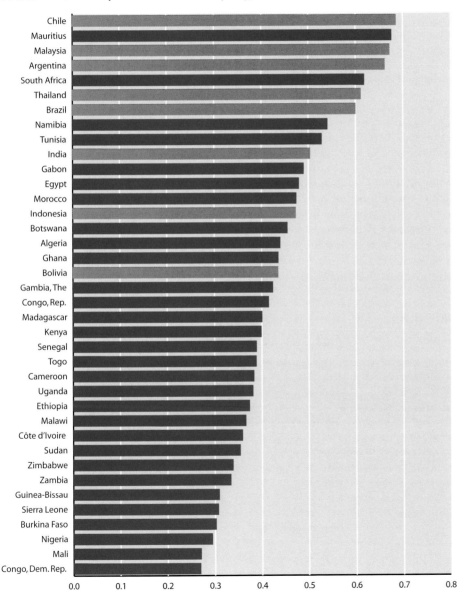

Note: *Blue represents African countries and black comparator Asia and Latin American countries.*

Source: *Calculations by ECA*

Improved macroeconomic stability and institutional quality are enabling trade in Africa

The two dimensions of the TEI are the macroeconomic environment and institutional quality. The Macroeconomic Environment Index, which includes average tariff rates, real GDP growth, inflation, interest rates, real effective exchange rates and domestic credit to private sector, assesses whether macroeconomic conditions are stable and trade policy sound. The Institutional Quality Index is measured by five political risk components: corruption, rule of law, government stability, bureaucratic quality, and democratic accountability (see box 3.1).

Table 3.2 shows that Africa's trade-enabling environment has improved over the last two decades. Approximately 82% of African GDP is produced in countries with moderate or high trade-enabling environments. Only Côte d'Ivoire and Zimbabwe have experienced significant deterioration of their TEI scores in the 1990s; by 10% and 6% respectively (see box 3.2).

Several significant changes in rankings have taken place over the last two decades. Between the second half of the 1980s and the end of the 1990s, eight countries improved their TEI ranking by more than five places. Ethiopia and the Gambia moved up from the low TEI cluster to become highly competitive; Mali, Malawi and Uganda rose from the low TEI cluster to become moderately competitive, Tunisia and Morocco moved up from the moderate TEI cluster to join the highly competitive cluster, and Egypt stayed in the moderate cluster but improved its ranking by six positions.

Table 3.2

TEI clusters for 30 African countries, 1980-2001

Period	High cluster		Moderate cluster		Low cluster	
	Number of countries	GDP share (%)	Number of countries	GDP share (%)	Number of countries	GDP share (%)
1980-1984	0	0	2	10	28	86
1985-1989	4	36	12	43	14	15
1990-1994	3	34	12	35	15	24
1995-1999	7	45	16	38	7	10
1997-2001	8	46	15	36	7	11

Source: *Calculations by ECA*

Africa's most trade-enabling countries

The most trade-enabling countries are Mauritius, South Africa, Namibia, Morocco and Tunisia (see figure 3.3). Good macroeconomic conditions, coupled with a very high institutional quality rating, have ranked Mauritius as the most competitive country in terms of creating an environment conducive to trade, despite relatively high real interest rates.

Similarly, South Africa has consistently had low average tariff rates, its domestic credit to the private sector (in terms of GDP) has been the highest in Africa over the last two decades, and its real effective exchange rate is competitive. Accordingly, this is mirrored in its TEI. While its growth rate has been relatively low, with real GDP per capita increasing by a mere 0.6% over 1997-2001, its real interest rates and inflation place it in the middle field. These factors increased the favourable setting for trade.[3] This combined with a high institutional quality rating has earned South Africa an extremely competitive TEI ranking.

Namibia has made enormous progress in improving the quality of its institutions in the 1990s. In fact, it has the highest institutional quality score with a perfect score in rule of law, and strong government stability and democratic accountability. However, it has also experienced setbacks in terms of bureaucratic quality and corruption, whose scores have deteriorated in the 1990s. Morocco and Tunisia alternate between the third and the seventh place for macroeconomic environment and institutional quality. The two countries' TEI rankings followed a similar evolution, with a big improvement at the end of the 1980s, driven by considerable progress in creating better quality institutions, which were further consolidated in the 1990s.

Good macroeconomic conditions, coupled with a very high institutional quality rating, have ranked Mauritius as the most competitive country in terms of creating an environment conducive to trade

Africa's least trade-enabling countries

The least trade-enabling countries, at the bottom of the TEI, are the Democratic Republic of Congo, Guinea-Bissau, Sierra Leone, Sudan and Nigeria (see figure 3.3). Nigeria is in this group because it ranks poorly in terms of institutional quality. This combined with moderate macroeconomic performances – high interest rates and low growth rates – has created an environment not particularly conducive to trade. Sudan, Sierra Leone, Guinea-Bissau, and the Democratic Republic of Congo are characterized by political instability and civil unrest in the recent past. These institutional constraints have compromised meaningful progress in creating a favourable environment for business and trade. In fact, these countries rank last in terms of institutional quality.

The prospects for countries looking to improve their trade-enabling environment improve greatly when political upheaval and civil war decrease, as the more recent progress of two formerly low TEI performers, Algeria and Uganda, indicates (see box 3.3).

Africa's comparators are not all doing well

Comparison with the eight comparator countries gives mixed results. Contrary to the case of the PRI, the TEI performance is not highly dominated by the comparator countries.

Box 3.3

The impact of crisis and recovery in Algeria and Uganda

> *The most trade-enabling countries are Mauritius, South Africa, Namibia, Morocco and Tunisia*

Whereas Uganda has experienced significantly improved TEI scores since the 1980s, Algeria witnessed a decline of its TEI in the late 1980s and early 1990s, followed by an improvement since the late 1990s.

Algeria's TEI score fell from 0.62 to 0.55 between the periods 1980-1984 and 1990-1994. It has fallen back several ranks in institutional quality and macro environment for which it ranked 16th and 23rd respectively in the period 1990-1994. This situation is undoubtedly a result of the severe political crisis that afflicted Algeria after the cancellation of the December 1991 parliamentary elections – preceded by violent rioting in 1985 and 1988. Indeed, the prospect of an Islamic party in control of Parliament pushed the secular and military elite to force President Benjedid to resign, suspend Parliament and halt the electoral process. Algeria plunged into a political crisis marked by extremely violent terrorist acts and political assassinations, which had devastating consequences on the economic environment. Signs of gradual and fragile recovery have appeared since the second half of the 1990s. As a result of recent progress in the macroeconomic environment, the rule of law and government stability, Algeria's TEI improved in the last period from 0.55 to 0.60, even though this does not translate into an improvement in ranking.

Uganda, on the other hand, was still bearing the legacy of Idi Amin's dictatorship at the beginning of the 1980s. Macroeconomic management was poor, inflation was in triple digits, and the economy was contracting at 5.2% a year by 1985, and real interest rates were negative. In addition, institutional quality indicators were extremely weak. Since then, the Ugandan economy has turned around with the end of its principal internal conflict in 1986 although conflict has remained a problem in northern and parts of eastern Uganda. Uganda managed to consistently increase its TEI ranking by 11 positions, from the third from last position at the beginning of the 1980s, to 17th in 2004. Although they are still low, the institutional quality indicators – especially the rule of law – and macroeconomic conditions have improved, leading to an increase in Uganda's ranking and a moderate TEI ranking. Prudent macroeconomic management coupled with reforms that have addressed supply constraints has kept inflation at single digit levels. Economic growth has remained above 5% a year. The Government has recognized that good governance and the rule of law are crucial in enhancing accountability and transparency in government operations, suppression of corruption, and in boosting private sector confidence. It has put in place a comprehensive framework to increase public oversight through increased transparency, education and awareness; to strengthen the enforcement of laws and penalties; and to strengthen existing anti-corruption institutions, through capacity building and the provision of additional budgetary resources. In spite of these efforts, implementation remains an issue, the future of some of the oversight institutions has become uncertain, and Uganda still ranks as one of the countries with the highest public corruption indicators.

Source: ECA, from official sources

Investigation of the components of the TEI reveals that some comparator countries do not perform particularly well in terms of macroeconomic environment, especially Brazil and Argentina, which rank respectively below 16 and 18 out of 30 African countries. This reflects the Latin American currency crises. Brazil's poor TEI performance, ranking 19th, is driven by low credit to the private sector, high lending rates resulting from the economic crisis witnessed at the end of the 1990s, and a weak institutional quality score (ranking 18th out of 38), especially high corruption, weak rule of law and low bureaucratic quality. While Indonesia's low score is essentially due to low institutional quality scores, for which it ranks below 18 out of 30 African countries, Argentina was able to compensate its low macroeconomic environment score with strong performance in institutional quality, especially the rule of law and democratic accountability and ranked 9th overall.

Figure 3.3

Trade-enabling Environment Index (TEI), 1997-2001

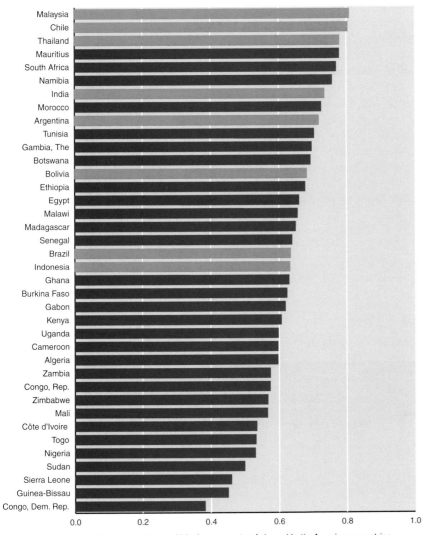

Note: *Blue represents African countries and black comparator Asia and Latin American countries.*

Source: *Calculations by ECA*

Africa's productive resources are moderately competitive and relatively stable

Africa's Productive Resources Index has not significantly changed during the last two decades

The PRI captures the availability of direct productive inputs in a country. It consists of two sub-indices: human resources – called the Labour Force Index – and other natural resources and geographical factors that affect a country's productive base – called the Geography Index. The Labour Force Index traces the availability and quality of human resources and takes into account the size, the skill level and the health status of the labour force. The Geography Index captures factors that are relevant for the major economic sectors – agriculture and manufacturing – and therefore includes the geographical location of the country – whether it is landlocked – the existence of arable land and renewable water resources. The Labour Force Index is an important input for all economic sectors and is more directly under the control of policymakers (see box 3.1)

Cluster analysis reveals that countries with a moderate PRI ranking dominate the picture – about half of the 30 African countries fall in the moderately competitive cluster (see table 3.3). Overall, Africa's PRI has not significantly changed during the last two decades (1980-2001) although country rankings have changed across the five-year periods being considered. During the period 1985-89, Egypt moved up from the low cluster to the moderate cluster and Ethiopia moved down to the low cluster. During the period 1990-1994, the Democratic Republic of Congo and Guinea-Bissau fell from the moderate PRI cluster to the low cluster, South Africa and Tunisia joined the countries with high PRI scores while Algeria become moderately competitive. As a result, both the high and low clusters increased.

The second half of the 1990s saw an improvement of Africa's PRI with Côte d'Ivoire moving to the moderate cluster and Togo moving to the high cluster. Finally, the period 1997-2001 witnessed a further improvement of Africa's PRI with the Democratic Republic of Congo, Guinea-Bissau and Sudan improving their rankings (see figure 3.4).

Table 3.3

PRI clusters for 30 African countries, 1980-2001

Period	High cluster		Moderate cluster		Low cluster	
	Number of countries	GDP share (%)	Number of countries	GDP share (%)	Number of countries	GDP share (%)
1980-1984	3	2	15	60	12	34
1985-1989	3	2	15	67	12	25
1990-1994	5	38	12	38	13	17
1995-1999	6	38	12	40	12	15
1997-2001	6	38	15	43	9	12

Source: Calculations by ECA

Strong performers have more productive labour

Gabon occupies the first place as it has the most productive resources in terms of labour force and is fourth in terms of geography. Mauritius follows because it has the second place in geography and is third in labour force competitiveness. The Republic of Congo follows at the third place despite a seventh place in labour force, because it has the best score in geography. Tunisia is at the fourth place due to its labour force competitiveness, which is the second highest among the 30 African countries in the sample, and its performance is compared with that of Ethiopia in box 3.4. South Africa comes in fifth place due to its strong performance in terms of labour force – ranking fourth – which compensates for its weak geography score.

> *Gabon occupies the first place in the Productive Resources Index*

Landlocked countries rank low

Regarding the countries with the least productive resources, Botswana's low performance in the PRI (i.e. fifth to lasg) rank order as per fig. 3.4 partly reflects its strong reliance on mineral resources that are not included in the Geography Index. Indeed, its weak performance in geography (it ranks last) overshadows its labour force score, for which it ranks eighth. Burkina Faso, Mali, Zambia, Malawi and ranked lowest in the PRI because they sccored poorly in terms of geography; being landlocked with a low availability of arable land and renewable water resources. Burkina Faso and Mali have also very low labour force scores with low educational enrolment rates.

Box 3.4

How Ethiopia and Tunisia compare in labour force education and skills

Ethiopia ranks 23rd out of 30 African countries in the PRI, while Tunisia ranks 4th in 1997-2001. The gap in the PRI score between the two countries is due to the difference in their labour force competitiveness. Indeed, Ethiopia has the least productive resources in terms of labour force with a score more than three times lower than Tunisia's, which ranks second. Ethiopia's adult literacy was estimated at 38% in 2000, and gross enrolment rates are among the world's lowest. Moreover, gender parity in primary education – measured as the ratio of gross primary enrolment of girls to that of boys – is among the lowest in Africa. The underlying reasons for Ethiopia's poor performance include late enrolment, extremely low enrolment in rural areas, and low female attainment or completion rates, especially in rural areas. There is however a noticeable improvement of Ethiopia's enrolment rates at all levels from the 1990s. In addition, the shares of education spending in total public spending rose in the 1990s (except during the war with Eritrea); yet because spending has not grown faster than the population, per capita spending on education has steadily declined (ECA, 2002).

Tunisia's PRI ranking substantially increased between 1980 and 2001 (from 0.43 to 0.58) despite the fact that its Geography Index score remained almost unchanged around 0.47. The improvement in Tunisia's PRI score is driven by its labour force ranking, which is the second most competitive. Tunisia has made impressive achievements in its educational policy with a literacy rate close to 100%. Currently, gross enrolment rates are above 100% in primary and around 80% in secondary. Primary completion rate reached 98% in 2002, increasing from 75% in 1990, indicating the success of the educational reforms. The female enrolment rate is equal to that of the male rate in primary education, while it exceeds male enrolment at the secondary level. Regional disparities tend to narrow with a dropout rate declining from 7.1% in 1987/88 to 1.5% in 2001/02. Education is essentially provided by the public sector particularly at the primary level, although the private sector is becoming increasingly active in the provision of specialized training. Education expenditure amounts to around 7% of GDP and 22% of the government budget, demonstrating that it is a national priority. The educational system, and particularly higher education, is subject to strong pressures with the annual increase in the number of students. Around 26% of the 18-24 age group was expected to enrol in universities in 2003, a rate that might reach 43% by 2010, higher than the average of OECD countries, which stands at 40%. A major concern is to ensure a quality of teaching that can improve graduates' chances of finding jobs easily on the labour market.

Source: ECA, from official sources

Comparators do well in the PRI

It transpires from the PRI scores that seven out of eight comparator Asian and Latin American countries have higher PRI scores than 26 African countries, with only Bolivia scoring lower than half of the African countries in the sample (see figure 3.4). This result is surprising as Africa is often thought to have more abundant resources. However, as noted earlier, the PRI does not capture non-renewable non-productive resources such as mineral resources.

With the exception of India, comparator countries score higher than the African countries in terms of the Labour Force Index, while the results are mixed for the Geography Index. The lower quality of Africa's labour force than in seven of the comparator countries helps to explain its lower PRI rankings.

Infrastructure has been improving but is still poor in too many countries

The II comprises four sub-indices that encapsulate the infrastructure base required for the development of economic activities in general and internal and external trade in goods and services in particular. The sub-components are telecommunications, energy, transport network and access to information (see box 3.1).

Africa's infrastructure has improved between 1980 and 2001 but still half the countries surveyed remain in the low cluster (see table 3.4). During the 1980s, Africa's infrastruc-

Figure 3.4

Productive Resource Index (PRI), 1997-2001

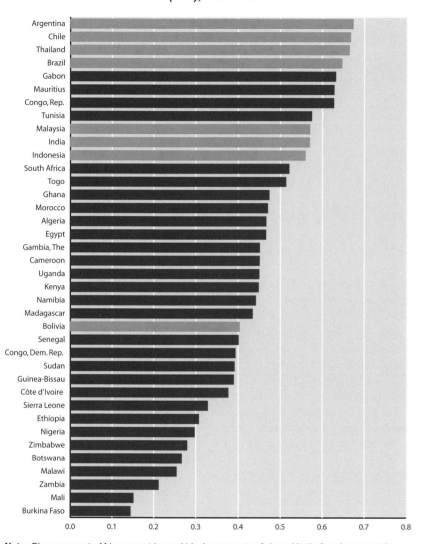

Note: *Blue represents African countries and black comparator Asia and Latin American countries.*
Source: *Calculations by ECA*

ture slightly improved, with Côte d'Ivoire moving from the low cluster to the moderate cluster. This improvement became more significant in the first half of the 1990s, with 16 countries moving up to the moderate cluster and Namibia jumping to the high competitive cluster by tripling its score. During the second half of the 1990s, the trend was reversed despite the fact that Mauritius became highly competitive, with the Gambia, Guinea-Bissau, Sudan and Uganda going back to the low cluster.

Table 3.4

Infrastructure Index clusters for 30 African countries, 1980-2001

Period	High cluster		Moderate cluster		Low cluster	
	Number of countries	GDP share (%)	Number of countries	GDP share (%)	Number of countries	GDP share (%)
1980-1984	1	39	2	10	27	47
1985-1989	1	35	3	14	26	45
1990-1994	2	33	18	45	10	15
1995-1999	3	33	13	42	14	18
1997-2001	4	34	11	42	15	17

Source: Calculations by ECA

Countries leading the way in infrastructure

Looking at the most competitive African countries in terms of infrastructure for trade, some conclusions can be drawn (see figure 3.5): Mauritius' first place is explained by the fact that it has the most developed telecommunications and highest access to information in Africa. South Africa ranks second because it has the most competitive energy infrastructure by far; it follows Mauritius in access to information and possesses well-developed transport and telecommunications networks. Namibia's third place is explained by a high transport network score.

Botswana has dramatically improved its ranking from 20th to fourth place with its developed telecommunications and transport networks; the country's progress is examined in box 3.5. Egypt follows with high scores in access to information and telecommunications.

Countries struggling to keep up

At the other end of the scale, Mali has had persistently uncompetitive infrastructure. Mali's large landmass is mostly a desert – arable land was 3.79% of land area in 2000 – making it difficult to develop a sound infrastructure. Guinea-Bissau's poor infrastructure score is mostly due to limited access to information and telecommunications resources despite a relatively developed transport network. Nigeria's 28th rank is due to a deterioration of its telecommunications ranking (from 24th to 29th). It has moderate scores and rankings in its transport network and access to information. Nigeria's low infrastructure score and ranking might appear surprising but is explained by its limited provision of infrastructure per capita given its large population.

With the exception of its transport network, Congo ranks in the bottom five in all the other infrastructure indicators and its rankings have been consistently deteriorating despite improvements of its infrastructure scores in absolute terms. The Democratic Republic of Congo (DRC) is the third African country in terms of landmass. This poses a

Box 3.5

The telecommunications revolution in Botswana

Botswana's infrastructure score is ten times higher than in the period 1980-1984, and as a result its ranking rose from 20th to fourth place in the II. This achievement is mostly driven by the expansion in telecommunications, which ranks second in Africa for the period 1997-2001. The improvements have resulted from both the steady increase of mainline fixed telephones and the rapid expansion of mobile telephones since 1999 (see figure below). With the Telecommunications Act of 1996, Botswana became the first country in Africa to establish an independent regulatory body, the Botswana Telecommunications Authority (BTA), and it adopted a new telecommunications policy based on gradual liberalization. Since the introduction of mobile phone services in 1998 – with two private operators – the mobile phone market has experienced exponential growth.

Botswana: Telephone density, 1990-2002

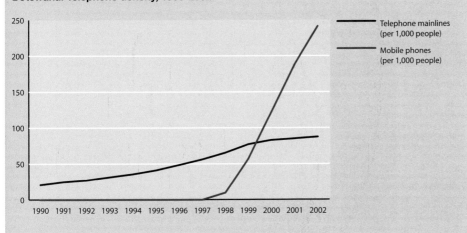

Botswana's commitment to improving the level and quality of basic telecommunication services, backed by strong policy strategies, brought increased competition, diversification, and efficiency to the sector. Botswana uses digital microwave and fibre-optic systems with digital exchanges, providing high-quality services. Botswana's success is attributed to its commitment to ongoing reform and dynamic policies that are open to private ownership and competition. There is a continuous search for quality service and reduced tariffs. The regulatory agency is empowered to control power abuse, while competition has led to reduced prices and an increase in the number of subscribers (Wallsten, 2001).

Source: ECA, from official sources

challenge to the development of its infrastructure network essential in building economic and social ties between the provinces, effective government control the territory, as well as the unity of the country. Unfortunately, decades of bad governance and misguided policies, followed by civil war have hindered new development and/or destroyed the existing infrastructure.

Figure 3.5

Infrastructure Index (II), 1997-2001

> *Decades of bad governance and misguided policies, followed by civil war, have hindered development and damaged the existing infrastructure in the DRC*

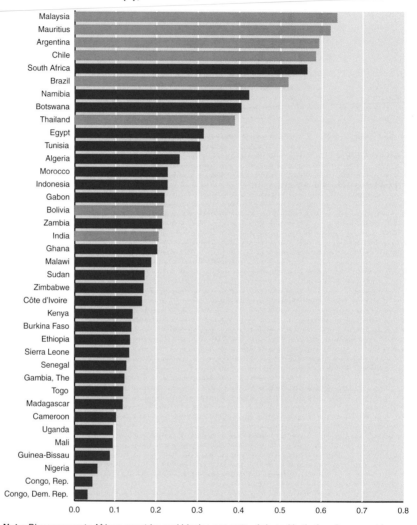

Note: *Blue represents African countries and black comparator Asia and Latin American countries*

Source: *Calculations by ECA*

Some African countries are ahead of the comparators

Some African countries are more developed, in terms of infrastructure, than most of the comparator countries. This is the case of Mauritius, which outperforms seven of the eight comparator countries in 1997-2001 in terms of infrastructure. South Africa, which outperforms five comparator countries, dominates all in terms of transport networks and energy, four of them in telecommunications, and three of them in access to information for the period 1997-2001. Bolivia and India rank below nine and ten African countries respectively in terms of infrastructure.

Competitiveness clearly improves trade performance

The TCI is constructed to capture important underlying factors for trade performance. Accordingly, the TCI's relevance can be tested by examining its relationship with past and current patterns of trade. As shown in figure 3.6, the TCI has a significant positive correlation (of 0.52) with exports volumes for the period 1997-2001 – a relationship which is also confirmed for the other four periods (although not reported here). This indicates that the TCI is a relevant measure of trade competitiveness; the more competitive countries tend to have higher export – to – GDP ratios.

> *Tests indicates that the TCI is a relevant measure of trade competitiveness*

Figure 3.6

Relation between TCI and exports of goods and services for 30 African countries, 1997-2001

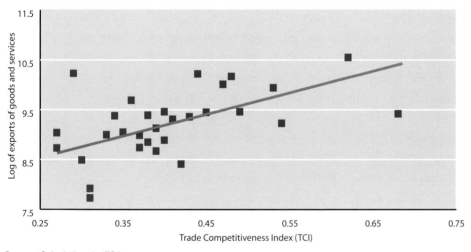

Source: *Calculations by ECA*

Africa's overall weak trade performance has often been blamed on the continent's inability to diversify its exports base to a large extent still dominated by unprocessed raw agricultural and mineral products. Examination of the relationship between the TCI and the Hirschman-Herfindahl Index[5] reveals that increased trade competitiveness is negatively correlated with exports concentration (see figure 3.7). This significant correlation implies that competitive countries rely on a larger number of products for their export revenues.

Examination of the correlations between horizontal diversification – measured as the opposite of the Hirschman-Herfindahl Index – and the three dimensions of the TCI, presented in table 3.5, shows that horizontal diversification for the 20 African States is negatively correlated with the PRI at 60%; the correlation is significant at the 1% level.

Table 3.5

Correlations between the Hirschman-Herfindahl Index (HHI) and the TCI dimensions,1997-2001

	Hirschman-Herfindahl Index	
	Coefficient	P-Value
Productive Resource Index (PRI)	- 0.60	0.01
Trade-enabling Environment Index (TEI)	- 0.35	0.18
Infrastructure Index (II)	- 0.24	0.36

Source: *Calculations by ECA*

> *Competitive economies rely on a larger number of products for their export revenues*

This suggests that both the lack of skilled labour force and unfavourable geographical conditions are two of the factors responsible for Africa's failure to increase its exports base and break its over-reliance on a limited number of products for its exports revenues.

Figure 3.7

Relation between TCI and the Hirschman-Herfindahl Index for 20 African countries, 1997-2001

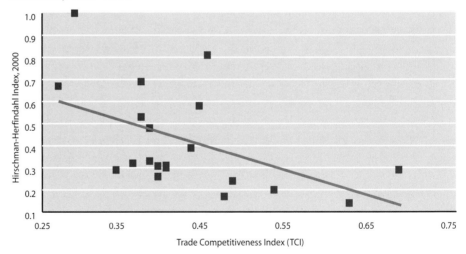

Source: *Calculations by ECA*

High TCI rankings are associated with higher export shares of manufactured goods, as figure 3.8 shows. The significant correlation of 0.73 between export shares of manufactured goods and the TCI for the period 1997-2001, suggests that those African countries that are more competitive in terms of trade have also managed to achieve more vertical diversification by moving from raw agricultural products exports to manufacturing exports.

Figure 3.8

Relation between TCI and manufacturing exports as a share of merchandise exports for 22 African countries, 1997-2001

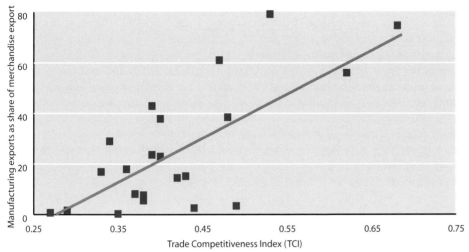

Source: *Calculations by ECA*

> *African countries that are more competitive have managed to move from raw agricultural products exports to manufactured exports*

The manufacturing exports of the 22 African States measured in figure 3.7 are also more closely related to TEI scores than to PRI or II rankings, as shown in table 3.6. This suggests that Africa's low vertical diversification is primarily a matter of policy. African countries' failure to diversify is more a reflection of institutional and policy failures – captured by trade policy, macroeconomic policy, and institutional quality sub-indices – than of a lack of skilled labour force support. In addition, the correlation between the shares of manufactured exports and the II suggests that unusually high (policy-induced) transaction costs are the main source of most of Africa's comparative disadvantage in manufactured exports (Collier, 1997).

Table 3.6

Correlations between the TCI dimensions and manufacturing exports as a share of merchandise exports, 1997-2001

	Manufacturing Exports	
	Coefficient	P-Value
Trade-enabling Environment Index (TEI)	0.73	0.00
Infrastructure Index (II)	0.68	0.00
Productive Resource Index (PRI)	0.48	0.05

Source: *Calculations by ECA*

Conclusions

> *Lack of skilled labour is responsible for many African countries to break their over reliance on a limited number of export products*

Overall trade competitiveness – as captured by the TCI – has been improving in Africa over the last two decades and is currently higher in the 30 African countries measured than it was two decades ago. However, half of the sample African countries fall in the moderately competitive cluster, making it clear that they are not sufficiently competitive on a global scale. The continent's top performers, Mauritius, South Africa, Namibia, and Tunisia, are more competitive than only three of the comparator countries, India, Indonesia, and Bolivia. Indeed, Bolivia, which is itself among the five poorest countries of Latin America and the Caribbean, is more competitive than 20 out of the 30 African countries in the sample.[5]

A few broad lessons can be drawn from the analysis of trade competitiveness and its sub-components. These can provide an insight into what needs to be done, as well as sketch strategies for improving Africa's trade competitiveness, and ultimately increasing its trade performance and integration into the global economy.

Africa's poor labour force is a major source of its low competitiveness

One important finding is that Africa's weak trade competitiveness compared to other regions is largely the result of a significant labour force gap: the PRI is the only sub-index where the Asian and Latin American comparator countries dominate the 30 African countries so strongly. The driving factor behind this performance is their labour force advantage. African populations are less healthy and less well educated than their counterparts in Asia and Latin America. Africa loses a higher proportion of their skilled labour force to the developed countries through "brain drain". Thus, the highest-scoring comparator country, Argentina, scores 25% higher with 0.91 points on the Labour Force Index than the highest-scoring African country, Gabon, which scores 0.73.

Labour force education and skills are also relevant in explaining the differences in trade competitiveness among some African countries. This is particularly true for countries such as Ethiopia and Tunisia. Indeed, Ethiopia has the lowest labour force score of all 30 African countries, ranking 23rd in terms of the PRI and 19th in the overall TCI. In Tunisia, progress in school enrolment during the last decades raised its labour force score to the second place from 0.39 at the beginning of the 1980s, where it ranked 14th out of 30 African countries in the sample, to 0.68 in 1997-2001, resulting in an improvement in the PRI and the overall TCI respectively from 0.43 to 0.58 and from 0.26 to 0.53.

Such labour differences will play an increasing role as Africa's experience and our results suggest that the lack of a skilled labour force is responsible for many African countries' failure to break their over-reliance on a limited number of products for their exports revenues and to increase their exports base – horizontal diversification – by producing and exporting goods requiring skilled labour. African countries need to increase access to education for their populations and improve their health if they are ultimately going to compete in global markets.

Institutional quality is vital for Africa

Having a trade-enabling environment is a key determinant of competitiveness among African countries. In fact, four of the five African countries which have the best TEI rankings are also the most competitive African countries in terms of the overall TCI. A closer look at country performances reveals that differences in institutional quality – proxied by corruption, the rule of law, bureaucratic quality and democratic accountability – are critical in intra-African performances. Mauritius, South Africa, Namibia, and Tunisia, besides having a relatively sound macroeconomic environment, have high institutional quality scores, while Zimbabwe and Côte d'Ivoire, which are currently in the middle of institutional crises, are among the least competitive countries.[6] In both cases, significant deteriorations of democratic accountability and bureaucratic quality as well as rises in corruption in the political system have been witnessed in the 1990s. The decline in democratic accountability shows that these governments are less responsive to their people and makes a violent fall of government more likely. This finding is confirmed by Fosu (2003), who examines the impact of political instability on export performance on 30 African countries and finds that the lack of a stable political environment adversely influences export performance via competitiveness and has been more deleterious to exports than to overall GDP growth. Therefore, improving political stability through better institutional quality is not the *non plus ultra* but rather the first step towards improving the trade-enabling environment, and ultimately trade competitiveness, in weakly performing African countries.

Africa's unusually high transaction costs poses major comparative disadvantage to exports of manufactured goods

Improving infrastructure is a major priority

Intra-African trade, as well as trade with other regions, is hampered by inadequate infrastructure. Africa faces unusually high transaction costs related to infrastructure. This is a major source of comparative disadvantage in manufactured exports, which are more "transaction-intensive" than primary products, and it therefore inhibits efforts to achieve greater vertical diversification (Collier, 1997). Therefore, if African countries are to reduce their reliance on exports of raw materials and move up the value chain producing manufactured goods or processed raw materials, critical steps include addressing inadequate infrastructures such as energy, a topic dealt with in Chapter 4. Finally, the correction of Africa's weak performance in trade and diversification will depend on African policy makers' ability to harness an environment and institutions that are conducive to trade. If African countries want to ease the flow of goods and services across the continent, much more trade facilitation is required, as discussed in Chapter 5.

Annexes

A3.1 Ranking of Countries Across Sample Periods

Table 1

Overall Trade Competitiveness Index (TCI) scores and ranks

Country Name	1980-1984		1985-1989		1990-1994		1995-1999		1997-2001	
	Score	Rank	Score	Rank	Score	Rank	Score	Rank	Score	Rank
Algeria	0.34	4	0.34	14	0.39	10	0.42	9	0.44	9
Botswana	0.19	22	0.36	8	0.42	7	0.43	8	0.45	8
Burkina Faso	0.14	25	0.24	27	0.22	28	0.27	28	0.30	27
Cameroon	0.25	8	0.36	12	0.35	18	0.38	16	0.38	17
Congo, D.R.	0.17	24	0.23	28	-0.12	30	0.25	30	0.27	30
Congo, Rep.	0.34	3	0.42	5	0.41	8	0.40	11	0.41	12
Côte d'Ivoire	0.23	16	0.36	9	0.36	16	0.35	22	0.36	21
Egypt	0.24	12	0.36	10	0.42	6	0.43	7	0.48	6
Ethiopia	0.11	29	0.18	29	0.22	27	0.35	21	0.37	19
Gabon	0.34	5	0.44	4	0.45	4	0.48	5	0.49	5
Gambia, The	0.25	10	0.34	16	0.39	11	0.39	12	0.42	11
Ghana	0.14	26	0.30	19	0.37	13	0.41	10	0.43	10
Guinea-Bissau	0.24	11	0.25	25	0.29	24	0.29	27	0.31	25
Kenya	0.23	14	0.37	7	0.35	17	0.39	14	0.40	14
Madagascar	0.23	15	0.36	13	0.37	14	0.38	15	0.40	13
Malawi	0.21	19	0.29	20	0.32	21	0.36	20	0.37	20
Mali	0.12	28	0.17	30	0.20	29	0.25	29	0.27	29
Mauritius	0.48	1	0.52	2	0.54	2	0.63	1	0.68	1
Morocco	0.24	13	0.36	11	0.40	9	0.45	6	0.47	7
Namibia	0.28	6	0.45	3	0.49	3	0.54	3	0.54	3
Nigeria	0.14	27	0.25	26	0.30	22	0.29	26	0.29	28
Senegal	0.23	17	0.33	17	0.34	20	0.37	17	0.39	15
Sierra Leone	0.21	18	0.28	22	0.28	25	0.31	25	0.31	26
South Africa	0.43	2	0.58	1	0.60	1	0.62	2	0.62	2
Sudan	0.09	30	0.25	24	0.28	26	0.31	24	0.35	22
Togo	0.25	9	0.34	15	0.34	19	0.39	13	0.39	16
Tunisia	0.26	7	0.38	6	0.44	5	0.49	4	0.53	4
Uganda	0.17	23	0.29	21	0.36	15	0.37	18	0.38	18
Zambia	0.20	21	0.27	23	0.29	23	0.32	23	0.33	24
Zimbabwe	0.21	20	0.32	18	0.37	12	0.36	19	0.34	23

Source: Calculations by ECA

Table 2

Trade-enabling Environment Index (TEI), scores and ranks

Country Name	1980-1984		1985-1989		1990-1994		1995-1999		1997-2001	
	Score	Rank	Score	Rank	Score	Rank	Score	Rank	Score	Rank
Algeria	0.62	2	0.57	11	0.55	16	0.59	19	0.60	19
Botswana	0.31	7	0.73	3	0.68	3	0.67	7	0.69	7
Burkina Faso	0.26	16	0.53	17	0.49	21	0.59	20	0.62	14
Cameroon	0.30	9	0.59	6	0.56	15	0.60	16	0.60	18
Congo, D.R.	0.09	27	0.27	30	-0.76	30	0.33	30	0.38	30
Congo, Rep.	0.34	6	0.56	14	0.50	20	0.56	21	0.57	21
Côte d'Ivoire	0.30	8	0.58	9	0.59	10	0.55	23	0.53	24
Egypt	0.26	17	0.55	15	0.64	5	0.64	8	0.66	9
Ethiopia	0.21	25	0.41	24	0.39	27	0.64	9	0.68	8
Gabon	0.28	12	0.58	10	0.57	13	0.61	15	0.62	15
Gambia, The	0.28	11	0.52	18	0.59	12	0.67	6	0.70	6
Ghana	-0.06	29	0.40	25	0.56	14	0.61	14	0.63	13
Guinea-Bissau	0.37	4	0.37	26	0.40	26	0.42	29	0.45	29
Kenya	0.27	14	0.63	5	0.60	8	0.63	11	0.61	16
Madagascar	0.22	24	0.58	8	0.52	18	0.60	18	0.65	11
Malawi	0.26	19	0.48	19	0.47	22	0.62	13	0.66	10
Mali	0.22	23	0.36	29	0.44	24	0.54	24	0.57	23
Mauritius	0.63	1	0.71	4	0.73	2	0.77	3	0.78	1
Morocco	0.27	13	0.56	12	0.61	6	0.69	4	0.73	4
Namibia	0.35	5	0.80	1	0.66	4	0.78	2	0.76	3
Nigeria	0.12	26	0.42	23	0.52	17	0.52	26	0.53	26
Senegal	0.29	10	0.59	7	0.59	11	0.64	10	0.64	12
Sierra Leone	0.26	18	0.46	20	0.36	28	0.42	28	0.46	28
South Africa	0.37	3	0.76	2	0.78	1	0.79	1	0.77	2
Sudan	-0.10	30	0.36	28	0.36	29	0.47	27	0.50	27
Togo	0.25	20	0.45	21	0.43	25	0.53	25	0.53	25
Tunisia	0.25	21	0.55	16	0.60	9	0.67	5	0.70	5
Uganda	0.07	28	0.37	27	0.51	19	0.60	17	0.60	17
Zambia	0.24	22	0.43	22	0.46	23	0.56	22	0.57	20
Zimbabwe	0.27	15	0.56	13	0.60	7	0.63	12	0.57	22

Source: *Calculations by ECA*

Table 3

Productive Resource Index (PRI), scores and ranks

Country Name	1980-1984		1985-1989		1990-1994		1995-1999		1997-2001	
	Score	Rank	Score	Rank	Score	Rank	Score	Rank	Score	Rank
Algeria	0.28	22	0.32	20	0.39	14	0.43	12	0.47	9
Botswana	0.22	27	0.26	26	0.26	25	0.27	26	0.27	26
Burkina Faso	0.17	28	0.17	28	0.12	29	0.14	29	0.14	30
Cameroon	0.41	12	0.43	10	0.41	10	0.42	13	0.45	12
Congo, D.R.	0.40	13	0.40	14	0.34	17	0.35	20	0.39	18
Congo, Rep.	0.67	1	0.67	1	0.63	1	0.60	3	0.63	3
Côte d'Ivoire	0.33	19	0.34	19	0.33	19	0.35	18	0.38	21
Egypt	0.34	18	0.35	18	0.41	9	0.44	7	0.47	10
Ethiopia	0.09	30	0.11	30	0.14	28	0.28	25	0.31	23
Gabon	0.61	2	0.61	2	0.62	2	0.62	2	0.63	1
Gambia, The	0.38	14	0.41	13	0.39	15	0.42	14	0.45	11
Ghana	0.42	8	0.45	8	0.40	11	0.44	9	0.47	7
Guinea-Bissau	0.36	17	0.37	17	0.32	20	0.35	19	0.39	20
Kenya	0.42	10	0.44	9	0.40	13	0.41	15	0.45	14
Madagascar	0.42	9	0.42	11	0.37	16	0.39	16	0.43	16
Malawi	0.24	26	0.25	27	0.21	27	0.26	27	0.25	27
Mali	0.15	29	0.16	29	0.09	30	0.13	30	0.15	29
Mauritius	0.58	3	0.61	3	0.60	3	0.62	1	0.63	2
Morocco	0.37	15	0.40	15	0.41	8	0.44	8	0.47	8
Namibia	0.41	11	0.42	12	0.43	7	0.43	10	0.44	15
Nigeria	0.25	25	0.28	24	0.28	23	0.30	22	0.30	24
Senegal	0.37	16	0.38	16	0.34	18	0.36	17	0.40	17
Sierra Leone	0.31	20	0.32	21	0.28	24	0.30	23	0.33	22
South Africa	0.47	4	0.49	4	0.52	4	0.53	5	0.52	5
Sudan	0.28	21	0.30	23	0.29	21	0.34	21	0.39	19
Togo	0.45	5	0.46	6	0.46	6	0.51	6	0.51	6
Tunisia	0.43	7	0.46	7	0.50	5	0.55	4	0.57	4
Uganda	0.44	6	0.46	5	0.40	12	0.43	11	0.45	13
Zambia	0.26	24	0.26	25	0.22	26	0.21	28	0.21	28
Zimbabwe	0.27	23	0.31	22	0.29	22	0.29	24	0.28	25

Source: *Calculations by ECA*

Table 4

Infrastructure Index (II), scores and ranks

Country Name	1980-1984		1985-1989		1990-1994		1995-1999		1997-2001	
	Score	Rank	Score	Rank	Score	Rank	Score	Rank	Score	Rank
Algeria	0.11	8	0.14	8	0.24	6	0.25	6	0.25	7
Botswana	0.04	20	0.09	16	0.32	3	0.34	4	0.40	4
Burkina Faso	-0.01	29	0.00	30	0.05	30	0.10	23	0.14	17
Cameroon	0.04	19	0.05	19	0.07	27	0.11	21	0.10	24
Congo, D.R.	0.02	22	0.02	27	0.06	29	0.06	28	0.03	30
Congo, Rep.	0.02	23	0.03	23	0.10	24	0.05	30	0.04	29
Côte d'Ivoire	0.06	17	0.16	4	0.16	17	0.14	16	0.16	15
Egypt	0.13	3	0.18	3	0.23	8	0.22	7	0.31	5
Ethiopia	0.02	26	0.04	21	0.14	21	0.14	17	0.13	18
Gabon	0.12	4	0.14	6	0.16	19	0.20	10	0.22	9
Gambia, The	0.07	13	0.09	15	0.19	14	0.08	27	0.12	21
Ghana	0.06	16	0.04	22	0.15	20	0.17	13	0.20	11
Guinea-Bissau	0.00	28	0.01	28	0.16	18	0.09	25	0.09	27
Kenya	0.02	25	0.03	25	0.07	28	0.11	22	0.14	16
Madagascar	0.06	15	0.07	18	0.21	10	0.16	15	0.12	23
Malawi	0.12	5	0.15	5	0.27	5	0.19	11	0.19	12
Mali	-0.01	30	0.01	29	0.07	26	0.09	24	0.09	26
Mauritius	0.22	2	0.25	2	0.29	4	0.48	2	0.62	1
Morocco	0.09	10	0.11	11	0.19	13	0.21	9	0.23	8
Namibia	0.08	11	0.13	9	0.38	2	0.40	3	0.42	3
Nigeria	0.04	21	0.05	20	0.11	23	0.06	29	0.06	28
Senegal	0.02	24	0.03	24	0.09	25	0.12	20	0.13	20
Sierra Leone	0.07	14	0.08	17	0.20	12	0.21	8	0.13	19
South Africa	0.45	1	0.49	1	0.49	1	0.55	1	0.56	2
Sudan	0.10	9	0.09	14	0.18	15	0.14	18	0.17	13
Togo	0.05	18	0.12	10	0.12	22	0.12	19	0.12	22
Tunisia	0.11	7	0.14	7	0.22	9	0.26	5	0.30	6
Uganda	0.01	27	0.03	26	0.18	16	0.09	26	0.09	25
Zambia	0.12	6	0.10	12	0.21	11	0.19	12	0.21	10
Zimbabwe	0.08	12	0.09	13	0.23	7	0.16	14	0.17	14

Source: *Calculations by ECA*

A3.2 Value-added of the TCI vis-à-vis alternative indices

A number of indices have been presented, assessing economic performance in general and competitiveness in particular. In fact, given the number of indices, this section will only discuss a small, non-exhaustive selection, focusing on those with a trade and/or African element. It will emerge that ECA's Trade Competitiveness Index (TCI), being a trade-specific and Africa-focused index, and capturing the underlying factors of competitiveness, is a unique tool for understanding African countries trade performances.

The Global Competitiveness Index

The Global Competitiveness Report 2003-2004, published by the World Economic Forum, contains two competitiveness indices. The first, called the Growth Competitiveness Index (GCI), was developed by Jeffrey D. Sachs of Columbia University and John W. McArthur of Earth Institute and was presented in *The Global Competitiveness Report 2001-2002*. The second index, now labelled the Business Competitiveness Index (BCI), was developed by Michael Porter of Harvard University and was first introduced in *The Global Competitiveness Report 2000*. These two indices are different from the TCI in the sense that they are not trade-oriented.

In fact, the GCI aims to "measure the capacity of the national economy to achieve sustained economic growth over the medium term, controlling for the current level of economic development" while the BCI is based on the micro-foundations of a country's competitiveness, and refers "... mainly to an economy's effective utilization of its current stock of resources" (WEF, 2002, Executive Summary, page xii). The World Economic Forum's Overall Competitiveness Rankings, which "encapsulate the relative strengths and weaknesses of growth within each economy", combine the two results.

Up to 2002, the GCI and the BCI included only eight African countries out of a total of 80 countries. However, the 2003 edition added 17 African countries. The GCI is a useful tool, and extending its coverage to 25 African countries is the main innovation of the 2003 GCI; but the GCI cannot replace the TCI simply because it measures growth potential, which is a concept different from trade competitiveness. The BCI is closer to the TCI but it focuses on companies' productivity, while the TCI is a broader and more trade-oriented concept.

The Trade Performance Index

The most recent indicator on competitiveness related to trade is the Trade Performance Index (TPI) presented by the International Trade Centre of the United Nations Conference on Trade and Development (UNCTAD) and the World Trade Organization (WTO). This index covers a total of 184 countries and 14 export sectors; it consists of 22 quantitative indicators of trade performance. The TPI aims to improve the traditional measures of trade performance, which are characterized by crude indicators such as the level of openness (total trade in goods and services divided by GDP) or growth of exports over a given period, by introducing an indicator of trade performance based on various criteria such as the type of product available, the level of market and economic diversification, the positioning on quality ladders etc. This makes the TPI an improved measure of observed trade performances – which is rather the outcome of competitiveness – while the TCI captures the underlying factors that explain those performances and trade patterns.

The Export Performance Index

The Export Performance Index was created by the World Bank in the early 1990s, and consists of four indicators pertaining to exports. However, the sample only covered a short period, spanning 1989-1993 and in addition only spanned 21 transition economies, including 15 states of the Former Soviet Union. Hence, it bears little relevance to Africa.

A3.3 Methodology

Each index is computed separately for selected African countries, and the three together form the TCI. As the previous sections suggest, construction of the three indicators, hence the overall TCI, is data-intensive. The set of indicators used in constructing the indices was assembled in two steps. Having selected indicators relevant to each sub-index, the collected set was investigated to see which indicators could be used that would enable a substantial coverage of the African continent. While many additional variables could be considered highly relevant and call for inclusion, the benefit had to be weighed against the cost of potentially reducing the number of countries in the overall sample. Thus, data with few observations were dropped from the sample, despite their potential relevance to the index. Investigation also yielded the necessity to remove several countries from the sample. In fact, 23 countries could not be included without limiting the dataset severely. However, of these 23 countries, only Angola and Tanzania contribute more than 1% to African GDP. Thus, the remaining 30 countries capture about 95% of African GDP. Vis-à-vis indicators, 31 indicators are used in computing the indices.

Data availability restricted the timeframe under consideration to the period 1980-2001. Hence, the TCI and its sub-components were computed covering five-year intervals starting from 1980, with an additional five-year interval to cover the most recent data (1997-2001). This last interval is presented in the text while a detailed ranking across time spans can be found in A3.1.

After data-collection, the variables were normalized, using the following formula:

$$x_{it} = \frac{x_{it} - \underline{x}_t}{\overline{x}_t - \underline{x}_t}$$

where x_{it} denotes the observation of variable i at time $t= 1980, 1981,\ldots, 2001$ and

$\overline{x}_t$ and $\underline{x}_t$ denote the maximum and minimum values of x_{it} for the African countries for the period 1997-2001. Hence, the normalized indicators for African countries lie in the interval [0,1] for the period 1997-2001. Accordingly, the normalized indicators for the comparator countries as well as for the African countries for the periods other than 1997-

2001 can lie outside the interval [0,1]. For the seven indicators that are defined in such a way that ordinal increases represent deteriorations (such as landlocked, average tariff rate, average cost of a local phone call, etc), appropriate adjustments were made (see box 3.1 for a complete list of the indicators used).

All the indicators - besides the ones defined below – are derived from the 2003 World Development Indicators (WDI) CD-ROM. For their definitions see the 2003 WDI (http://devdata.worldbank.org/dataonline).

Additional sources include:

Urban population (% of total): Population Division of the Department of Economic and Social Affairs of the United Nations Secretariat, *World Population Prospects: The 2002 Revision and World Urbanization Prospects* (http://esa.un.org/unpp).

Actual renewable water resources, total (in cubic kilometres) 1977-2001: Earth Trends – The Environmental Information Portal, World Resources Institute (http://earthtrends.wri.org).

Average tariff rate (taxes on international trade divided by the imports of goods and services): ECA computation using the following data from the WDI: taxes on international trade (% of current revenues), current revenues, excluding grants (% GDP), GDP (current $US), and imports of goods and services (current $US).

Real effective exchange rate: ECA computation using monthly real effective exchange rate from International Monetary Fund's International Financial Statistics (IFS) CD-ROM.

Corruption index: International Country Risk Guide ratings – Political Risk Components. Corruption refers to corruption in the political system. The value ranges from 0 to 6. The higher the value of the corruption index, the lower the level of corruption. In other words, countries that have lower level of corruption have a higher value of the index and vice versa.

Rule of law index: International Country Risk Guide ratings – Political Risk Components. Law and order is an assessment of the strength and impartiality of the legal system as well as the popular observance of law. It ranges from 0 to 6.

Government stability index: International Country Risk Guide ratings – Political Risk Components. Government stability is an assessment of both the government's ability to carry out its declared programmes and its ability to stay in office. The components include government unity, legislative strength and popular support. The variable ranges from 0 to 12.

Bureaucratic quality index: International Country Risk Guide ratings – Political Risk Components. Bureaucratic quality measures the institutional strength and quality of bureaucracy. This measure is expected to be a shock absorber that minimizes reversions of policy when government changes. High points are given to countries where the bureaucracy is autonomous from political pressure and have an established mechanism for recruitment and training. The variable ranges from 0 to 4.

Democratic accountability index: International Country Risk Guide ratings – Political Risk Components. Democratic accountability measures how responsive the government is to its people, on the basis that the less responsive it is, the more likely it is that the government will fall, peacefully in a democratic society, but possibly violently in a non-democratic society. It ranges from 0 to 6.

Notes

[1] Physical capital, which is usually part of the production function, forms part of the Index.

[2] The classification procedure used is a K-means cluster analysis: means of selected characteristics are used to classify countries into relatively homogeneous clusters, countries are iteratively assigned to the nearest cluster centre using the simple Euclidean distance. To ease comparison across the periods, the cluster centres for 1997-2001 are used as reference points.

[3] The recent appreciation of the rand lies outside the sample period and is not included in the analysis.

[4] The Hirschman-Herfindahl index normalized to obtain values ranking from 0 to 1 (maximum concentration), according to the following formula:

$$H_j = \frac{\sqrt{\sum_{j=1}^{239} (x_i / X)^2} - \sqrt{1/239}}{1/ - \sqrt{1/239}}$$

Where H_j is the country index, x_i is the value of exports of product i, $X = \sum_{j=1}^{239} x_i$ and 239 represents the number of products at the three-digit SITC, Revision 2 level. Therefore, it is equal to 1 when a single product generates all the exports revenues and approaches 0 when exports revenues are evenly distributed over a large number of products. **Source** UNCTAD Handbook of Statistics Online Database.

[5] Bolivia is among the five poorest countries in terms of GDP per capita of all 38 Latin American and Caribbean countries with data in the World Bank Development Indicators 2003.

[6] However, note that low political and economic risk should not necessarily be equated with good governance and political freedom.

References

Asea, P. and Lahiri, A. (1999), "The Precious Bane," *Journal of Economic Dynamics and Control,* 23 (5-6), pp823-49

Collier, P. (1997), "Policy Commitment Arrangements for Africa: implications for aid, trade and investment flows". Paper presented at African Economic Research Consortium (AERC) workshop on Africa and the WTO, November 1997, AERC, Nairobi

Fosu, A. K. (2003), "Political Instability and Export Performance in Sub-Saharan Africa," *Journal of Development Studies*, 39 (4), pp67-83

Gyimah-Brempong, K. (2003), "Political Instability," in E. Nnadozie (ed), *African Economic Development,* Academic Press

International Country Risk Guide ratings – Political Risk Components (http://www.icrgonline.com)

Pourgerami, A. and Djeto, A. (1989), "The Inflation-Growth Trade-off in an Export-Oriented Rural Economy: the case of Ghana," *Eastern Africa Economic Review*, 5, pp32-41

Rodrik, D. (1998), "Where Did All the Growth Go? External shocks, social conflict, and growth collapses", draft version of paper (same title) published in *Journal of Economic Growth,* December 1999

Sachs, J. and Warner, A. (1999), "Natural Resource Intensity and Economic Growth," in Mayer, Chambers and Farooq (eds), *Development Policies in Natural Resource Economics,* Edward Elgar Publishing, Cheltenham

Savvides, A. (1995), "Economic Growth in Africa," *World Development*, no 23, pp449-458

World Economic Forum (WEF) (2002), Global Competitiveness Report 2002-2003, Geneva

Poor Energy Infrastructure Hobbles Export Diversification

t is evident from the previous chapter that most African economies are still some distance from providing a competitive trade environment. Many countries are saddled with a commodity-dependent and largely static export base, which has tended to decline in relation to the growth in global trade. Only a very few African countries have managed to increase their market share of the Organization of Economic Co-operation and Development (OECD) imports since the 1960s. If more countries are to achieve continuing diversification of their exports they will need to improve local conditions for business and to identify the major obstacles to business development and remove them.

Countries that want to compete effectively in the international market have to keep investing in improving their physical and communications infrastructure on all fronts. In particular, and highlighted in this chapter, African countries vitally need good and efficient electrical power infrastructure; this will help them move more rapidly into resource-based manufacturing and commodity processing, as well as trade in services. Even the efficiency of the agricultural sector will be greatly enhanced by the provision of reliable energy supplies, both at the local and national levels.

Nature has endowed the African continent with the widest-possible range of energy resources and yet its power sector remains severely underdeveloped in all countries. According to the International Energy Agency, sub-Saharan Africa has the lowest electrification of any major world region: in terms of world electricity production, Africa's power generation represents a mere 3.1% . Only 23% of Africa's population have access to electricity, and much of the available supply is unreliable and subject to power rationing and/or unscheduled power cuts. With the conditions prevailing in many countries, it is clear that Africa's export diversification drive is simply being hobbled by poorly functioning energy infrastructure. Much needs to be done to address the backlog of problems in the power sector, including its poor technical and financial performance. Although reforms undertaken in some countries have managed to reduce technical losses and power outages, such measures have not yet begun to increase the general level of electrification. New investment is urgently required.

Solving Africa's power sector problems requires not only greater energy efficiency and sustainability, but also a reduction in the dominant role of the State in its management. A significant step towards freeing up the sector is the transformation of power companies into independent and self-reliant corporations where feasible. What determines the success and efficiency of power companies is the extent to which they incorporate economic decisions in their operations.

> *Africa's power generation represents 3.1% of world production*

Ensuring and sustaining private participation in the provision of electricity services in Africa will require concrete national strategies aimed at addressing problems affecting domestic business development. Good and credible regulation is necessary to address any ill effects associated with private sector participation and to prevent any abuse of monopoly power. For effective performance, it is essential that regulatory bodies are independent, and distanced from political, corporate, and other pressures.

Energy efficiency is vital, both to reduce operating costs and to improve the productivity and international competitiveness of energy-consuming companies. Efficient pricing of electricity is also important for the power sector's own development. To ensure economic efficiency, price distortions must be minimized, and the principles of consistency, transparency, clarity and cost-effectiveness must be promoted.

Finally, the promotion of regional and subregional integration in energy services would help promote the development of Africa's power sector. This integration can enhance the sector's development by reducing power costs and by minimizing the operating costs of existing subregional networks. The development of regional and subregional markets in energy would require common regulations for all international exchanges.

Diversification is the way forward

Many African countries continue to depend on very few export commodities for a large proportion of their export earnings. Between 1996 and 2000, broad primary commodities accounted for about 85% of total exports from Africa. Primary commodity dependence can have three impacts on economic development (Collier, 2002):

- First, because primary commodity prices are highly volatile, countries have had to cope with large shocks. Evidence suggests that the largest of these shocks were poorly managed, with negative shocks causing substantial reduction in economic growth.
- Secondly, the rents generated by primary commodities have been associated with poor governance for various reasons (Sachs and Warner, 1995; Pritchett et al., 2002).
- Thirdly, primary commodity dependence has been associated with a substantially higher risk of civil war (Collier and Hoffler, 2002; Yartey, 2004).

Given these problems, export diversification is desirable and on the average most developing regions of the world have massively diversified their export structures over the past few decades. Africa, however, has experienced very little diversification and remains heavily dependent on primary commodities.

In comparing the export structures of developing countries by region, certain important features are worth mentioning (see figure 4.1). Commodity dependence was widespread in all regions between 1966 and 1970. Thirty years later, primary commodities

> *South Africa, Morocco, Tunisia, Egypt and Zimbabwe have managed to diversify their export structures*

still represented a significant component of the merchandise export of all regions with the exception of Asia. Africa alone still depended on these commodities for about 85% of total exports, falling from about 93% 30 years before. This suggests that very little change has taken place in the export structure of African countries (Bonaglia and Fukasaku, 2003).

Figure 4.1

Commodity dependence by world regions, 1966-1970 and 1996-2000 (average percentage share of broad primary products in total exports)

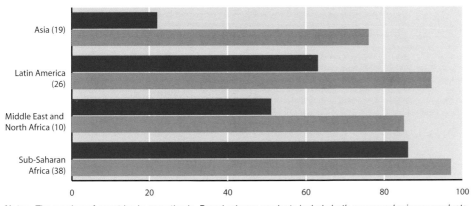

Notes: *The number of countries in parenthesis. Broad primary products include both processed primary products and unprocessed primary products.*

Source: *Bonaglia and Fukasaku, 2003*

Figure 4.2 uses the Hirschman-Herfindahl index (HHI) to examine the extent of export concentration in Africa. Accordingly, export concentration is lowest in countries such as South Africa, Morocco, Tunisia, Egypt and Senegal, implying that these countries export a wide range of products. On the other hand, countries such as Nigeria, Angola, Comoros and Botswana have the highest degree of export concentration and are dependent primarily on a single commodity for their export revenues.

The table in annex A4.1 uses OECD 'mirror' data to summarize the degree of commodity export diversification in selected African countries for two five-year periods, 1966-1970 and 1996-2000. (It is called mirror data because it uses OECD import trade statistics to look at the export performances of developing countries for the sake of data reliability.) There are 98 countries in the OECD mirror data. The countries currently consist of 52 low-income countries and another 46 countries classified as developing at the beginning of the 1970s for the sake of comparison. To make the exercise consistent throughout the period, the aggregate import value of 23 high-income OECD countries is taken to represent total merchandise exports of the individual countries under consideration. The 23 high-income OECD countries received in total roughly 60% of total merchandise exports of these 98 countries in the OECD mirror data between 1996-2000 (IMF, 2002).

Figure 4.2

Export concentration in selected African countries: the Hirschman-Herfindahl Index for exports (HHI), 2000

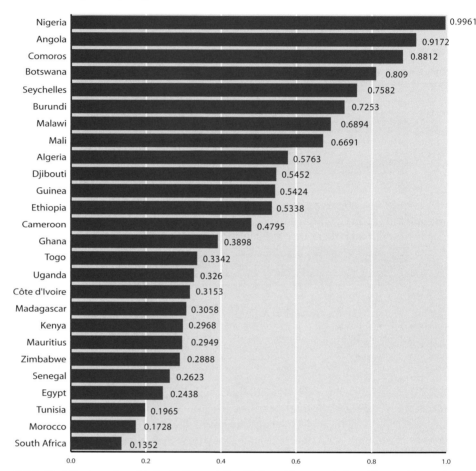

Notes: *The index ranges from 0 to 1, with the most diversified countries nearer to 0, and the countries most dependent on single commodities nearer to 1. When a single export product produces all the revenues, HHI is equal to 1 and when export revenues are evenly distributed over a large number of products, HHI approaches zero. 1990 values for Angola, Egypt, Madagascar, Mali, Malawi, and Seychelles.*

Source: *UNCTAD, 2003*

Africa starts from a low base...

Analysis of the OECD mirror data confirm that the degree of export diversification in most of SSA is low. Only a limited number of African countries (Botswana, Lesotho, Mauritius, Tunisia and Zimbabwe) managed to increase their market shares of high-income OECD imports between 1966 and 2000. Thirty-four out of 46 African countries in the data account for about 1.37% of high-income OECD imports, falling from 3.21%

30 years ago. The OECD market constitutes the single most important export market for all developing countries so that a rise in market shares can be seen as an important indicator of policy success. More specifically, a rise in the market share of high-income OECD countries imports is taken to represent diversification into manufacturing. In fact, almost all countries that were able to increase their OECD market shares were also able to reduce substantially their dependence on primary commodity exports and have moved into manufacturing. The OECD mirror trade data suggest that many different routes to diversification exist, including resource-based manufacturing and primary processing.

Most of the diversification that has taken place in Africa involves primary commodity processing and the identification of new products such as fish, salt and cut flowers. Diversification toward manufacturing is not the only possibility. African countries could also pursue a different route to diversification by developing of resource-based manufacturing and commodity processing, as well as trade in services. Examples are provided by Ghana and Uganda, which have adopted a modest but generally successful approach to the diversification of their exports. Ghana is now operating "Presidential initiatives" to develop local production of garments, starch, palm oil and salt for export (ECA, 2003). In Uganda, the development of flower and fish exports has helped to boost non-traditional activities and to reduce dependence on coffee, although there are still fluctuations in export revenues (Dijkstra, 2001).

> *Only 5 African countries managed to increase their market shares in high-income OECD countries*

...but there's evidence of progress

At the end of 2000, nine of the 46 countries in the data were deriving more than 25% of their exports from the manufacturing sector. Among the countries that are less dependent on primary commodity exports, the efforts of Mauritius, Lesotho, Madagascar and Tunisia are worth mentioning.

Mauritius has managed to build a thriving export-oriented manufacturing sector starting from a sugar-dependent economy. Mauritius' success has been built on the development of good infrastructure. The country has one of the highest levels of telephone penetration in Africa. In 2000, there were 280,900 connected lines giving a telephone density of 23.53 per hundred people. Mauritius also has well-developed energy infrastructure. Per capita electricity consumption in 2000 was 995.83 kWh representing one of the highest in Africa. The Export Processing Zone (EPZ) is based on a set of statutory and tax provisions that have enabled Mauritius to diversify its economy by exploiting its political stability, good infrastructure, flexible labour force and attractive investment climate. The EPZ presently contributes about 85% of total export earnings and about 13% of GDP.

Lesotho offers another example. By exploiting its geographical location to transport South African products during the apartheid era, the country made a significant move into manufacturing and since then has been a focus of FDI in the clothing sector. Lesotho has also taken advantage of the trade privileges and the duty-free access to the US market offered under the AGOA. Lesotho is one of the few countries in the region to attract significant FDI in export-oriented manufacturing for OECD markets. As a result, Lesotho now derives some 70% of its exports from manufactures.

In the case of Madagascar, manufacturing exports grew by 233% between 1980 and 1993, and by 109% between 1992 and 1999. There has been a transformation of exports structures at the expense of primary commodities such as vanilla, spices, cotton and tea (UNDP, 2002). The liberalization of the economy has further enhanced Madagascar's export competitiveness. Over 200 investors, particularly garment manufactures, have located in the country's free-trade zone since it was established in 1991. In 1999 entrepreneurs invested about $51 million in textile firms, while agro-processing amounted to approximately $9 million (Cadot and Nasir, 2002).

Tunisia has also managed to build a thriving export sector. Its rise as a garment exporter started when the 1972 investment code opened the country to FDI. Since then, hundreds of foreign companies have established wholly or partly owned garment factories in Tunisia. It's export success has been built on its outward processing trade with the EU, under which companies in developed countries can export fabrics or parts of garments, and then re-import them as finished garments. The EU's outward processing arrangements have brought Tunisia considerable foreign investment. Today the textile industry accounts for about 50% of all industrial jobs and 46% of national exports.

These examples provide some useful lessons for African countries in their export diversification drive. First, export diversification does not come about by itself. As discussed in chapter 2, it requires concrete national, sector-level and enterprise-level strategies based on a realistic assessment of supply capacities and international demand, as shown by the cases of Tunisia and Madagascar. Secondly, diversification does not necessarily deliver success in exports in terms of either higher share of OECD markets or reduced volatility. Finally, a well-developed and reliable infrastructure, particularly energy services, is critical for export development, as shown by the case of Mauritius.

Export diversification depends on good infrastructure...

The low competitiveness of African products in global markets can be attributed in part to the continent's inadequate infrastructure development. Adding value to exported commodities through manufacturing is important for export diversification and sustained export growth, but depends vitally on the available infrastructure. figure 4.3 indicates the positive correlation between the Infrastructure Index (as introduced in chapter 3) and export diversification in 2000.

Infrastructure quality has been identified as the dominant explanatory factor in both manufacturing and competitiveness. Enterprise-level surveys conducted in several countries show that infrastructure costs and problems of unreliability rank high among issues of concern to businesses (Reinikka and Svensson, 1999). Table 4.1 provides an overview of the state of infrastructure in Africa and other developing countries. The table clearly shows that in all categories, sub-Saharan Africa (SSA) has relatively less infrastructure than other developing regions. In 2000, per capita electricity consumption in SSA was 432 kWh. The Middle East and North Africa, Latin America and the Caribbean consumed three times more per capita than SSA.

Infrastructure costs and problems of unreliability rank high among issues of concern to businesses in Africa

Figure 4.3

Correlation between infrastructure and export diversification, 2000

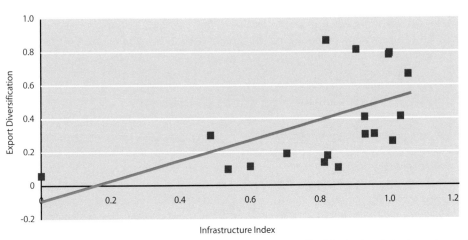

Notes: *Export diversification is measured as 1 minus the HHI index. The Infrastructure Index is made up of transport, energy, telecommunication, and access to information. Data are available for 18 countries in the Trade Competitiveness Index database. The countries are Algeria, Argentina, Bolivia, Brazil, Cameroon, Chile, Ethiopia, Ghana, Indonesia, Kenya, Malaysia, Morocco, Nigeria, Senegal, South Africa, Thailand, Tunisia, and Zimbabwe. The correlation is significant at the 5% level of significance – with a correlation coefficient of 0.405 and a p-value of 0.05.*

Source: *ECA Trade Competitiveness Index data*

There is an especially sharp contrast between Africa and East Asia. In a little over three decades, a number of East Asian countries have invested heavily in their infrastructure – between 6-8% of GDP per year, compared to 4% for the average developing country. In Taiwan, the rate of investment has sometimes been above 10% of GDP a year. Thailand developed its automotive industry on its eastern seaboard by investing in good rail and road networks and port facilities, supported by electricity, water and communications (Mody and Walton, 1998).

Table 4.1

Infrastructure indicators in Sub-Saharan Africa and other developing regions, 1995-2001

	Sub-Saharan Africa	Middle East & North Africa	Latin America & Caribbean	East Asia & Pacific
Electricity consumption per capita (kWh) in 2000	432	1,346	1,528	760
Paved roads (percentage of total road network) 1995-2000	12.9	66.3	26.9	21.2
Telephone mainlines (per 1,000 people) 2001	14	100	165	110

Source: *World Bank, 2003a*

Because quality is not taken into account, the numbers shown in table 4.1 do not indicate the real extent of the infrastructure gap between Africa and other developing economies. For instance, electric power failures are frequent in many parts of SSA, and paved as well as unpaved roads are often in poor condition. For example, the Ethiopian Minister of Trade and Industry has pointed out that "about 65% of the population lives half a day away from roads and basic infrastructure" (World Bank, 2003b).

> *Expenditure on standby generators represented 25% of total firm investment in equipment and machinery in Uganda*

Unreliable power hobbles diversification

Good and reliable energy infrastructure is a prerequisite for export diversification and sustained growth. It is vital for resource-based manufacturing and commodity processing, as well as trade in services. Reliable energy is also needed to increase efficiency in the agricultural sector and to develop non-traditional exports. That reliable energy infrastructure is important for diversification is further supported by the fact that most African countries that have moved into manufacturing started with the manufacturing of garments (e.g. Lesotho, Mauritius and Tunisia) The available evidence shows that textile production is a highly energy-consuming process. Average consumption lies between 54 and 72 MJ/kg (Megajoules per kg). Energy consumption increases with the switch from yarn to fabric finishing and from synthetic to natural fibres (Schmidt, 1999).

ECA independently verified the correlation between export diversification and per capita electricity consumption and electricity production per worker. Per capita electricity consumption was used as a proxy for energy cost (both direct and indirect costs). Countries with high per capita electricity consumption are expected to have lower energy costs and vice versa. The exercise found that export diversification is positively associated with per capita electricity consumption and electricity production per worker with correlation coefficients of 0.39 and 0.43 respectively. Both correlations are significant (at the 5 per cent level) implying that countries that have more access to electricity tend to have a relatively lower cost of energy and are more diversified.

The inability of many African countries to provide good and adequate energy services has been a major constraint to their export diversification. Under protectionist regimes, firms can actually absorb and even pass on higher costs they incur when they are forced to provide their own energy services. As a result, the inability of government to provide energy services may not be an important barrier to trade promotion but, when some form of trade liberalization takes place, firms with export potential will be unable to compete because they are saddled with inefficient production structures that were created as they attempted to substitute the private provision of energy in response to the failure of the public sector (Gugerty and Stern, 1997).

The poor energy services that characterize most of SSA also reduce the overall level of private sector investment. The links between energy provision and export diversification are illustrated in figure 4.4. A 1999 survey of firms in Senegal cited power failures, transport costs and other infrastructure problems among the top four operational problems, with the strongest impact on small-and medium-sized firms (SMEs). Three of the largest companies assessed the resulting costs from the power outages (electric generators, operating costs, loss of production and material deterioration) at approximately 10% of their total sales. A similar study by the World Bank's Regional Programme on Enterprise Development (RPED) in Madagascar in 2002 found power supply to be a major burden on enterprise development. Whereas electric power appeared to be adequate in the capital city, firms reported that voltage fluctuations and outages were increasing and that they planned to buy standby generating plants. Outside Antananarivo, the study found that the electricity infrastructure was in an even worse condition.

Figure 4.4

Energy–diversification linkages: the micro picture

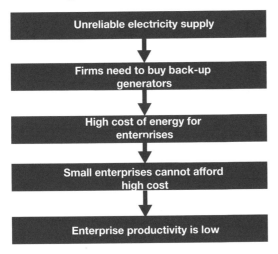

Further evidence points to inadequate electricity supply, increasing business costs and dissuading potential investment. For instance in Uganda, a survey of 243 firms conducted in 1998 showed that they did not receive electricity from the public grid for 89 operating days a year, on average, resulting in 77% of large firms (in addition to 44% of medium-sized and 16% of small-sized firms) purchasing generators, representing 25% of their total investment in equipment and machinery (Reinikka and Svensson, 1999). In Tanzania and Malawi, firms that took the initiative to buy generators, to compensate for the faulty public power supply, have been affected by high costs of fuel (Confederation of Tanzania Industries, 2002; Privatization Commission of Malawi, 2000). Finally, in Ghana as many as 75% of the exporters surveyed said that they had suffered financial losses due to power fluctuations (Edjekumhene et al., 2001).

Small firms are worst hit

Public utility companies provide most of the electric power in SSA. Public utilities supply electric power inefficiently, at high costs, and with a low degree of reliability. The resulting high costs reduce export competitiveness. While it is possible to substitute private power for public power, this is often achieved at a cost that reduces profitability.

Further, there is evidence that the effort to substitute private power for public power have differential effects on SMEs and large firms. Lee and Anas (1992) examined the cost to Nigerian firms of providing their own power needs. They found that small firms cannot afford to make costly capital investments to meet their power needs. Given that SMEs are greatly affected by unreliable power supply, the growth of these firms and the generation of employment are negatively impacted. The high dependence on electricity supply of Ghana's new data processing sector is discussed in box 4.1.

Box 4.1

Data processing in Ghana: electricity is a critical factor

A new area where Ghana's low-cost labour force and investment incentives have attracted investors is labour-intensive data processing. For example, one foreign company, Affiliated Computer Services, has been set up to process data by satellite to service such US companies such as UPS, Aetna and American Express. The company employs about 220 workers and is planning in its initial phase to grow to 1,000. If things go well, the firm may expand to other areas of the country and employ up to 4,000 processors and perhaps even move into software programming.

For data processing, electricity supply is critical. The industry depends on turnaround times; batches of data received have to be turned around in three hours. If these turnaround times cannot be met, the data processing businesses in Ghana will be in jeopardy. An erratic electricity supply, with four or five cuts a day, also leads to power surges, which damage critical equipment.

Source: World Bank, 2001c

There is evidence that SMEs can make a significant contribution to export development and job creation. Lee (1989) finds that SMEs generated about 60-80% of new jobs created in Asia and Latin America. Berry (1992) finds that the export potential of SMEs is limited to the processing of primary products, the manufacture of traditional products using labour-intensive indigenous technology, products which cannot be standardized and specialized products with small total market. Thus, while most SMEs may not be important exporters of manufactured products, they can serve as suppliers of "indirect exports", that is, as producers of parts used by major exporters (Gugerty and Stern, 1997). Lack of adequate and reliable energy prevents such developments. Kessides (1993) finds that small firms tend to start up near urban centres with easy access to good utilities. Cities with poor infrastructure are unable to offer this "incubator" function to new small firms. As a result, the potential links between SMEs and larger firms, including exporters, fail to develop.

Africa's power sector today — untapped potential and challenges

Africa possesses an abundant and wide range of energy resources. As table 4.2 indicates, the exploitable hydropower capacity in Africa is massive, with over 1,888 Terawatt-hours per year (TWh/yr). The region has an estimated 10,122 million tons of petroleum, 11.4 trillion cubic metres of proven natural gas reserves, and over 55 billion tons of bituminous coal (WEC, 2003). However, the distribution of the energy potential across the continent is highly uneven. Conventional resources such as oil and gas are concentrated in North and West Africa while hydroelectric potential is mainly located in Central and East Africa and coal in Southern Africa.

Only 23% of Africa's population have access to electricity

Table 4.2

Africa's vast energy potential

Energy resources	Total	% of global reserves
Oil reserves	10,122 millions of tons	7.1
Gas reserves	11.4 trillion m3	7.5
Bituminous coal reserves	55,000 millions of tons	10.6
Uranium reserves	613 kilotons	18.7
Hydroelectric capacity (Technically exploitable)	Over 1,888 TWh/yr	33 (13)

Note: *1 Terawatt = 1 million Megawatts*
Source: *World Energy Council, 2003*

Despite the abundance of substantial energy resources, less than 30% of sub-Saharan Africans have access to electricity. This is a very low figure, when compared to other developing countries in Asia and Latin America, which are able to supply more than 70% of their population with electricity (Karekezi, 2002). Africa's electricity generation was 479.8 TWh in 2001, representing about 3.1% of the world's electric production (see figure 4.5). The Middle East has approximately the same share with a population almost five times smaller (IEA, 2003).

Africa's electricity generation capacity is mainly concentrated in two regions, subregions, North Africa and Southern Africa. Combined, these two regions alone account for 82% of total power generating capacity in Africa. The DRC (Central), Kenya (East), and Nigeria (West) are the leaders in power-generating capacity for Africa's other subregions. Most countries have an installed capacity below 1,000 Megawatts (MW). The largest producers are Egypt, with installed generating capacity of 17,000 MW, and South Africa, where the utility company, Eskom, has installed capacity of about 40,000 MW (EIA, 1999).

Electricity is largely generated from thermal stations such as large coal-fired power stations in South Africa and oil-fired units in North Africa and Nigeria. For the rest of the continent, hydroelectricity represents the primary source of electricity. The major hydropower stations are situated on Africa's great rivers (Congo, Niger, Nile, and Zambezi). Reliance on hydropower is 80% or greater in Cameroon, the DRC, Mozambique, Rwanda, Uganda, and Zambia. (EIA, 1999).

Figure 4.5

World regional shares of electricity generation in 2001

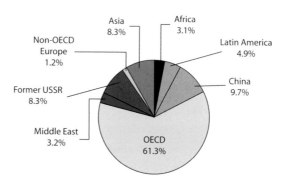

Notes: *Electricity generation excludes pumped storage; Asia excludes China, Japan and Korea*
Source: *International Energy Agency, 2003*

Access to a central power grid is a major challenge for Africa. Outside of Southern Africa (and to a lesser extent, North Africa), electricity demand on a per capita basis is very low, especially in Central, East, and West Africa. As figure 4.6 indicates, the average electricity consumption per capita in Africa is estimated to be about 515 kilowatt-hours (kWh). This is the lowest figure in the world, compared to other regions. Excluding South Africa and North Africa, this figure would drop to 126 kWh per capita (World Bank 2001a, Karekezi 2002). Africa's consumption per capita is about three times less than the per capita consumption in Latin America and five times less than per capita consumption in the Middle East.

A number of problems have limited the ability of the sector to power Africa's export diversification drive. These include:

- High system losses, in transmission and distribution;
- Unsustainable tariffs;
- Climatic fluctuations ;
- Poor technical and financial performance;
- Low level of private investment; and
- Failure to supply rural areas.

Figure 4.6

World regional shares of electricity consumption, 2001 (kWh p/capita)

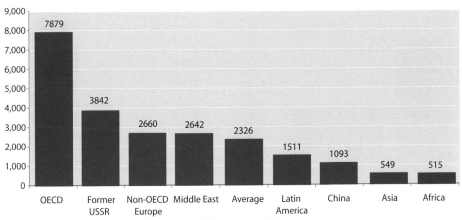

Power losses at transmission and distribution levels exceed 30% in many African countries

Notes: *Electricity consumption for Asia excludes China, Japan and Korea*
Source: *International Energy Agency, 2003*

High system losses

Power transmission and distribution losses are those that occur in transmission between sources of supply and points of distribution to consumers. As figure 4.7 shows, some of the power systems in Africa record total system losses sometimes exceeding 30%, while the international standard is between 10-12% (World Bank, 2003a; Karekezi, 2002). In South Africa, system losses are close to international standards (8.2%). When a line is too thin, energy is lost in terms of heat because of high pressure, and this is referred to as a technical loss. But the bulk of losses at transmission and distribution level in Africa are non-technical, usually because of illicit connections, theft of equipment, metre tampering and old/faulty meters. Large investments in upgrading and reinforcement of transmission and distribution networks and retrofitting of plants with more efficient auxiliary devices are the keys to reducing these inefficiencies.

Unsustainable tariffs

Most African governments have subscribed to the view that low-priced electricity can contribute to achieving economic and social development. Consequently, electricity tariffs in some African countries can tend to reflect a political agenda rather than an economically sound management policy. As a result, tariffs are often below marginal costs, requiring high levels of subsidies to keep the utilities afloat. On the other hand, countries in West Africa, particularly the francophone countries, seem to record very high tariffs that could have a detrimental impact on low-income consumers (Karekezi and Kimani, 2002). One promising solution to tariff problems is the pricing of electricity through a regulatory process. Indeed such a process can seek to eliminate monopoly pricing to protect the interests of end-users, as well as provide a fair return to network owners.

Figure 4.7

Electric power transmission and distribution losses, selected sub-saharan Africa countries in 2000 (percentage of output)

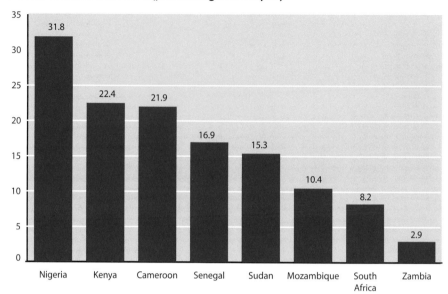

Source: World Bank, 2003a

Climatic factors

Hydroelectricity represents the primary source of electricity for SSA countries, especially those not endowed with fossil fuels. During times of drought, however, some countries experience power shortages because of insufficient hydropower generation. Climatic fluctuations can thus have a direct impact on electricity supply and generation costs, and the overall economy. For instance, Zimbabwe's 1992 drought caused electricity shortages that cost it $235 million in lost export earnings, equivalent to nearly 3.5% of GDP (EAGER 1998; World Bank, 2003a). In Kenya, where hydropower accounts for approximately 80% of power production, low dam reservoir levels led to reductions in generation; water and power rationing devastated the country's economy in 1999 and 2000. The cost of unmet electricity demand was equal to 3.8-6.5% of GDP (World Bank, 2000). In Ghana, sustained low rainfall over 18 months in 1997-1998 resulted in power rationing and power cuts affecting domestic and industrial consumers alike. The level of GDP growth for 1998 was estimated to have been cut by three percentage points as a result (Edjekumhene et al., 2001). In vulnerable countries, electricity generation sources need to be diversified to include thermal stations.

Poor financial and technical performance

Financially, debt owed by customers is often a sizeable amount, leading to deterioration of the cash flow situation and company losses (Karekezi, 2002; AFREPREN, 2001). In many cases, customers (particularly governments) fail to pay their bills on time. In Tanzania the debt collection period, standing at 64 days in 1990, reached 315 days in 1998 (AFREPREN, 2001). In 1997, the Tanzanian Government owed its national utility, TANESCO, about $47.62 million, representing 26% of the company's annual turnover (Kibanga, 1997). At the beginning of 2002, the Kenyan Government owed Kenya Power and Lighting Company (KPLC) about 2.5 billion Kenyan shillings (Wamukonya, 2003), equivalent to nearly 9% of its annual turnover. Further, throughout SSA, energy theft, ineffective metering and billing practices all contribute to low revenue collection.

Technical and managerial performance of African utilities is often poor, resulting in a low quality of supply and services and an inability to meet growing electricity demand. Little improvement in refurbishment and maintenance has taken place is SSA's power plants over the last ten years. Fuel and lubricant consumption tends to be high in diesel power plants, partly because of poor maintenance. In many instances, engines last only a fraction of their normal lifetime, greatly increasing capital costs per unit of production. In several countries, average engine lifetimes are as low as five to ten years (World Bank, 1992).

Private investment in electricity in sub-Saharan Africa was less than 2% of all private electricity projects in developing countries

Low levels of private investment

African governments have been able neither to finance the expansion or refurbishment in the power sector nor to attract private sector investment. The International Finance Corporation (IFC) estimated that FDI in the power sector in SSA was only 6% of all infrastructure FDI inflows into the region between 1990 and 1998. In comparison, telecommunications accounted for 89% of all FDI inflows in this period. Far more popular destinations for the electric sector are East Asia and the Pacific, and Latin America and the Caribbean.

Between 1990 and 1999, private investment in electricity in SSA was $2.9 billion, representing less than 2% of all private electricity projects in developing countries (see table 4.3). The bulk of private investment in electricity was in Latin America and Caribbean, with almost 40% of the total. More private investment is essential to mobilize resources for the development of the sector and, more importantly, alleviate the budgetary burden on African state-owned power utilities.

Failure to supply rural areas

In most African countries, the provision of electricity is largely confined to the urban areas. Urban electrification levels are still well below 50% (AFREPREN, 2001). Statistics show that even in urban areas, with the exception of Zimbabwe and South Africa, the percentage of households served with electricity is still small. Household electrification is especially low in the rural areas of SSA, and yet the majority of the population in Africa (80%) resides in the rural areas. For instance, rural electrification levels in Malawi, Mozambique, and Kenya are just 0.05%, 0.7%, and 2.0% respectively (AFREPREN, 2001). The agricultural sector in Africa accounts for a large proportion of the GDP. This heavy dependence on agriculture is likely to continue being the norm for most of SSA.

Table 4.3

Private investments in electricity projects in developing countries, 1990-1999

	1990	1991	1992	1993	1994	1995	1996	1997	1998	1999	Total
Sub-Saharan Africa	49	0	27	1	84	42	1,014	503	709	455	2,884
Middle East and North Africa	0	0	0	0	225	0	217	4,679	0	715	5,837
Europe and Central Asia	85	0	1,041	0	1,332	3,369	3,507	2,128	504	688	12,655
South Asia	169	735	37	1,186	3,081	3,193	4,934	2,319	926	2,227	18,805
East Asia and the Pacific	55	454	4,622	5,592	7,291	7,492	11,677	12,437	4,833	1,945	56,398
Latin America and the Caribbean	1,204	23	2,497	3,298	2,924	5,788	8,750	20,629	12,720	6,287	64,120
Total	1,562	1,212	8,225	10,077	14,936	19,884	30,100	42,694	19,692	12,317	160,698

Source: *World Bank Private Participation in Infrastructure (PPI) database*

With low levels of electrification in rural areas, the increase in productivity in large farms as well as in the agro-industry for export diversification will be very limited. Secure and low-cost supplies of electricity and other forms of energy are crucial if economic development, and social progress are to be realized. Furthermore there are gender implications in the failure to supply rural areas. Box 4.2 shows that women rely on the use of biomass because they have very limited access to modern sources of energy such as electricity and this affects competitiveness.

Reforming the sector through restructuring and competition

Power sector reforms are designed to introduce competition, where feasible, in the upstream production and downstream supply functions of the industry structure, and to use economic regulation of the wholesale and retail power markets to promote competition and protect consumer interests (AFREPREN, 2001). Reforms broadly consist of the following elements:

Box 4.2

Energy, gender and competitiveness

African women are engaged in a number of energy-demanding economic activities that can generate income through national, regional and international trade. In their contributions to the economy, women are the major producers of food and most of them are involved in income- or potential income-generating activities such as sewing, knitting, making handcrafts, food preservation, processing and retailing. In Zambia, for instance, women are also engaged in bakery, pottery, fish smoking, oilseed processing, beer brewing, soap making and maize milling, all of which have great export potentials. Experience in countries such as Uganda and Ghana shows that these types of commodities can become exports under the US Africa Growth and Opportunity Act (AGOA) system. However, in order to increase production and to exploit the full trade potential presented by trade liberalization, adequate and reliable sources of energy are necessary. Most of these industries owned by women depend on the use of biomass, especially firewood. With the provision of other forms of energy such as electricity, women can become more productive because they would spend less time searching for wood.

The table below shows how the use of wood fire by Zambian female entrepreneurs is still very important, accounting for a high percentage of output. For example it takes 9 kilograms of wood to produce 1 kilogram of flour!

Enterprises	Energy Use
Beer brewing	2 kg wood/1 litre of brew
Pottery	1.4 kg wood/1 kg of clay
Oil seed processing	0.24kg wood/1 kg seed
Bakery (Dover)	2.6 kg wood/1 kg of flour
Bakery (Dug out kiln)	9 kg wood/1kg of flour

The cost of producing potentially tradable goods is high in Africa and will translate into higher prices on the world market, creating a competitive disadvantage for many goods sold by African women. Heavy reliance on biomass as the only or major source of fuel cannot be sustained. Traditional energy sources not only have lower energy efficiency when compared to modern energy sources such as electricity and solar energy but they engage women in a downward spiral of environmental degradation. Women's access to new and affordable sources of energy such as electricity is crucial to improving their competitiveness and their contribution to economic development and social progress.

Sources: ECA, from official sources; ZERO, 1998

- Obliging electricity enterprises to operate according to commercial principles;
- Introducing of competition to improve sector performance in terms of efficiency, customer responsiveness, innovation and viability;
- Restructuring the electric power supply chain to enable the introduction of competition;
- Privatizing of unbundled electricity generators and distributors under dispersed ownership, as competition is unlikely to develop properly among entities that are under common ownership – whether State or private;

- Applying economic regulation of the power market transparently, through an agency that operates independently from influence by government, electricity suppliers or users; and

- Focusing the government's role on policy formation and execution, with divestiture of state ownership in generation and distribution.

Power sector reform in most of Africa has been recommended by the international financial institutions, which have been the traditional sources of finance for the sector. In Ghana, for instance, the national power company used to rely almost exclusively on guaranteed loans from foreign governments and donor agencies to finance generation and transmission projects (Edjekumhene et al., 2001). Since 1993, power sector reform has been a condition for lending to the power sector (World Bank, 1993). Mismanagement, poor operational performance, distorted tariffs resulting in poor economic efficiency and low returns on investment have been cited by the international financial institutions as essential reasons for the reform.

Compared to the other regions of the world, Africa's power sector reforms have been very slow to materialize, especially those reforms designed to minimize or reduce government control of the power sector, whether through establishing independent regulatory agencies, amendments to the electricity law, restructuring, or fully privatizing the generation and transmission sub-sectors. The Energy Sector Management Assistance Programme (ESMAP) of the World Bank surveyed 115 countries in 1998 to see how many of them had taken key reform steps in the power sector and whether there were important differences between regions (see table 4.4). Most countries in Latin America and the Caribbean appeared to have reformed their power sectors by 1998. South Asia was the next most reformed region. SSA appeared to have the least number of countries undertaking reforms, and the least reform measures – in fact only 15% of them. Only two countries in SSA had privatized their existing assets and only four had restructured the sector. It was clear that very little reform has taken place in the power sector in SSA, with the exception of the corporatization of the state utilities, and to a lesser extent the introduction of independent power producers (IPPs) in 19% of countries as opposed to the global figure of 40% of countries (AFREPREN, 2001).

An important factor for the acceptance of power reform processes in Africa is public education, whether through consultations or the use of the electronic and print media. For instance, Uganda's success in its privatization drive is based on regular consultation with consumers to ensure public awareness and support (Redwood-Sawyerr, 2002). Privatization is always likely to result in increases in electricity tariffs, and it is important that the rationale for increases is always well explained and discussed, if the support of the public is to be gained.

Mixed progress so far

A review of the impact of the few power sector reforms undertaken in Africa shows mixed results. Power sector reform has resulted in a reduction in technical losses among many reformers in Africa because of improvements in management and maintenance. Power losses in Côte d'Ivoire decreased from 19.8% to 17.4% between 1990 and 1998 (Bacon and Gutierrez, 1996). Curtailing of theft and illegal connections by using technical devices that

Table 4.4

Developing countries' power sector reform measures as of 1998, by number of countries per region

Reform Step	Region (number of countries)					
	Africa (48)	East Asia and the Pacific (9)	Europe and Central Asia (27)	Latin America and the Caribbean (18)	Middle East and North Africa (8)	South Asia (5)
Corporatization	15 (31%)	4 (44%)	17 (63%)	11 (61%)	2 (25%)	2 (40%)
Amendments to electricity law	7 (15%)	3 (33%)	11 (41%)	14 (78%)	1 (13%)	2 (40%)
Establishment of independent regulatory agencies	4 (8%)	1 (11%)	11 (41%)	15 (83%)	0 (0%)	2 (40%)
Introduction of independent power producers (IPPs)	9 (19%)	7 (78%)	9 (33%)	15 (83%)	1 (13%)	5 (100%)
Restructuring	4 (8%)	4 (44%)	14 (52%)	13 (72%)	3 (38%)	2 (40%)
Privatization of electricity generation	2 (4%)	2 (22%)	10 (37%)	7 (39%)	1 (13%)	2 (40%)
Privatization of electricity distribution	2 (4%)	1 (11%)	8 (30%)	8 (44%)	1 (13%)	1 (20%)
Reform indicator	0.88 (15%)	2.44 (41%)	2.70 (45%)	4.28 (71%)	1.00 (17%)	3.00 (50%)

Source: AFREPREN, 2001

prevent such tampering contributed significantly to the loss reduction. Power outages in Côte d'Ivoire decreased from 50 hours to 19 hours per month over four years, but at higher consumer prices (Girod and Percebois, 1996). In Kenya and Senegal, power rationing was an acute problem in 2001 because of drought, but also as a result of reform-associated factors (Wamukonya, 2003). One study in Kenya showed that electricity supply no longer ranked as such a major concern as in the past among multinational corporations, mainly because 60% of them had invested in full standby generators (*Daily Nation*, 2002).

Despite the successes attributed to the reforms in some countries, overall they have had very little impact on improved electrification levels, especially among the rural and urban poor.

This is partially due to the limited attention given to the distribution end. The rural electrification programmes initiated by governments have not been able to mobilize adequate funds or to ensure a timely release of rural electrification funds collected from electricity customers. Rural electrification programmes in the majority of East and Southern African countries appear to have stagnated, with the exceptions of those in South Africa and Zimbabwe.

Political and economic interests still have control over the power sector in many African countries. It is a situation that has generally resulted in high inefficiency and bad management. It is, however, important to note that no single model of reform appears to provide a panacea for the range of problems faced by African countries. African governments have done little so far to monitor the impact of the reforms they have already undertaken in order to ensure that they are working well and that consumers are starting to benefit from them. Power sector reform in SSA countries appears to have been concentrated more on alleviating the generation capacity shortfalls than on the serious deficiencies in distribution (AFREPREN, 2001). For the reforms to have a greater impact on the power sector, they need to concentrate on improving the technical and financial performance of power companies, as well as promoting access to electricity by rural dwellers and the urban poor.

A new agenda for Africa's power sector

The potential for African countries to achieve energy sustainability is enormous, provided the problems affecting the power sector are effectively addressed. The success of any strategy to develop the energy sector depends on solutions originating from governments and the private sector across the continent. This section explores key elements of a strategy to remedy the imbalance in energy supply and demand, including the promotion of energy efficiency; making power companies more efficient; promoting rural electrification; encouraging private participation in the power sector; effective regulation; realistic pricing; and undertaking subregional integration in energy services.

Energy efficiency

Energy efficiency seeks to cut operating costs, enhance economic efficiency and improve the productivity and international competitiveness of energy-consuming companies. Energy use in the modern sector in Africa is extremely inefficient, offering large, unused energy conservation potential (World Bank, 1992). Experience from other developing countries has demonstrated that technically proven, cost-effective energy conservation and efficiency measures can save between 10% and 30% of energy consumption. In Ghana, for example, the low energy efficiency of the manufacturing sector could be increased by at least 15% through "housekeeping" measures alone, for instance, changing the way equipment is used (World Bank, 1993).

Energy efficiency measures the amount of GDP generated by one unit of energy use. Indeed, most African countries lag behind in terms of energy efficiency when compared to the rest of the world. Figure 4.8 indicates that for the year 2000, Tanzania, Zambia,

Nigeria and had the lowest level of energy efficiency in Africa, with respectively $1.3, $1.2 and $1.1 for one unit of energy use. By contrast, Namibia and Morocco recorded one of the highest levels of energy efficiency in the world, with respectively $12 and $9.5 for one unit of energy use. Low energy-efficiency levels in countries such as Nigeria and Zambia are due in large part to the virtual absence of energy conservation measures in their industrial sectors (Nilecom Technology, 2003).

Although the average African uses far less energy than the world average, producing a dollar's worth of GDP uses more energy in Africa on the average than the rest of the world. Increasing the efficiency of current supply and utilization should be the top-most priority of strategies for power sector development. Power sector reform to increase the efficiency and reliability of energy supplies and promote efficient use of energy is the cheapest solution with the greatest short-term benefits. This is particularly relevant in large parts of Africa where installed capacity is lagging behind demand.

Producing a dollar's worth of GDP uses more energy in Africa than in the rest of the world

Figure 4.8

GDP per unit of energy use selected African countries, 2000 (PPP US$ per kg of oil equivalent)

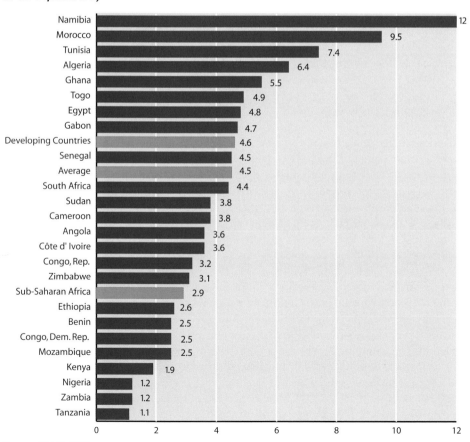

Namibia	12
Morocco	9.5
Tunisia	7.4
Algeria	6.4
Ghana	5.5
Togo	4.9
Egypt	4.8
Gabon	4.7
Developing Countries	4.6
Senegal	4.5
Average	4.5
South Africa	4.4
Sudan	3.8
Cameroon	3.8
Angola	3.6
Côte d' Ivoire	3.6
Congo, Rep.	3.2
Zimbabwe	3.1
Sub-Saharan Africa	2.9
Ethiopia	2.6
Benin	2.5
Congo, Dem. Rep.	2.5
Mozambique	2.5
Kenya	1.9
Nigeria	1.2
Zambia	1.2
Tanzania	1.1

Source: UNDP, 2003

An energy efficiency programme needs to include:

- Promotional and information dissemination activities to increase energy conservation awareness;
- Technical support for industry and commerce through the provision of diagnostic energy services, energy conservation installations and retrofits;
- Promotion of energy-efficient technologies such as electric motors, heating and lighting systems;
- Financial interventions to assist energy users in acquiring energy efficient technologies;
- Development and promotion of alternative energy sources such as solar, water heaters, mini-hydro for local grids, biomass powered plants, etc.; and
- Establishment of a body to advocate and implement energy conservation measures.

> *Promoting energy efficiency is the cheapest solution with the greatest short-term benefits*

The success of any energy-efficiency initiatives depends on how information on the latest technologies and methods, as well as the benefits of energy efficiency, gets to energy consumers. The Ghana Energy Foundation, for instance, has an elaborate programme of action to educate the public through seminars and workshops, electronic media campaigns and billboards. The results of such campaigns confirm that given the right information at the right time, Ghanaian consumers could reduce their electricity consumption by between 25-75% (Ofosu-Ahenkorah, 2003).

Better-managed power companies

It is increasingly being argued that power sector reforms should concentrate on distancing the sector from the interests of political leaders and the State bureaucracy and on introducing incentives, to both managers and workers, to provide the most efficient electricity services to the consumer. A significant step is to transform power companies that are under government ownership into independent and self-reliant corporations, where feasible. As the corporate culture gains root, some form of commercialization can be introduced to impose the discipline of corporate law and the expectations of the market (Chiwaya et al., 1996).

Public ownership does not necessarily mean inefficiency; neither does private ownership guarantee economic efficiency. Continued public ownership may be justified where state-owned power companies are working well and governments can mobilize the financing for their investments without crowding out other priorities. For example, South Africa's State utility, Eskom, has provided a good quality of electricity supply in recent years and will maintain a dominant role in the generation sector for the foreseeable future, while independent power producers will be licensed so that greater competition in generation can be encouraged (Clark, 2001). However, in some other countries, where private investment is badly needed, because of both management and funding problems, continued government ownership of electric power companies may hamper progress. Mauritius provides an example of the potential of local private participation in the power sector. Close to 25% of annual electricity generation comes from local privately owned and operated cogeneration plants within the sugar industry (Deepchand, 2001).

The success and efficiency of power companies will depend to a large extent on how they incorporate economic considerations into their operations. This may require tariffs based on real cost, effective and efficient collection of revenues, minimization of loss and waste in the delivery of energy services, internally generated reinvestment in technological upgrading and new capacity creation (Mkhwanazi, 2003). An example of successful transformation has been provided by Uganda, which essentially addressed the separation of generation, transmission and distribution before the unbundling of its operations. By the end of 1999, it had seen a remarkable increase in most performance indicators, such as increased revenue collection (from 83% to 94 % in 1998), increased billing for consumption of about 12%, a better debt collection rate and a more attractive business profile (Bidasala-Igaga, 2001).

In Cape Verde wind energy represents 10 to 15% of all electricity produced

The challenge of rural electrification

Rural electrification has great potential to enhance Africa's export diversification and to promote economic growth through the processing of agricultural products for export. Direct economic benefits would be expected to flow from the use of electricity in productive applications, such as irrigation, crop processing and food preservation, as well as greatly improved social services (WEC, 1999). The ongoing restructuring of the power sector in Africa has not really taken into account the realities in rural areas where the extension of energy services does not keep pace with population growth. Private companies will probably be reluctant to invest in rural electrification because of the limited financial benefits, and so there is a need for public investment. This can be done if governments play a more aggressive and transparent role of promoting smaller village-based energy systems. Recent solar and wind power developments in Kenya and Cape Verde have, however, shown that there is also an important role for commercial initiatives in forms of electrification beyond the scope of national grid systems (see boxes 4.3 and 4.4).

Empirical evidence shows that some rural electrification programmes have been an economic success when measured by returns on investment. Diesel generators for local supplies or diesel engines for pumping may in some cases be more viable than universal grid coverage. In general, rural electrification is more likely to succeed when it is based on, or accompanied by, complementary social and economic infrastructure development (e.g. rural water supplies, health programmes, primary and secondary education, and regional and feeder roads).

Rural electrification, especially where it can support export expansion and diversification, is important in any full power sector development strategy. Emphasis should be placed on decentralized power generation and renewable energies. Small or micro power generation systems are viable alternatives to over-reliance on the centralized national grid, which rarely serves rural areas. There is, however, a need for more financing from the international development institutions for such projects (Bamenjo, 2002).

Box 4.3

Solar power in Kenya

Photovoltaic (PV) technology converts sunlight directly into electricity. In such a system, power is produced when sunlight strikes the semiconductor material and creates an electric current. The Kenya PV industry provides a model of sustainable, commercially driven and off-grid rural electrification, worthy of consideration by other countries in Africa. It is estimated that some 200,000 PV solar home systems have been installed since the early 1990s totalling more than 3.5 MW of installed capacity. Since the 1990s, sales of solar modules have remained over 20,000 systems per year, representing a PV market worth more than ★6 million a year.

Currently the PV industry in Kenya has a number of players including importers, installers, battery charging stations and appliance sellers, many of whom have an annual turnover of more than ★500,000. Most people who purchase PV systems are members of the rural middle class who have little hope of gaining access to the national grid. People who purchase PV systems are interested in gaining power for TV, lighting and music systems. Even though low-cost provision of PV solar home systems has been successfully developed by the private sector in Kenya, a number of problems (such as lack of awareness and affordability) have prevented PV systems from reaching the rural poor.

Source: Hankins, 2001

Box 4.4

Wind power in the Cape Verde Islands

The ten islands that constitute the Republic of Cape Verde rely heavily on imported fuel for their electricity needs. ELECTRA, the State-owned utility, is facing serious difficulties in meeting growing demand for electricity in the archipelago, which has no primary energy resources except firewood, which meets 57% of household energy needs; wood is increasingly scarce as forests are depleted. The country, however, has an excellent wind energy potential, which is a suitable and technically viable substitute for high-cost diesel generation. Wind energy has always been used in Cape Verde Islands for water pumping, but it is only since 1994, when wind farms with a total capacity of 2.6 MW were installed, that wind energy has come to represent 10-15 % of all electricity produced.

The World Bank/GEF (Global Environment Facility) project added an additional 7.8 MW at a cost of ★9 million. The project's objective is to mitigate carbon emissions resulting from power generation. By making it possible for ELECTRA's strategic private partner to develop the first commercial wind farms, the project allows wind energy projects to be implemented on a fully commercial basis. Promoting renewable energy with the help of the private sector will save foreign exchange otherwise spent on imported fuel. Wind power also facilitates activities in agriculture and tourism. For a country with such a dry environment and scarce vegetation, preservation has a real meaning.

Sources: World Bank, 2001b; Monteiro Alves et al., 2000

Attracting the private sector

Power sector development in Africa has been constrained by a lack of public resources and by the difficulty of attracting bilateral and multilateral development assistance or FDI for investment in the sector. Private sector participation in the power sector can potentially bring substantial benefits to African governments. It offers new skills, technology and management techniques to the power sector, resulting in more efficient operations and management of resources and, most importantly, continued funding for renewal and expansion.

The main forms of private sector participation in the development of the energy sector include:

- Service contracts to contract out responsibility for delivering particular services;
- Management contracts to transfer responsibility for certain operations;
- Build Own and Operate (BOO)/Build Operate and Transfer (BOT) and other concessions for financing new investments; and
- Divestiture and sale of existing electricity businesses.

Table 4.5

Options for private participation in the energy sector

Option	Asset ownership	Operation and maintenance	Capital investment	Commercial risk	Typical duration
Service contract	Public	Shared	Public	Public	1-2 years
Management contract	Public	Private	Public	Public	3-5 years
Lease	Public	Private	Public	Shared	8-15 years
Concession	Public	Private	Private	Private	25-30 years
BOO/BOT scheme	Shared	Private	Private	Private	20-30 years
Divestiture	Private	Private	Private	Private	++

Source: *World Bank, 2002*

The range of options for private participation in the energy sector is outlined in table 4.5. Most of these forms of involvement are already taking place in most African countries. At the individual country level, the best strategy to encourage private sector participation in the power sector is the provision of a good business environment, in which private firms can operate with less uncertainty and instability. Governments should commit themselves to implementing energy reforms and restructuring in order to allow more competition and private entry into the market. The potential role of local stock markets is discussed in box 4.5. At the regional and subregional level, African countries should aim for greater integration by organizing subregional markets and strengthening cooperation in energy.

Box 4.5

Financing the power sector in Africa: the role of stock markets

Perhaps the greatest problem facing the power sector in Africa is the inability to meet capital requirements. The increased use of energy will require capital – a factor that is very scarce in most African countries. For electric power alone, the average annual investment cost for an African country lies between ★60-100 million, depending on assumptions regarding the rates of growth, improvement in end-use energy efficiency, and pricing.

The prospect for any significant increase in aid for power sector development is very slim. In addition to the constraint on international concessionary credit and commercial bank finance, the resources of the public sector are limited. In fact, the public sector in Africa is already overburdened with the need to meet investment in health and social services, and cannot find the billions needed to finance the power sector. This leaves domestic and international capital markets as the main sources of finance for the power sector. However, domestic capital markets are either non-existent or underdeveloped in Africa. Africa's stock markets are generally very small, illiquid and poorly regulated.

The development of local capital markets can, nevertheless, lead to a boost in finance for the power sector. In many advanced countries the financing of infrastructure by attracting private savings helped stimulate their capital markets. The history of European and North American stock markets reveals that the issuing of securities by large public companies, many of which can be classified today as utility companies, was a foundation of the capital markets' growth. Local capital markets can offer substantial benefits. For the government, the existence of a local interest in power finance can ease many political problems, as well as act as a springboard for attracting FDI.

Sources: World Bank, 1989; Yartey, 2002

A critical role for good regulation

Good, credible and consistent regulation of the power sector is a necessary condition for effective service delivery. In general, a regulatory body is expected to provide mechanisms for monitoring, supervision, areas of intervention, objectives and targets for development of the sector and financial and best business/industrial practice. Adequate regulation will be able to reduce the ill effects associated with monopolistic elements in the power sector. The possibility of regulating prices by applying price cap-type measures, as well as the progressive introduction of competition, would help prevent any abuse of monopoly power and limit price increases. To perform effectively, it is essential that regulatory bodies are independent, and distanced from political, corporate and other pressures. This is not an easy matter, however, and the kinds of problems that may arise before independent regulation is achieved are illustrated in box 4.6.

The autonomy of regulatory bodies depends on the expertise of its membership in legal and technical issues as well as the government's commitment to recognize the authority of this body. However, many of the regulatory agencies in Africa have to report to their respective Ministers of energy, and most lack independent sources of finance.

The regulators' decisions, particularly on tariffs, have not always been adhered to and this is a further indicator of the constraints on their power. For example, after the Uganda Electricity Board raised tariffs by as much as 158%, consumer outrage forced the country's President to seek tariff reductions (*East African Standard*, 2001).

Box 4.6

Autonomous regulation in Kenya?

Kenya's Electricity Power Act of 1997 established the Electricity Regulatory Board (ERB) to regulate the power industry. However, another statute, the State Corporation Act, effectively placed the Electricity Regulatory Board under the Ministry of Energy and provided for its dissolution. ERB has been defined as a State corporation and therefore its autonomy is suspect. For instance, although the ERB is supposed to provide licences for the construction of electrical works, the Ministry of Energy has continued to do so. Moreover, the ERB can only advise the Minister of Energy on matters relating to granting, suspension and revocation of licences. It is the Minister rather the ERB that has the power to fine a licensee in breach of conduct. In 2001, the entire board of ERB was replaced under State Corporation Act provisions. The main source of finance for the ERB is a levy imposed by the Ministry of Energy on electricity sales. While so far this funding has been sufficient, there is no provision for ERB to seek external funding in the case of any shortfall.

Source: *Nyoike and Okech, 2002*

> *Regulatory bodies should be independent, and distanced from political, corporate and other pressures*

The example of India shows that regulators can succeed in keeping control over tariffs (Balakrishna, 2000). In some states, notably Orissa and Maharashtra, regulators have been reluctant to allow increases in tariffs without evidence of reduced losses. Regulatory decisions on tariffs have not gone unchallenged. In Orissa, the World Bank explicitly urged the Regulatory Commission to approve tariff increases to provide comfort to investors just before privatization, a request that they rejected. In Madhya Pradesh, the regulatory agency refused to allow tariff increases, a decision that was challenged by the state government (Indiapoweronline.com, 2000).

Regulation in Africa should at first be limited to correcting market imperfections that arise from unregulated markets, and it should not impede the development of the power sector itself. Considering that rules and regulations can become so stringent that they stifle private initiative, there is a need for a balanced approach.

Ways to make pricing realistic

The essential nature of the service that electricity provides to all sectors of the economy requires that its prices be set prudently and efficiently. If electricity prices are held below the cost of production, it can result in negative results in terms of over-consumption, environmental degradation and wasted natural resources. On the other hand, if prices are held artificially high, industrial competitiveness will suffer and some consumers may be deprived of an essential service.

Figure 4.9

Cost of 1 kWh in Tunisia compared to selected ECOWAS countries (in CFA francs)

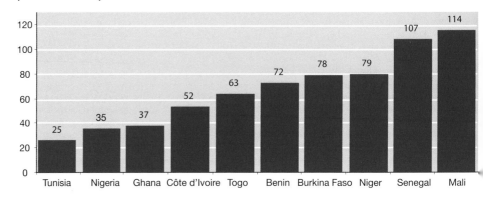

Source: *ECA, from official sources*

> *Producing 1 kilowatt hour of electricity in Mali and Senegal is four times more expensive than in Tunisia*

Within Africa, there are wide variations in the cost of producing electricity, as figure 4.9 shows, and these variations inevitably pose problems in achieving efficient pricing systems. In essence, efficient pricing of electricity allows for economically optimal behaviour by each consumer and avoids system overload without having to resort to rationing because the price of electricity changes as system conditions change. Joskow and Schmalensee (1983) argued that wholesale and retail power prices are not generally based on marginal cost-pricing principles, even in advanced economies. Hourly, daily and seasonal variations in marginal costs are lost in the fixed annual rates. The variability of system marginal costs over time means that the rate of return will fail to transmit to consumers the true marginal cost of the power they consume at any time. In most of Africa, it will not be possible to introduce more efficient marginal cost-pricing mechanisms until ongoing reforms become sufficiently established.

Electricity pricing mechanisms are typically complex and vary across countries and regions. Different countries have different regulatory regimes and policy frameworks, as well as different energy policy goals and objectives. In African countries, energy policies commonly subsidize, cross-subsidize and impose import tariffs, taxes and levies as well as prescribe required standards and other regulations. The subsidies on energy products results in market distortions, leading to lower economic efficiency and misallocation of resources. To ensure economic efficiency, it is important that price distortions are minimized and that the principles of consistency, transparency, clarity, and cost effectiveness are promoted. A balanced approach is needed in most African countries, by staged phasing-out of subsidies over a period of time, as new privately-funded plants are put in place. An interesting example of electricity pricing in the context of private investment in energy supply is provided by Malaysia, as discussed in box 4.7.

Given that monopolistic tendencies still dominate the African power sector, competition is not perfect, and information is asymmetric, marginal cost pricing cannot deliver the necessary benefits. In the short term, African governments should keep electricity prices regulated. However, as power sector reforms intensify, and competition is fully introduced, marginal cost pricing should be the ultimate objective.

Box 4.7

Pricing of electricity in Malaysia

Malaysia has developed a very successful independent power producer (IPP) programme. It is based on a bankable Power Purchase Agreement (PPA), backed by an indigenous fuel supply arrangement, making it possible for project financing in local currency. By 2000, the total installed generating capacity of the IPPs reached 4,149 MW, all in gas-fueled gas turbine plants. Tenaga Nasional Berhad (TNB), the national utility, continues to maintain dominance through its control of most of the generating capacity, the transmission network and distribution system. Under the current tariff structure, 100% of the peninsular population is supplied with electricity. This is achieved by having a tariff structure that allows TNB to cross-subsidize the electricity price. The determination of the tariff is subject to the approval of the government, based on the following considerations:

- Energy prices that reflect the economic or true cost of supply;

- Adequate revenues that allow for the development of the power sector;

- Competitiveness of Malaysia's industries and services;

- Diversification of energy resources, with greater use of indigenous resources; and

- Alignment with the social and economic objectives of the government.

Source: Onn, 2000

Regional and subregional energy integration

Africa has a rich abundance of commercial energy resources, but they are distributed unevenly. Inadequate energy transportation facilities, such as pipelines and transmission lines to move energy from abundant regions to deficient ones, have been cited as a major constraint to energy sector development in Africa. Regional and subregional cooperation and integration in energy services can help to create a viable export sector and promote economic growth. Simply because of the small size of national markets, many projects are only feasible and profitable in more regional and subregional dimensions. Subregional economic communities are, however, now beginning to encourage and strengthen cooperation in the energy trade through the joint interconnections of electricity grids, and collective oil and gas pipeline projects.

If well managed, regional cooperation should reduce power costs, minimize the operating costs and reduce system expansion costs through regional planning. The Southern African Power Pool (SAPP) is already in operation and there are bilateral pooling arrangements between some countries of East and Central Africa. The development of regional markets in energy services requires mechanisms for the use of interconnections, for operational security and for power purchase operations. This constitutes a major challenge for African energy authorities to take up.

A stronger commitment from African countries is needed to develop regionally integrated solutions. A study by the Southern African Development community (SADC) and the World Bank suggested that an estimated saving of $1.6 billion over ten years could be realized through optimal use of regional electricity resources and installation in Southern Africa. The SAPP, for instance, has recorded reductions in both capital and operating costs through the cooperation of its members, who have been able to recover their costs and share equitably in the resulting benefits (ECA, 2003). There has also been a reduction in the operating reserve requirement. Before the pooling arrangements, members carried a 30% reserve margin; currently, SAPP requires members to carry reserves of 10.2% for hydro and 7.6% for thermal. The power pool has also provided a forum for regional solutions to electricity problems in individual SADC countries.

> *1.6 billion dollars could be saved through optimal use of regional electricity resources in Southern Africa*

Conclusions

This chapter has focused on the need for Africa's energy sector managers and policy makers to work towards harnessing the continent's massive energy resources. Good energy management can be a basis for broader economic development as well as for export diversification. The greatest challenge is to make the development and utilization of energy as efficient as possible, in addition to ensuring that it is socially and economically beneficial. Governments have to commit themselves to restructuring their domestic energy sectors, both by allowing more competition and private investment into the market, and by strengthening subregional and regional cooperation in energy.

The key policy issue for Africa is how to provide adequate and reliable energy to meet the growing population in an efficient and affordable manner. The current energy infrastructure in many African countries is simply insufficient to support export diversification or ultimately to promote sustainable economic development. Growing demand for power supply needs to be met promptly and in a well-regulated manner. Pricing mechanisms must be effective and fair. If countries are to compete in the global marketplace, then governments and private investors must keep investing in expansion and renewal of the energy sector. To maintain this momentum, however, the role of the State will almost certainly have to be reduced.

The substantially higher cost of electric power in Africa compared to other regions has negatively affected the region's competitiveness in international markets. The relatively small size of many African countries suggests that more aggressive regional integration initiatives merit greater attention. Stronger emphasis should be placed on integrated energy supply networks based on regional initiatives, and especially in gas and electricity.

Annexes

A4.1 The Structure of Exports in Selected African Countries, 1966-2000

Countries	1966-1970		1996-2000		Diversification with Growth	Primary Processing
	PC Share	OECD Share	PC Share	OECD Share		
Algeria	98	0.5	88	0.31	D	A
Angola	99	0.17	100	0.1	C	C
Benin	99	0.01	83	0	D	D
Botswana [a]	99	0	86	0.01	A	A
Burkina Faso	99	0	77	0	D	D
Burundi	100	0.02	99	0	D	D
Cameroon	99	0.11	97	0.05	D	A
Central African Rep. [b]	99	0.01	97	0	C	C
Chad	100	0.01	94	0	D	D
Comoros	68	0	65	0	D	A
Congo, Rep.	88	0.03	96	0.03	B	C
Congo, Dem. Rep.	99	0.37	95	0.03	D	D
Côte d'Ivoire	99	0.24	94	0.08	D	A
Djibouti	83	0	51	0	D	D
Egypt	89	0.13	58	0.1	D	A
Equatorial Guinea	99	0.01	97	0.01	D	D
Ethiopia	97	0.06	86	0.01	D	D
Gabon	94	0.12	97	0.06	C	C
Gambia	99	0.01	97	0	D	D
Ghana	98	0.17	88	0.04	D	A
Guinea [a]	98	0.02	99	0.02	B	C
Guinea-Bissau [a]	97	0.01	94	0	D	A
Kenya	90	0.09	88	0.03	D	D
Lesotho [c]	28	0	20	0	A	D
Liberia	93	0.15	47	0.02	D	A
Madagascar	93	0.05	55	0.02	D	D
Malawi	99	0.02	98	0.01	D	A
Mali	96	0	83	0	D	D
Mauritania	99	0.05	98	0.01	D	A
Mauritius [a]	97	0.03	29	0.04	A	D
Mozambique	96	0.09	93	0	D	D
Morocco	95	0.26	38	0.17	D	D
Niger	100	0.02	91	0	D	A

A4.1 The Structure of Exports in Selected African Countries *(continued)*

Countries	1966-1970		1996-2000		Diversification With Growth	Primary Processing
	PC Share	OECD Share	PC Share	OECD Share		
Nigeria	98	0.42	98	0.31	C	C
Rwanda [a]	99	0.01	98	0	D	A
Senegal	98	0.08	92	0.01	D	D
Sierra Leone	99	0.06	69	0	D	A
Somalia	97	0.01	73	0	D	A
South Africa [a]	86	0.73	67	0.47	D	D
Sudan	99	0.09	93	0.01	D	A
Tanzania [a]	94	0.05	91	0.01	D	D
Togo	99	0.03	90	0	D	D
Tunisia	89	0.08	18	0.14	A	D
Uganda	100	0.09	98	0.01	D	D
Zambia	99	0.43	83	0.01	D	D
Zimbabwe	93	0.02	73	0.03	A	A

Notes: PC share is the share of primary commodities in total export. OECD share indicates the country's share in OECD imports. Data cover the period 1966-2000 except few countries for which data are only available from (a) 1970, (b) 1975, (c) 1976 and (d) 1978. Countries for which data are available after 1975 are excluded from figure 4.1. The 23 high-income OECD countries are Australia, Canada, EU (15), Iceland, Japan, New Zealand, Norway, Switzerland, and the United States. Columns 1 and 3 provide information on the share of primary commodities in total exports over the relevant period. Columns 2 and 4 summarize information on the share of total exports in OECD imports.

Column five summarizes the direction of change in both export diversification and market share. Countries that managed to increase both the share of manufactures and their weight in OECD imports are classified as A. A smaller share of manufactures coupled with bigger weight in OECD imports is classified as B. A lower share of manufactures coupled with a smaller weight in OECD imports is designated as C. Countries that were able to diversify away from primary products but had their share in OECD imports decreased are designated as D.

Column six summarizes the change in share of manufactures exports in total exports and processed primary products in total exports. Countries that both increased these shares are classified as A. B represents lower manufactures exports combined with higher processed primary exports. Countries that experienced a reduction in both are designated as C. D represents higher manufactures exports combined with lower processed primary products.

Source: Bonaglia and Fukasaku (2003), based on OECD Foreign Trade Statistics Database, 2002

References

African Energy Policy Research Network (AFREPREN) (2001), "Power Sector Reform in Africa," proceedings of a regional policy seminar, 24-25 April 2001, Nairobi

Bacon, R. and Gutierrez, L.E. (1996), "Global Reform Trends and Institutional Options for Sub-Saharan Africa," Symposium on power sector reform and efficiency improvement in Sub-Saharan Africa, Energy Sector Management Assistance Programme (ESMAP) report, no 182/96, World Bank, Washington DC

Balakrishna, P. (2000), "Power Regulators Grapple with Tariff Issues," July 2000, available online, accessed March 2002 (www.indiapoweronline.com)

Bamenjo, J. N. (2002), "Energy Sector Privatization in Africa: what perspectives for rural electrification?" presentation to the Second International Conference, Energy for Sustainable Societies, Bogota, 25-27 July 2002

Barberton, C. and Clark, A. (1999), "Barriers Inhibiting Investment in DSM in South Africa," Energy and Development Research Centre, University of Cape Town

Berry, R.A. (1992), "Firm Size in the Analysis of Trade," in Gerald Helleiner (ed), *Trade Policy, Industrialization and Development: New Perspectives*, Oxford, Clarendon Press, pp46-88

Bidasala-Igaga, H. (2001), "Power Sector Reform and Privatisation in Uganda," African Energy Policy Research Network (AFREPREN) occasional paper no 5, Nairobi

Bonaglia, F. and Fukasaku, K. (2003), "Export Diversification in Low Income Countries: an international challenge after Doha," Organisation for Economic Co-operation and Development (OECD) Technical Paper no 29, Paris

Cadot, O. and Nasir, J. (2002), "Madagascar: incentives and obstacles to trade, lessons from manufacturing case studies," Report of Regional Programme on Enterprise Development, World Bank, Washington DC

Chiwaya et al. (1996), "Reforming the Power Sector in Africa" in M.R. Bhagavan (ed), *African Energy Policy Research Network*, Zed Books, London

Clark, Alix (2001), "Power Sector Reforms in South Africa: plans and progress," briefing papers on power sector reform, International Energy Initiative (IEI), University of Cape Town, June 2001, only available online (www.energypublicbenefits.com/outputs_aug2002/southafrica/SouthAfrica_Clark.pdf)

Collier, P. (2002), "Primary Commodity Dependence and Africa's Future," World Bank, Washington, DC

Collier, P. and Hoffler, A. (2002), "Greed and Grievance in Civil Wars," Centre for the Study of African Economies (CSAE) Working Paper, 2002-01, University of Oxford

Confederation of Tanzania Industries (2002), "CTI Submits to the Government Tax Policy Proposals for the Year 2002/3 Budget," newsletter no 71, 28 March 2002

Daily Nation (2002), "Firms Plan to Move Out of Kenya," 30 April, Nairobi

Deepchand, K. (2001), "Bagasse-Based Cogeneration in Mauritius: a model for eastern and southern Africa," occasional paper no 2, African Energy Policy Research Network, (AFREPREN) Nairobi

Dijkstra, T. (2001), "Export Diversification in Uganda: developments in non-traditional agricultural exports," Working Paper 47/2001, African Studies Centre, Leiden University, Netherlands

Equity and Growth through Economic Research (EAGER) (1998), "Modeling Electricity Trade in Southern Africa," Eager Report, Issue 7/Summer, Washington DC (http://www.eagerproject.com/7e2.html)

East African Standard (2001), "Ugandans Oppose New Electricity Tariffs," 11-17 June, Nairobi

Economic Commission for Africa (ECA) (2003), *Economic Report on Africa 2003: Accelerating the Pace of Development*, Addis Ababa

Edjekumhene et al. (2001), "Power Sector Reform in Ghana: the untold story," Kumasi Institute of Technology and Environment (KITE), Ghana

Energy Information Administration (EIA) (1999), "Energy in Africa," Washington, DC (http://www.eia.doe.gov/emeu/cabs/africa.html)

Girod, J. and Percebois, J. (1996), "The Electric Power Sector in SSA: current institutional reforms," Symposium on Power Sector Reform and Efficiency Improvement in Sub-Saharan Africa, Johannesburg, Energy Sector Management Assistance Programme (ESMAP), Report no 182/96, World Bank, Washington DC

Gugerty, M. K. and Stern, J. J. (1997), "Structural Barriers to Trade in Africa," Harvard Institute for International Development (HIID) discussion paper, Boston

Hankins, M. (2001), "Energy Services for the World's Poor," World Bank, Washington DC

International Energy Agency (IEA) (2003), *Key World Energy Statistics*, Paris

International Monetary Fund (IMF) (2002), Direction of Trade Statistics, Washington DC

Joskow, P. L., and Schmalensee, R. (1983), *Markets for Power: An Analysis of Electric Utility Deregulation*, MIT Press, Cambridge MA

Karekezi, S. (2002), "The Status of Power Sector Reforms: a global overview with emphasis on reforms in Africa," African Energy Policy Research Network (AFREPREN), Nairobi

Karekezi, S. and Kimani, J. (2002), "Status of Power Sector Reform in Africa: impact on the poor," African Energy Policy Research Network (AFREPREN), Nairobi

Kessides, C. (1993), "The Contributions of Infrastructure to Economic Development: a review of experience and policy implications," World Bank Discussion Paper 231, Washington DC

Kibanga, P. (1997) "World Bank Says Pay Up Before Divesting TANESCO," *East African*, 4-10 August, Nairobi

Lee, K. S. (1989), *The Location of Jobs in a Developing Metropolis: Patterns of Growth in Bogotá and Cali, Colombia*, Oxford University Press for the World Bank, New York

Lee, K.S. and Anas, A. (1992), "Cost of Deficient Infrastructure: the case of Nigerian Manufacturng," *Urban Studies* 29 (7), pp1071-92

Mahloele, T. (2003), "Mobilizing Funds for Africa's Power Projects," *ESI Africa*, issue 2 (http://www.esi.co.za/last/esi_2_2003/032_28.htm)

Mkhwanazi, Xolani (2003), "Power Sector Development in Africa," Document prepared for the workshop for African Energy Experts on operationalizing the NEPAD Energy Initiative, 2-4 June, Dakar

Mody, A. and Walton, M. (1998), "Building on East Asia's Infrastructure Foundations," *Finance and Development*, 35 (2), International Monetary Fund (IMF), Washington DC

Monteiro Alves, Luis M., Costa, A. L., and Carvalho, M. da G. (2000), "Analysis of Potential for Market Penetration of Renewable Energy Technologies in Peripheral Islands," *Renewable Energy*, 19, pp311-317

Nilecom Technology (2003), "Africa: energy and carbon intensity," available online (http://www.teconinc.com/nts/information/intensity.html)

Nyoike, P. and Okech, B. A. (2002), "Is the Kenyan Electricity Regulatory Board Autonomous?" African Energy Policy Research Network (AFREPREN) newsletter 33, January, pp1-3, Nairobi

Onn, Lim Man (2000), "Pricing Electricity in Developing Countries: APEC experience," Integrity Consulting Services, Kuala Lumpur

Privatization Commission of Malawi (2000), *Annual Report 2000*, Lilongwe

Pritchett, L., Isham, J., Woolcock, M. and Busby G. (2002), "The Varieties of Rentier Experience: how natural resource export structures affect the political economy of economic growth," Von Hugel Institute working paper no 2002-05, University of Cambridge

Redwood-Sawyerr, Jonas A. S. (2002), "Widening Access in the Context of Power Sector Reform: an overview of the institutional challenges in Africa," Power Sector Reform and Sustainable Development Brainstorming Meeting, UN Environment Programme, Nairobi

Reinikka, Ritva and Svensson, J. (1999), "Confronting Competition Investment Response and Constraints in Uganda," Development Research Group, World Bank, Washington DC

Sachs, Jeffrey D. and Warner, A. M. (1995), "Natural Resource Abundance and Economic Growth," National Bureau of Economic Research (NBER) working paper no W5398, December, New York

Schmidt, L. (1999), "Zur Ökologischen Produktbewertung in der Textil-und Bekleidungsindustrie-Theoretische Grundlagen und Praktische Umsetzung," Fakultät für Umweltwissenschaften. Schriftenreihe Umwelttechnik und umweltmanagement, Band 21, Witten, Private Universitat Witten/Herdecke

United Nations Conference on Trade and Development (UNCTAD) (2003), *Handbook of Statistics*, online database, Geneva

United Nations Development Programme (UNDP) (2003), *Human Development Report 2003: Millennium Development Goals: A Compact Among Nations to End Human Poverty*, Oxford University Press, New York

Wamukonya, Njeri (2003), "African Power Sector Reforms: some emerging lessons," *Energy for Sustainable Development*, VII (1), March

World Bank (1989), "Financing of the Energy Sector in Developing Countries," Washington DC

———— (1992), "World Bank Study of Key Problems in Diesel Electric Power Projects," EPUES (Electric Power Utility Efficiency Study) report, Washington DC

———— (1993), "The World Bank's Role in the Electric Power Sector," World Bank Policy Paper, Washington DC

———— (2000), *Can Africa Claim the 21st Century?* Washington DC

———— (2001a), *African Development Indicators,* Washington DC

———— (2001b), "Developing Countries and Hybrid Energy Systems: a World Bank perspective," paper presented at the National Energy Technology Laboratory, Morgantown, West Virginia, 7-8 August, 2001

———— (2001c), "Ghana's International Competitiveness: opportunities and challenges facing non-traditional exports," macroeconomics 4, Africa Region, Washington DC

———— (2002), "Energy Chapter of the Poverty Reduction Strategy Paper Sourcebook", Washington DC

———— (2003a), *World Development Indicators*, Washington DC

———— (2003b), "Trade for Development: the stakes for African economies in the current WTO trade round," Brussels, August 2003

World Energy Council (WEC) (1999), *The Challenge of Rural Energy Poverty in Developing Countries,* London

———— (2003), "The Potential for Regionally Integrated Energy Development in Africa," discussion document, London

Yartey, C.A. (2002), "Financial Liberalization, the Stock Market and Long Run Economic Growth," unpublished paper, Faculty of Economics and Politics, University of Cambridge

———— (2004), "The Economics of Civil Wars in Sub-Saharan Africa," Forthcoming in Jean Clement (ed), *From Conflict to Reconstruction: Main Lessons and Challenges*, International Monetary Fund, Washington DC

ZERO Regional Environment Organization (1998), "Energy and Sustainable Rural Industries: issues from pilot studies in Tanzania, Zambia, Botswana and Zimbabwe," ZERO, Harare

Trade Facilitation to Integrate Africa into the World Economy

Facilitating increased trade between African countries and the rest of the world is essential for Africa's future economic well-being, and it is an objective that deserves the serious attention of governments, subregional organizations, the African Union and NEPAD alike. In improving the continent's ability to trade, governments and subregional organizations need not only to make the energy sector more efficient, as was discussed in the previous chapter, but they have to tackle other persistent constraints, most particularly the poor state of the continent's transport infrastructure and the labourious customs and payments procedures prevailing in many countries – factors that result in the very high costs of overland transport for exports and imports, most especially for Africa's 15 landlocked countries. These hindrances severely constrain the continent's trade growth, and they have become a major disincentive to the kinds of private investment that are essential to keep the continent's economies on the path of closer integration into the world economy.

High costs of overland transport limit Africa's trade potential

This chapter explains how a well-planned and well-managed trade facilitation process will be of direct benefit to the conduct of both business and government. Traders must be given the opportunity to reduce their costs, through fewer delays in the movement of goods, faster customs clearance and a more transparent framework for competition. For their part, governments can only benefit from the resulting improved economic performance, higher revenue yields, more efficient deployment of resources, more effective regulation and improved trader compliance with the rules. Trade facilitation is a matter of huge importance for all developing countries, just as it is an objective generally supported by the international business community. WTO has sought to identify the central issues, each of which is examined here in terms of its relevance to conditions in many African countries, including those that are landlocked.

Most trade facilitation initiatives undertaken so far in Africa have not shown much success. Generally, this has been attributed to factors such as non-compliance with the agreements, poor programme implementation, lack of coordination among and between countries, lack of cooperation among relevant agencies within countries, inadequate skilled labour and, most importantly, the absence of a multisectoral approach to trade facilitation. Africa is still faced with very high transaction costs resulting from the blockages and delays prevailing in so many countries, although these are sometimes aggravated by the difficulty of meeting increasingly stringent international trade standards.

Tackling the challenges of opening up to international trade requires a comprehensive and coordinated approach by African countries that needs to include improvements in infrastructure; provision of efficient and competitive services in the areas of roads, railways, ports, information and communications technology; the removal of illegal and reduction of check points that constitute a *de facto* tax on trade; the simplification and harmonization of customs and border procedures; the use of new technology by customs agents; and the strengthening of regional trade facilitation initiatives.

> " *International trade values were 50 times greater in 1999 than in 1960* "

The growing importance of trade facilitation

In recent years, the volume of goods that move across borders has increased exponentially thanks to changes in the international trading environment, which stem from the global integration of modern production systems, new forms of electronic commerce and the development of containerized transport. This has allowed large cost reductions in cargo handling and has increased cargo transhipment. Indeed, the value of international trade was 50 times higher in 1999 than it was in 1960.

However, African countries have not yet benefited from the increases in international trade. Their poor performance is partly due to high transaction costs, which significantly contribute to the cost of tradable goods and consequently determine the degree of integration of a country into the world economy. These costs generally fall into two categories: direct costs, which include transportation and the cost of compliance associated with the collection and processing of information; and indirect costs or time-sensitive costs, which are brought about by administrative and customs procedures that delay goods, leading to increased transportation fees and inventory charges.

As liberalization continues to reduce artificial trade barriers, transaction costs are becoming higher than the cost of tariffs. For instance, the effective rate of protection provided by transport costs is now, in many cases, considerably higher than that provided by tariffs (Amjadi and Yeats, 1995). For some countries, such as Chile and Ecuador, transport costs exceed by more than twenty times the average tariffs they face with US markets (Clark et al., 2001). In many instances, the cost of complying with customs formalities has been reported to exceed the cost of the tariffs to be paid. SMEs, which are the dominant actors in developing countries, are the most affected by these high transaction costs.

The dramatic increase in the volume and complexity of world trade, both in terms of type of goods being traded and in the conduct of import and export transactions, makes it essential for administrations to provide simple, predictable and efficient customs procedures for the clearance of goods and movement of people while simultaneously tackling increasingly complicated national and international requirements to ensure compliance with national laws, international agreements and security demands.

These considerations and the need to reduce costs have pushed trade facilitation into the forefront of public policy discourse. Although several attempts have been made to define trade facilitation, to date no consensus has been reached on a standard definition. In a narrow sense, trade facilitation efforts address the logistics of moving goods through ports or the documentation associated with cross-border trade. More recent definitions have been broadened to include the environment in which trade transactions take place, that is, the transparency and professionalism of customs and regulatory agencies, as well as the effects of harmonization of standards and conformity with international or regional regulations. For instance, the International Chamber of Commerce (ICC) defines trade facilitation as "the adoption of a comprehensive and integrated approach to simplifying and reducing the cost of international trade transactions, and ensuring that the relevant activities take place in an efficient, transparent and predictable manner based on internationally accepted norms and standards and best practices".

Trade facilitation should therefore not only be perceived as a "transportation or customs problem", but rather as a broader issue, which straddles many aspects of weak capacities that exist in many developing countries – especially in Africa – inhibiting their effective participation in international trade. However, trade facilitation is not just the concern of developing countries. Indeed, developed countries are leading the clamour for trade facilitation measures in WTO. The international business community is increasingly demanding greater transparency, efficiency and procedural uniformity for cross-border transportation of goods, as well as the need for an efficient legal redress mechanism, proper co-ordination between customs and other inspection agencies, use of modern customs techniques and improvement of transit regimes. In response, WTO members added trade facilitation to the agenda at the Singapore Ministerial Meeting in 1996. The Singapore Ministerial Declaration called upon the Council for Trade in Goods to conduct exploratory research into cross-border barriers, and analyse the effects of these barriers on traders and consumers. The WTO Secretariat has circulated a "checklist of issues" that summarize the central issues of trade facilitation. These, include:

> *Transparency and efficiency are crucial to improving international trade*

- Physical movement of consignment (transport and transit) and border-crossing problems;
- Import and export procedures, including customs;
- Information and communications technology;
- Payments, insurance and other financial requirements that affect cross-border movement of goods in international trade; and
- International trade standards

Trade facilitation is in the interest of governments and the business community alike. Government benefits include increased effectiveness of control methods; more effective and efficient deployment of resources; correct revenue yields; improved trader compliance; accelerated economic development; and encouragement of foreign investment. Benefits to traders include reduced costs and delays; faster customs clearance and release, through predictable official intervention; a simple commercial framework for doing both domestic and international trade; and enhanced competition.

The following sections explore the central issues of trade facilitation in the WTO checklist, assessing and comparing, to the extent possible, the African situation with that of other regions of the world as well as outlining the special situation of landlocked countries. It also highlights current trade facilitation efforts in Africa using examples of national, bilateral, subregional and multilateral initiatives, and provides recommendations for the way forward to facilitate trade in Africa including a discussion of trade facilitation in a multilateral framework.

Africa's physical and procedural constraints on trade

The movement of goods in Africa is rendered difficult by a host of different factors. The continent has a generally inadequate road and rail network, its transport services operate at a low level of efficiency, many routes are subject to official and unofficial roadblocks, and there are slow and cumbersome border-crossing procedures. Transport costs in many African countries have been recorded as the highest in the world, and many of the factors are attributable to unnecessary delays and corruption.

The continental road network is not only poorly developed but also badly maintained. Very little of the network has been updated to accommodate larger vehicles, which can cause major damage on unsuitable surfaces. Inefficiency is equally manifest in the lack of care of vehicles, shoddy routine maintenance and poor operating practices. Vehicle operating costs are considerably higher in Africa than elsewhere in the world. Transport operators in turn shift the burden of their high costs onto their passengers and freight customers. Studies have shown, however, that allowing competition into transport services can lead to dramatic reductions in costs.

Another contribution to Africa's high transport costs comes from the proliferation of rules governing road transport, and the wide variations in technical standards adhered to by different countries, leading to uncertainty and a multiplicity of forms at national borders. Problems regularly arise with transit charges and visa requirements for transport crews. An additional and unnecessary burden is imposed by the roadblocks put in place on major roads in many countries. Different administrative services are deployed to control and in some instances collect payments from passing vehicles, payments that may include local or regional taxes, transit charges or simple bribes. Naturally enough, Africa's landlocked countries are especially disadvantaged by the long distances from their nearest seaports.

Escalating cost factors

Calculating overall transport costs to include both monetary and indirect costs related to conveyance, storage and handling of goods has demonstrated that transport costs in Africa are the highest in the world. A recent study by UNCTAD indicates that the freight cost as a percentage of total import value was 13% for Africa in 2000 compared to 8.8% for developing countries and 5.2% for industrial countries. At the subregional level, the freight cost for West Africa as a percentage of total import value was 14% while that for East and Southern Africa, including the Indian Ocean region, was 15.2%. The ratio for North Africa stood at 11% (UNCTAD, 2002). A study in the 1990s indicated that transport costs in SSA countries of Cameroon, Côte d'Ivoire and Mali were on average five or six times higher than in Pakistan (Rizet and Hine, 1993).

When transport costs are added, the consumer prices of imported goods are much higher than they would be elsewhere. Equally, high transport costs undermine the competitiveness of exports in foreign markets. This is why the level of transport costs can limit a country's participation in international trade. A study by Limao and Venables (2000), using a sample of countries from Africa and the rest of the world, indicates that in general a 10% increase in transport costs will lead to a reduction in trade volumes by approximately 20%. Booth et al (2000) share this view, arguing that high transport costs are the main reason why trade liberalization in Africa has not had the level of success experienced in Asia and Latin America. As liberalization continues to reduce artificial trade barriers, the effective rate of protection provided by transport costs is now, in many cases, considerably higher than that provided by tariffs (Amjadi and Yeats, 1995).

Africa in general, and SSA in particular, has the highest cost rates in the world, as shown by figure 5.1, and the lowest share of international trade. In 2000, Africa's share of world exports was only 2.7%, while SSA's share of exports fell from 1.9% to 1.4% during the 1990s (ADB, 2003) (see also Annex table A5.1).

> *Consumer prices are higher due to excessive transport costs*

Figure 5.1

Transport costs by world regional and country groupings, 2000 (freight cost as a percentage of total import value)

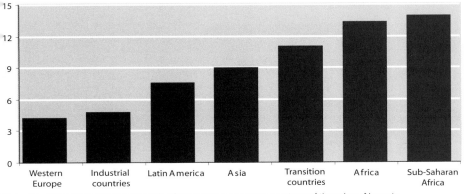

Note: The transport cost rate is the ratio of transport costs as a percentage of the value of imports.
Source: Calculations by ECA

Transport costs are incurred both in the shipping and in the inland movement of goods to and from the coastline. However, goods often incur more than half their total door-to-door transport times and costs in the course of the inland movement. For example, the total cost added to coffee in Côte d'Ivoire from producer to port is about 170%, and about 60% for cocoa, with transport accounting for a significant share in both cases (De Castro, 1996). Limao and Venables (2000) compared the transport costs of land and sea legs of a journey and found out that the former is around seven times more costly for the same distance.

Empirical evidence suggests that the burden of high transport costs is greater in landlocked African countries than elsewhere in the world. In 1995, the World Bank reported that the final prices of imported products in these countries were from 30% to 80% higher than the "free on board" (f.o.b.) value of goods. Hendeson et al. (2001) reported the range to be between 30% and 40%. UNCTAD has also reported values for specific landlocked African countries as follows: 55.5% for Malawi, 51.8% for Chad and 48.4% for Rwanda (UNCTAD, 2001).

Poor road and rail conditions

The current level of road density, or coverage, in Africa is estimated at 6.84 km per 100 sq km, far below that of Latin America (12 km/100sq km) and Asia (18 km/100 sq km). Roads also fail to reach enough of the continent's people. Africa's road network distribution is very low, at 2.71 km for 10,000 persons, resulting in poor accessibility, a low frequency of transport services and high transport costs. The road density and distribution of Africa's five subregions is shown in figure 5.2.

Figure 5.2

Africa's road network, by region and subregions, 2002 (density and distribution

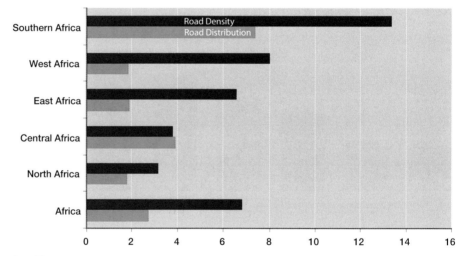

Note: *The network density is in km per 100 sq km. The distribution is in km per 10,000 inhabitants*
Source: *Calculations by ECA*

Although the road subsector accounts for 90% of inter-urban transport in Africa, it is generally in a deplorable state. The total length of roads in the region is 2.1 million km out of which only 29.7% is paved, the remaining portion being made of either earth or gravel. Figure 5.3 shows that the total length of unpaved roads is by far larger than that of paved roads in all the subregions of the continent, with the exception of North Africa where 55.27% of the network is paved.

In addition to its low density, distribution, and the fact that a large proportion is unpaved, much of Africa's road network is in a state of disrepair as illustrated by table 5.1 which shows the network conditions in the Central African Economic and Monetary Community (CEMAC) and the Common Market for Eastern and Southern Africa

Figure 5.3

Africa's road surfaces, by region and subregions, 2002 (length in km)

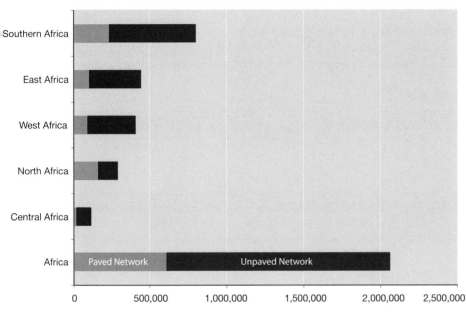

Source: Calculations by ECA

> "55% of Africa's mostly unpaved roads are in poor shape"

(COMESA) in 1999. In CEMAC, 34% of paved roads and 55% of unpaved roads were in poor condition in 1999. Similarly 34% of paved roads and 68% of unpaved roads in COMESA were in poor condition in the same period. Poor quality roads inevitably result in high vehicle maintenance costs, the burden of which is usually transferred to those requiring transport services (importers, exporters, local businessmen, ordinary commuters etc.), through high fares and fees.

Table 5.1

Road network conditions in CEMAC and COMESA, 1999

	Paved road network %			Unpaved road network %		
	Good	Fairly good	Poor	Good	Fairly good	Poor
CEMAC	32	34	34	20	25	55
COMESA	40	25	34	12	20	68

Source: ECA, from official sources

Most roads in Africa were not constructed to carry the heavy goods vehicles that are now commonly used. The excessive axle loads of large container-carrying vehicles can damage road surfaces, and this will only push the costs of transport even higher. A major challenge to African countries is how to maintain or rehabilitate existing roads while also expanding the network to isolated areas. The geometry of many existing roads (i.e. lane and shoulder widths, as well as vertical and horizontal alignments) has to be adjusted, taking into consideration the increased use of heavy goods and container vehicles.

Recent estimates by the World Bank have put the asset value of the African road network at $150 billion, and the cost to fully restore all roads on the continent that are classified to be in poor condition at $43 billion. The World Bank also estimates that the extra cost of insufficient maintenance in Africa amounts to about $1.2 billion a year (Heggie and Vickers, 1998).

The African rail network is currently estimated to be about 89,380 km long, with a density of 2.96 km per 1,000 sq km. Three railway width gauges predominate in Africa, i.e. 1.000m, 1.067m and 1.435m, and this inhibits the physical integration of the networks within and between the various subregions. The interconnection of the networks is poor, especially in both Central and West Africa, and the available rolling stock is of a generally lower standard than in other regions of the world. Disjointed railway networks result in frequent loading and off-loading of goods, which only increase delays and transport costs as well as the probability of pilferage. In an effort to improve rail connection in the region, the Union of African Railways (UAR) has recommended the following solutions, at the interconnecting points of lines with different gauges: transhipment of goods separately or in standardized containers; operating of passenger and goods train sets that cannot be divided; and use of rolling stock equipped with axles that have changeable gauges.

Some signs of improvement

Overall, density of infrastructure in Africa is still significantly below the rest of the world (see figure 5.4). As a point of reference, it is apparent that Latin America's overall infrastructure – including roads, railways, airports with paved runways and telephone lines – works out to be twice as dense as that of Africa. The gap is wider still with Central and Eastern Asia and Eastern Europe, where density is four times higher than in Africa.

There has, however, been some progress in Africa's infrastructure development. The length of Africa's surfaced road network grew by 128% between 1991 and 2000, from 242,000 km to 547,742 km. The development of the surfaced network confirms the importance African governments increasingly attach to improving the road network. The case of Ethiopia also shows that a road sector development programme can produce good results (see box 5.1).

Road Funds, created within the framework of the Road Management Initiative (RMI) of the Sub-Saharan African Transport Policy Programme (SSATP), a joint initiative of ECA and the World Bank, are playing a key role in improving Africa's road network. At least 20 SSA countries have established Road Funds, most of which have put in place independent auditing and transparency measures and are managed by boards of directors with a mixture of private and public sector representation. About half of the RMI members have been able to establish community-run road agencies to execute or manage roadworks. Road Funds provide a sustainable means of maintaining existing stocks of infrastructure.

Figure 5.4

Density of infrastructure by world regions and country groupings, 2002/03

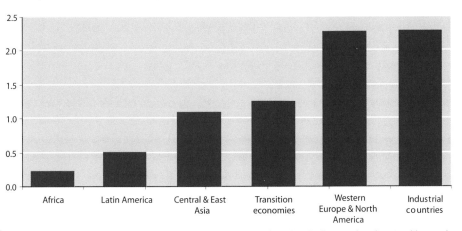

Note: *The index of infrastructure density is the average density of road and rail networks, airports with paved runways, and telephone lines.*

Source: *Calculations by ECA*

> *Independent road management funds gauge transparency levels*

Box 5.1

Road sector development in Ethiopia

Ethiopia has had quite a successful experience in its recent efforts to improve its roads. An evaluation in June 2002 of the country's Road Sector Development Programme (RSDP), launched in 1997, showed an increase in the total classified road network by 40% over a period of five years, with an increase of 107% in regional roads, including tertiary roads. There was also an increase in the proportion of roads in good condition from 18% in 1995 to 30% in 2002. The second phase of the RSDP is even more ambitious, and aims to increase road density to 34 km per 1,000 sq km by 2007 from the present density of about 30 km per 1,000 sq km. In addition the distribution by population is targeted to reach 5 km per 10,000 people in 2007. Another target of RSDP II is to increase the percentage of roads in good condition, from the current 30% to 45% by 2007.

Source: *Ethiopian Roads Authority, 2003*

Inefficient vehicle use and management

Inefficiency of transport services is manifested in several ways including high vehicle prices, lack of information about demand, existence of transport cartels, poor operating practices, inadequate routine maintenance and unnecessarily fast driving, all of which lead to high vehicle operating costs and low vehicle utilization. Transport operators usually transfer the burden of high vehicle operating costs to consumers by raising their fares. Similarly, operators increase their fares to offset low revenues because of low vehicle utilization.

Vehicle operating costs in Africa are significantly higher than elsewhere in the world. Table 5.2 shows that the vehicle operating cost per kilometre for two-axle trucks in Tanzania (50.1 US cents) is substantially higher than in Pakistan (21.0 cents) and Indonesia (19.7 cents). Higher fuel prices, maintenance costs, tire costs and overheads in Tanzania all help to explain the wide margin of difference.

> *Competition encourages better, safer and cheaper transport services*

Table 5.2

Estimated composition of operating costs for two-axle trucks (1995 US cents per km)

	Tanzania	Pakistan	Indonesia
Capital costs	10.6	1.8	2.7
Fuel	15.4	9.3	5.8
Crew	2.7	3.2	3.2
Oil	1.0	1.0	0.7
Maintenance	6.1	2.2	4.3
Tires	7.8	1.1	1.2
Overhead	6.5	2.4	1.8
Total	50.1	21.0	19.7

Source: *Ellis and Hine, 1998*

Levels of vehicle utilization are extremely important in determining the burden of vehicle capital costs and interest repayments. There is a significant difference between utilization in Africa and Asia. For example, the average annual utilization of two- and three-axle trucks in Tanzania was found to be 60,000 km compared to 80,000 km for Indonesia (Hine et al., 1997). According to other studies reported by Rizet and Hine (1993), annual utilization in Pakistan was found to be 123,000 km compared to an average of 50,000 km in the SSA countries of Cameroon, Côte d'Ivoire and Mali. Vehicles in the three SSA countries travelled empty for 34% of their journeys, compared to only 12% running empty in Pakistan. In this context, a national network of transport brokers who match loads with available vehicles can reduce empty running and increase vehicle utilization.

Transport costs are usually a measure of the degree of competition. A study in Cameroon showed that competition led to better, safer and cheaper services in the northern part of the country. In just two years after competition was introduced, transport charges dropped by 40%. No such improvement was observed in the south-west province of the country where strong syndicates were in control of vehicle parks, resulting in long waiting times at queues while available loads had to be shared amongst registered vehicles (Lisinge, 2001).

Excessive rules and regulations

A multitude of international agreements and protocols intended to simplify and harmonize trade and transport between States have been signed in Africa. These bilateral agreements tend to undermine regional and subregional agreements. For instance, it has been estimated that in West African Economic and Monetary Union (UEMOA), only 30% of the rules governing road transport are subregional, the remaining 70% being either bilateral or national. There are also more than 100 agreements between UEMOA member States in the area of transport. The proliferation of rules covering the same area leads to uncertainty and a multiplicity of forms and procedures (see box 5.2).

Box 5.2

Subregional road transport agreements in Africa

Several subregional-level agreements and protocols governing international transport exist in Africa. In West Africa, the two most important conventions on transport are the Inter-State Transport Convention (TIE) and the Inter-State Road Freight Transit Convention (TRIE). These conventions, both of which were signed in 1982, define the conditions of road transport between member States and provide for the transit, without interruption, of freight as well as the non-payment of customs and other fees, with the cover of a single TRIE document. In Central Africa, international road transport is governed by the Inter-State Convention for Road Transport of Miscellaneous Goods (CIETRMD), the inter-state convention for multi-modal transport of goods, the Inter-State transit for Central African countries (TIPAC) and the transport regulation for road transport of dangerous goods.

Other communities, including SADC and COMESA, also have transport protocols and there are transport corridor initiatives such as the Northern and Central Corridor initiatives, both in East Africa. Overall, 28 transit transport corridors have been identified in SSA.

Good examples of bilateral cooperation between transit and landlocked countries are those between Cameroon and its landlocked neighbours of Chad and the Central African Republic. These conventions identify the transit corridors that are jointly managed by the national land freight authorities of Cameroon and its neighbours; specify the percentage of freight to be transported by Cameroonian transporters and their counterparts from the landlocked countries; and stipulate that all vehicles in possession of specified documents plying the identified corridors should be subjected only to limited controls at jointly selected checkpoints.

Source: ECA, from official sources

> *Overlapping regional, subregional and bilateral agreements can cause confusion*

Variations in approved technical standards for vehicles – axle load limits and vehicle dimensions – height and width in different subregions of Africa are a block on free competition between transport operators. This is because vehicles that fail to meet the standards of a given subregion would be compelled to offload at border posts and have their goods transferred to vehicles that meet the approved standards. ECOWAS, CEMAC and COMESA all apply different vehicle standards from each other. table 5.3 shows that if these standards were applied, a 22m long truck operating in Nigeria (a member State of ECOWAS) would not be allowed to operate in neighbouring Cameroon (a member State of CEMAC) whose maximum allowable vehicle length is 18m. In Southern Africa, maximum authorized measurements are lower in Mozambique than neighbouring countries, which is a constraint on transport operators from Malawi, South Africa and Zimbabwe. While axle load limits are necessary to prevent damage of road surfaces, applying different standards in different subregions results in delays and additional expenses and discourages international trade.

Table 5.3

Technical standards for vehicles in Africa's different regional economic communities (RECs), 2004

| RECs | Axle load limit | | | Max. load | Max. length | Max. height | Max. width |
	Single axle (tonne)	Tandem axle (tonne)	Triple axle (tonne)	(tonne)	metres	metres	metres
CEMAC	13	21	27	50	18	4	2.5
COMESA	10	16	24		22		
ECOWAS	12	21	25	51	22	4	2.5

Source: *ECA, from official sources*

Transit charges constitute an additional burden for Africa's transport operators. At present, there are divergences in transit costs among member States in different African subregions, resulting in lack of transparency and high road user charges. COMESA has taken the lead in the harmonization of transit charges at the subregional level, and ECOWAS has also begun to consider establishing a common system for transit charges, basically for heavy vehicles.

Agreements regulating transport operations in the subregion do not always take into account questions relating to crew members, i.e. the driver and apprentices. These employees are confronted with administrative problems concerning their documents (driving licences, residence permits, work permits, etc.). The suppression of visas between ECOWAS countries has, however, improved the situation in most of West Africa. Other subregional agreements may be necessary.

Unnecessary roadblocks

Roadblocks pose a serious challenge to trade in Africa as they cause both delays and increased costs. In Cameroon, *The Economist* (2002) reported 47 roadblocks between Douala and Bertoua, a distance of about 500 km. Nearly all ECOWAS member states also maintain numerous checkpoints, where drivers are sometimes subjected to administrative harassment and extortion (see table 5.4).

Payments at checkpoints include, among other things, various taxes, transit charges and bribes. Such payments tend to vary with the type of vehicle, the type of goods transported and whether the transporter is a country national, and they may involve the police, customs officers and/or *gendarmes.* Furthermore, while some of these checkpoints are legal,

Table 5.4

Checkpoints along major ECOWAS highways, 2003

Highways	Distance (km)	Number of checkpoints	Checkpoints per 100 km
Lagos-Abidjan	992	69	7
Cotonou-Niamey	1,036	34	3
Lome-Ouagadougou	989	34	4
Accra-Ouagadougou	972	15	2
Abidjan-Ouagadougou	1,122	37	3
Niamey-Ouagadougou	529	20	4

Source: *ECOWAS official site, 2003*

> " *Transit corridors to seaports are basic trade requirements for landlocked countries* "

others are illegal. Added to the inconvenience is the risk of goods being diverted from their intended destinations. In some cases, containers are looted directly on the truck or train on which they are being transported.

The resultant loss of time and increase in vehicle operating costs from roadblocks are considerable. In theory, the trip from Bangui in the Central African Republic to Douala in Cameroon which could be done in 3 days, in actuality takes between 7-10 days. A study on transit transport in ECOWAS in 1999 revealed that enormous amounts of time and money are wasted each year at checkpoints in the region. Overall, lost revenue was estimated at 2 billion CFA.

The challenges for landlocked countries

The ability of landlocked countries to trade relies on the existence of efficient and easily accessible transit corridors. In addition to their own infrastructure, landlocked economies need good roads and railways in their neighbouring countries. Econometric evidence suggests that being landlocked constitutes a geographical disadvantage with relevant effects on transport costs and trade flows. For instance, Limao and Venables (2000) compute that transport costs for the median landlocked country are 50% greater than costs for the median coastal economy, after controlling for other determinants of transport costs. Figure 5.5 shows that for pairs of countries – one landlocked and the other non-landlocked – the cost of shipment of goods for similar distances is always greater for the landlocked country.

Africa has 15 landlocked countries, whose distance to the sea ranges from 220 km for Swaziland to 1,735 km for Chad. The generally low density and poor quality of infrastructure on the continent tends to aggravate these disadvantages further. Weak infrastructure imposes a large burden on competitiveness, not just against the average coastal economy but also against the average landlocked country in other continents (see figure 5.6). This is because of the poor average quality of infrastructure even in those countries with direct access to the sea.

Figure 5.5

Shipment costs in selected landlocked and non-landlocked countries

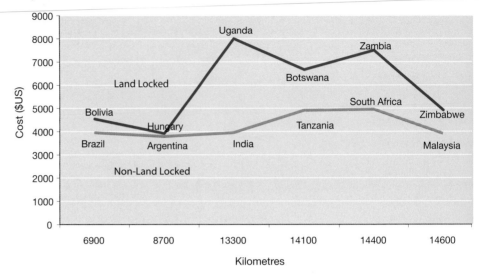

Source: *Calculations by ECA*

Figure 5.6

Infrastructure density in transit countries, a comparison between Africa and the rest of the world (index of infrastracture density)

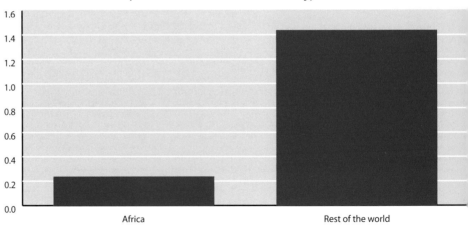

Notes: *The index of infrastructure density is the average density of road and rail networks; airports with paved runways, and telephone lines. The index is computed from a sample of African countries and other countries of the world and ranges from 0.03 to 7.5, with an average of 1.15. The higher the index, the denser the infrastructure network.*

Source: *Calculations by ECA*

The infrastructure gap between African landlocked countries and landlocked transition economies in Europe is particularly evident. As one example, the transit countries of the Czech Republic are Austria, Germany and Italy. For these three countries the average index of infrastructure is 3.3. In Africa, Malawi has transit through Botswana, Mozambique, South Africa, Zambia, and Zimbabwe, with an average transit infrastructure density of 0.22. Further, Burundi has transit through Kenya, Tanzania, Rwanda and Uganda, whose average value of infrastructure density does not reach 0.14.

Africa's pervasive customs barriers

Customs inefficiencies hinder the integration of developing countries into the global economy and can also severely impair import–export competitiveness and inflows of FDI. The key problems that plague customs operations in developing countries in general, and African countries in particular, include excessive documentary requirements; outdated official procedures; insufficient use of automated systems; a lack of transparency; predictability and consistency in customs activities; and inadequate modernization of, and cooperation among, customs and other governmental agencies.

> *Customs inefficiencies can impair import-export competitiveness*

According to estimates by UNCTAD, an average customs transaction in Africa involves 20-30 different parties, 40 documents, 200 data elements (30 of which are repeated at least 30 times) and the re-keying of 60-70% of all data at least once. Frequently, documentation requirements are ill-defined and traders are not adequately informed on how to comply with them, thus increasing the potential for errors. This problem is even worse at borders, especially as border posts and customs offices, in most cases, are physically separated. In essence, there are two complete sets of controls for each border post, with each having a multitude of forms and documents to be filled and checked.

The lack or insufficient use of automated processes is a major source of delays, costs and inefficiencies, as paper documents are usually presented at the time of border crossing, and verification of the information submitted takes place at that time. Experience in customs administrations that have increased the use of information technology shows that border-crossing times can be reduced considerably, while control and revenue collection functions are improved. African countries have recognized the need to simplify and speed up customs procedures by use of automated systems. The case of Tunisia TradeNet is a good example (see box 5.3). Other African countries have also introduced the use of the Automated System for Customs Data (ASYCUDA). See box 5.4.

Customs delays: causes and effects

Lack of transparency and predictability is a major source of uncertainty as regards costs and time involved for international trade transactions. When information on applicable regulations is not readily available, trade operators have to spend money to obtain the information. Enterprises operating in an environment that is not transparent frequently have to add expenses for bribes, penalties and administrative or judicial appeals. As these additional expenses do not vary according to the value of the goods or the volume of sales, they serve to increase the operational costs per unit and put firms in developing countries in a much weaker position than larger firms.

Box 5.3

Speeding up customs operations in Tunisia

Tunisia TradeNet (TTN) is an automated system, which can be accessed through a PC after subscribing, provides a one-stop trade documentation-processing platform connecting the principal actors of international trade. It serves as a tool for exchanging international trade documents, maritime community documents and other administrative documents and allows for payment of documentary credits and settlement of duty taxes. It is also a tool for business transactions such as processing purchase orders, shipment and delivery bills, invoices and transfer orders. In terms of international financial transaction, the TTN facilitates the exchange of bills of lading between Tunisian banks and European banks. In addition, it serves as a marketplace where offers and requests are made and transactions processed.

Prior to the creation of TTN in February 2000, the complexity of trade documentation processing in Tunisia meant delays in clearance of goods for imports. For example, the vessel turn-around time in Tunis varied from 5 to 17 days, with an average of 8 days, and port facilities were often overloaded. TTN is expected to reduce shipment clearance to 3 days. Overall, it is estimated that TTN will result in a productivity gain of 7%.

TTN was created with equity of ★2 million and is jointly controlled by the State (85%) and the private sector (15%). With investment of ★3.5 million, the corporation employs 40 personnel, including 20 engineers. Today, 100 subscribers use TTN. In the long run, about 2,000 companies are expected to use the system, with brokers being the main target.

The main challenge to its successful implementation is the unfamiliarity with its benefits on the part of customs agents and other professionals within the trade community. A customs training centre has been created to deliver courses to the principal actors in Tunisia's international trade.

Source: ECA, from official sources

Box 5.4

Automated System for Customs Data (ASYCUDA)

The Automated System for Customs Data (ASYCUDA) process was developed under UNCTAD's Special Programme for Trade Efficiency to assist in the clearance of goods. ASYCUDA aims to: (a) reduce the administrative costs of external trade control activities; (b) help governments to bring about more effective application of external trade regulations, leading in most cases to an increase in revenue; (c) accelerate the clearance of goods, while maintaining effective control of the flow of goods; and (d) produce timely and reliable data, as a basis for external trade statistics and management reports. ASYCUDA is available to UNCTAD member governments free of cost in the framework of an UNCTAD-executed technical assistance project. At least 29 African countries are known to have experience in the use of ASYCUDA.

At the subregional level, a project under the auspices of COMESA, for the computerization of customs operations using ASYCUDA, has been beneficial to customs administrations in the region, where the implementation of a standard system is seen as instrumental in the establishment of a customs union. Two different versions of the system are in use in the region. Kenya remains the only country along the main transit corridors in East Africa that does not use the system. The Kenya Revenue Authority is considering various options for its replacement, including ASYCUDA.

Source: ECA, from official sources

Customs departments and other government agencies involved in trade are often inefficiently structured internally. Common problems include inadequacies in physical infrastructure, training and education, inefficient emoluments of staff, and lack of co-ordination and co-operation between customs administrations and between customs and tax administration. In addition to ongoing difficulties in reducing corruption and bureaucracy in general, the current need for more stringent security procedures, especially those introduced for trade with the US, poses a new and serious challenge to customs administration (see box 5.5).

Box 5.5

New security measures increase customs delays and transaction costs

One of the most significant developments in the international transportation of goods since 2001 is the proliferation of security initiatives in maritime transport, most of which have been introduced for trade with the US. These initiatives have implications for transport costs and operations.

US security initiatives focus on customs treatment for incoming cargo, particularly in containers and include: the Container Security Initiative (CSI) and the Customs-Trade Partnership against Terrorism (C-TPAT) which brings commercial parties together, including importers, carriers, brokers, warehouse operators and manufacturers, to conduct trade in a secure environment. The International Maritime Organization (IMO) Maritime Safety Committee has also been involved in efforts to reduce the risk of terrorist attacks through maritime transport. To this end, the IMO has developed an International Code for Security of Ships and Port Facilities, which provides a platform on which ship operators and port authorities can cooperate to detect and deter acts of maritime terrorism.

The resultant additional costs that tight security entails may reduce demand for lower-value goods moving in containers. It may even make some products uncompetitive and could harm the trade of developing countries. UNCTAD has listed some likely outcomes of new security measures on developing countries, which include the following: (i) shipping companies operated by developing countries will see their costs and liabilities increase; (ii) ports in developing countries will need to undertake a port security assessment and prepare a port security plan (failure to do so could lead to vessels calling at these ports being barred from US ports); (iii) ports will need to expand their container inspection areas; and national customs may need to invest in costly container scanning systems.

Source: ECA, from official sources

The problem of delays at customs and border posts is well known throughout Africa. For instance, an enormous amount of time is wasted at border posts in Southern Africa, as table 5.5 illustrates. Waiting for up to 24 hours to cross a border appears to be the norm rather than the exception. The table shows that border delay is estimated at 36 hours at both the South Africa-Zimbabwe border post at Beitbridge and the Zimbabwe-Zambia border post at Victoria Falls. In East Africa, long delays are recorded in the transportation of goods along the Djibouti-Ethiopia corridor. Numerous stages in the process of clearing and transporting commercial goods in transit from the port of Djibouti to Addis Ababa often take more than 20 days.

Overall, delays at African customs are on average longer than the rest of the world: 12 days in countries south of the Sahara, compared to 7 days in Latin America, 5.5 days in Central and East Asia, and slightly more than 4 days in Central and East Europe (see figure 5.7). Such delays add costs for importers for each day that goods wait at customs' warehouses.

Table 5.5

Delays at selected border posts in Southern Africa, 2000

Corridor	Border post	Countries	Estimated border delay (hours)
Beira	Machipanda	Mozambique and Zimbabwe	24
	Zobue	Mozambique and Malawi	24
	Mutare	Mozambique and Zimbabwe	26
Maputo	Ressano Garcia	South Africa and Mozambique	6
	Namaacha	Swaziland and Mozambique	4
North-South	Beitbridge	South Africa and Zimbabwe	36
	Chirundu	Zimbabwe and Zambia	24
	Victoria Falls	Zimbabwe and Zambia	36
	Martins Drift	South Africa and Botswana	6
Trans-Caprivi	Kazungula	Botswana and Zambia	24
Trans-Kalahari	Buitepos	Namibia and Botswana	6
	Pioneer Gate	Botswana and South Africa	4
Tanzam	Nakonde	Zambia and Tanzania	17

Source: *World Bank, 2000*

The longest delays are observed in Ethiopia (30 days), Cameroon (20 days), Nigeria (18 days), Malawi (17 days) and Uganda (14 days). See also Annex table A5.1.

The effect of customs efficiency on trade facilitation is evident from the correlation between customs delays (measured in days) and trade volumes (measured as a percentage of GDP) (see figure 5.8). There are two important effects behind the direct linkage of these two variables. First is the increase in the cost of trade that results from having commodities stacked at the customs for several days or weeks, especially when they are perishable. The second effect is the uncertainty about the outcome of the procedures, as the delay gets longer. Uncertainty in turn is a powerful disincentive for individuals to trade. In one form or another, all African countries are affected by the problem of cumbersome customs and border procedures and this has a negative impact on trade development in the continent.

Figure 5.7

Delays at customs, compared by world regional and country groupings (days)

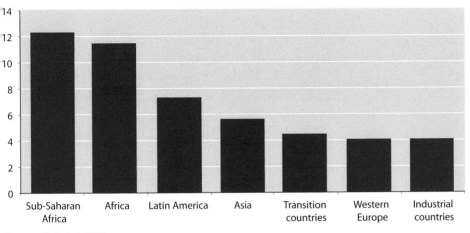

Source: *Clark et al., 2001*

> *Uncertainty is a powerful disincentive to individual traders*

Figure 5.8

Correlation between customs delays and trade volumes, 1990-2003 (log of days)

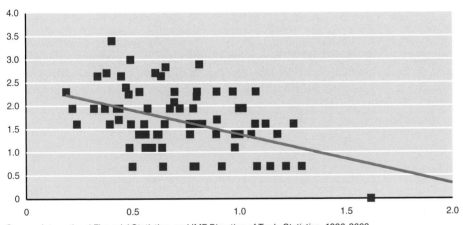

Source: *International Financial Statistics, and IMF Direction of Trade Statistics, 1990-2003*

Tackling corruption

Customs administrations are among the world's organizations most vulnerable to corruption. They are situated in the centre of the international supply chains and are strategically positioned to facilitate or hamper trade. In many countries, the major manifestation of corruption is the bribe to inspectors to do what they are paid to do (i.e. to ensure the timely entry of legitimate cargo). As customs officials are often underpaid, they consider bribes as a legitimate means to improve their income.

Bribes are a substantial cost factor to many producers and they therefore undermine competitiveness. However, as the marginal cost of customs delay is often higher than the bribe, importers or exporters are willing to pay to have their goods cleared without further inconvenience. For example, in a survey on Mozambican enterprises, 43% of the firms replied that corruption by customs officials is a major problem to their business (Biggs et al., 1999). In Nigeria, many firms do not attempt to fight the bureaucracy and corruption associated with exporting and they sell to traders and middlemen who export for them (Marchat et al., 2002).

Corruption by customs officials greatly hinders business

Establishing a reliable customs system with honest personnel needs to be closely coordinated with the rest of the trade liberalization process. The following actions can establish a foundation for a customs system characterized by integrity and competence (Lane, 1998):

- Pay a salary that is consistent with a professional position of honour and trust, which will attract high-quality personnel;

- Establish internal controls and audit systems, to prevent breaches of integrity and to leave trails that can identify and uncover violations;

- Publish standards for cargo clearance and all customs services, and provide appeals for customs decisions; and

- Develop a code of conduct and core values that address integrity at all levels of the organization.

Some countries have implemented successful reforms and reduced corruption by streamlining customs procedures and making them transparent. Peru is a successful example. With help from the Inter-American Development Bank, Peruvian customs fired corrupt employees, instituted a test for competence, provided training to remaining employees, hired new professionals, established standards for cargo clearance times, simplified tariffs and reduced duty rates. As a result, over a five-year period, imports doubled, revenue collections quadrupled, staffing was reduced by 30% and cargo clearance times were reduced from 15-30 days to 1 or 2 days (Lane, 1998). In Jamaica, corruption was fought by facilitating the customs-clearing mechanism and the introduction of a binding, comprehensive manual of procedures setting out all customs rights and responsibilities in export clearance. This manual was published, so that exporters and their agents know what the rules of the game are (Staples, 2002). In Mozambique, the Government selected Crown Agents, an international firm delivering capacity-building and institutional development services in public sector transformation to manage customs operations and to train customs staff. This measure has reduced corruption significantly (Nathan Associates, 2002).

As a temporary measure, pre-shipment inspection can counter inefficiency or corruption in the customs administration. These types of services are provided by private companies in the exporting country for verification of unit prices and for examination and reporting of the quantity and quality of exports before they are shipped to the importing country. PSI has not reduced tariff evasion and corruption in all countries where it was introduced (Anson et al., 2003). Thus, its effectiveness depends on how well it is implemented. Essentially, it needs to be combined with a comprehensive programme of customs reform and modernization.

Information and communications technologies

Although there are encouraging developments in countries such as Botswana, Mauritius, Namibia and South Africa, the African region as a whole lags behind others in the use of modern information technology in domestic as well as international trade activities. Telecommunications services are inadequate, inefficient and very expensive, availability of mobile cellular phones is very limited, prohibitively expensive and non-existent in some rural areas. Africa also has the lowest Internet diffusion in the world (see figure 5.9).

Figure 5.9

Internet diffusion worldwide, 2002/2003 (users per 1,000 population)

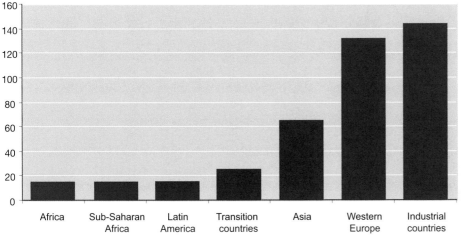

Source: *World Development Indicators, 2003*

While many African countries are not yet making full use of e-commerce systems, several are serviced by organizations that use e-commerce-oriented systems. The African Development Forum held at ECA in Addis Ababa in 1999 identified the following barriers to e-commerce in the continent:

- African infrastructure is not sufficiently e-commerce friendly: the physical infrastructure is inadequate; the electronic transaction infrastructure is deficient; and the legal and regulatory framework is undeveloped.
- The African e-commerce environment is not supportive: the level of awareness of e-commerce is not high enough; African entrepreneurs need training in using the Internet for business; and African Internet-support professionals need training.

As a result of poor quality but expensive telecommunications, businesses in Africa find themselves less competitive, especially as they lack up-to-date information on prices of goods, services and shipments; and they also incur all the costs of the unnecessary delays at ports and border posts.

Payment mechanisms

Capital controls limit business opportunities

Inefficient and cumbersome payment and credit arrangements, as well as costly insurance and customs security fees remain an obstacle to trade. First, different methods of payment are adopted in international sales transactions, depending mainly upon the relationship between seller and buyer. For example, if the seller and the buyer know each other and have a long-standing business relationship, they may transact business on trust and the seller may periodically send invoices to the buyer for settlement. Payment may also be made by other methods such as "cash with order", when the buyer sends a cheque or a bank draft with the order, or by "documentary credit", where payment is made against documents instead of against goods. The documents transfer title to the goods. The documentary credit is operated through banks: the seller sends the relevant documents to his bank for release of payments by the buyer's bank on the buyer's acceptance.

ECA studies in West, East and North Africa reveal that the documentary credit payment system is the most popular international payment system on the continent, but it is a practice characterized by cumbersome and complex procedures. The basis of the system is a series of checks, in which the progress of the goods towards the buyer is pinned to the progress of payment to the seller. The process is time consuming, requires physical movement of documents between different banking establishments in two different countries, is not well understood and is badly managed by many users. Indeed it has been reported that half of all requests for payment are rejected on grounds of documentary inconsistencies. In addition, the system is open to fraud.

Empirical evidence indicates that imposing restrictions on current payments and transfers (exchange controls) and on capital account transactions (capital controls) represent a notable non-tariff barrier to trade (Tamirisa, 1999). In particular, the effect of capital controls appears to be particularly strong for developing countries, tending to limit business opportunities for hedging foreign exchange risks, financing trade, and managing assets and liabilities. Exchange controls contribute to reducing trade by rationing the foreign exchange available for transactions.

Next, on average, insurance fees are around 2% of the value of trade and represent around 15% of total maritime charges. The conditions of many African countries, including socio-political instability and poor infrastructure, together with the long distances that separate such countries from international markets, imply high average insurance premiums, which have the effect of discouraging trade.

In most developing countries, international trade is performed on the basis of traditional commercial practice: exports are made on a "free on board" (f.o.b.) basis and imports on a "cost, insurance and freight" (c.i.f.) basis. Those who export tend to prefer selling their products on departure instead of taking an aggressive marketing position by selling on delivery terms. African businesses rarely get involved in negotiating insurance fees for maritime transport.

Finally, customs security is one of the major difficulties in freight transit between countries. There are financial guarantees and mechanisms designed to ensure that goods in transit do not enter the transit country market without the necessary taxes and customs duties being paid. Guarantee payments represent a high cost for transport operators. In Africa, however, no subregional organization has managed to put in place a satisfactory system. Texts have been adopted in subregions such as COMESA, but they have yet to be ratified. In the case of ECOWAS, texts are applied differently in different countries. Customs services in Côte d'Ivoire and Senegal, for example, require bank guarantees. Burkina Faso, Benin and Niger have all instituted guarantee funds, with the guarantee being cumulative (paid in each of the countries transited) and non-reimbursable. UEMOA and ECOWAS are exploring the possibility of regionalizing the guarantee fund but there are still diverging views on a number of points, including vehicle conformity, the guarantee fund subscription rate and the formalities required by the transit countries. The benefits of regional customs guarantees include: transport cost savings, a single customs bond that is accepted regionally, quicker clearance of vehicles at borders, and higher productivity of vehicles through quick transit and turnaround times.

Roadblocks represent a de facto tax on trade

International trade standards

In recent years, an increasing mass of standards and technical regulations governing the admissibility of imported goods into an economy has emerged. In principle, the purpose of such standards is to ensure that the products available on markets meet minimum requirements, whatever their origin is. Such requirements may refer to the safety of consumers (i.e. in the case of food products), or the protection of the environment (i.e. in the case of trade in manufactured goods), or other quality-related characteristics.

Standards and regulations impose higher production costs on firms seeking to export from developing countries. This follows from both technological and preference gaps *vis-à-vis* industrial economies. Demand for standards in advanced countries is highly elastic to income, meaning that standards are a luxury good whose demand rises with rising incomes. Associated with continued advances in scientific knowledge about health and environmental hazards, standards tend to change frequently and to become more and more stringent over time. In this respect, they obviously reduce the ability of developing countries to access international product markets. Empirical evidence suggests that stringent standards can have a negative effect on trade. For instance, a recent study reveals that African exports of cereals will decline by 4.3%, and that of nuts and dried fruits by 11% with a 10% tighter EU standard on contamination levels of aflatoxin (i.e. a dangerous mold that can be found in grains) in these products (Wilson et al., 2003). The EU has also estimated the costs of technical standards as being equivalent to the tax of 2% of the value of goods traded (Otsuki et al., 2001).

An issue of particular concern to African countries is the multiplicity of standards for agricultural products imposed by the EU, and its unilateral approach in developing these standards, which do not often conform to corresponding WTO standards. The high dependency of African exports on European markets makes them more susceptible to European regulatory reforms.

Facilitating trade for the future

Tackling the challenges of international trade in Africa requires a comprehensive and coordinated approach that entails improvements in infrastructure; provision of efficient and competitive services in the areas of roads, railways, ports, information and communications technology; the removal of illegal roadblocks that constitute a *de facto* tax on trade; the simplification and harmonization of customs and border procedures; and more stringent international trade standards. The gains and benefits of trade facilitation are related to the whole chain of processes.

One major new initiative that is helping African economies identify and deal with trade facilitation and related bottlenecks is the Integrated Framework initiative designed to tackle trade facilitation, which combines detailed diagnostic studies with follow-up implementation efforts, in order to alleviate the tremendous constraints facing many of these economies (see box 5.6).

Box 5.6

Integrated Framework Initiative to tackle trade facilitation and related bottlenecks

The Integrated Framework for Trade-Related Technical Assistance to Least Developed Countries (IF) is a multi-agency, multi-donor programme that assists the least developed countries (LDCs) to expand their participation in the global economy, thereby enhancing their economic growth and poverty reduction strategies.

The IF was inaugurated in October 1997 in response to the complexity of LDC trade-related problems by six multilateral institutions (the International Monetary Fund, International Trade Centre (ITC), UNCTAD, UNDP, World Bank and WTO, which, with their distinct areas of competence, could complement each other to deliver greater development dividends to LDCs in the multilateral trading system.

The objectives of the IF are, to mainstream trade into the national development plans of LDCs, and to assist in the coordinated delivery of trade-related technical assistance in response to needs identified by the LDC.

The IF process comprises three broad stages: (a) preparatory activities, including an official request by a country to participate in the initiative and a technical review of the request, the establishment of a National IF Steering Committee, and, to the extent possible, the establishment of a lead donor; (b) a diagnostic phase during which the key constraints to a country's integration into the multilateral trade system and global economy are identified, based on which a rational programme for technical assistance consistent with needs could be prepared; and (c) follow-up activities that start with the translation of diagnostic phase findings into the elaboration and validation of an action plan, which serves as basis for trade-related technical assistance delivery.

Box 5.6 *(continued)*

Integrated Framework Initiative to tackle trade facilitation and related bottlenecks

Several African countries including Burundi, Djibouti, Eritrea, Ethiopia, Guinea, Lesotho, Madagascar, Malawi, Mali, Mauritania and Senegal are part of the IF initiative. Implementation of the IF remains a "work in progress" and as such the concerned agencies are still in a process of learning from the lessons of on-going implementation. However, the fact that the IF process helps to identify constraints to international trade should serve as incentive for those African countries that are not part of the initiative to get on board.

Source: *www.integratedframework.org, accessed 08/04/2004*

An important message emerging from this report is the need for subregional and regional approaches and strategic partnerships to complement national measures to facilitate trade. This is because international trade involves the use of infrastructure and services of at least two countries. This is especially true for landlocked countries with key transit facilities lying outside their territorial boundaries. For example, imported goods for Rwanda and Burundi have to pass through Kenya and Uganda or Tanzania and Uganda, depending on whether the goods arrive at the port of Mombasa or Dar es Salaam. A subregional approach can be an efficient means of coordinating actions, setting priorities, reviewing progress, mobilizing resources, allocating funds and monitoring contribution levels, with regard to solving common problems.

Infrastructure priorities

Specific actions required in the road, rail, and ports sub-sectors include the following:

Roads subsector

- Maintain and rehabilitate existing roads;
- Expand road network to isolated areas; and
- Widen roads with narrow lane and shoulder widths, and where necessary, adjust horizontal and vertical alignments taking into consideration the increased use of heavy vehicles.

Rail subsector

- Increase connectivity of railway sections with different track gauges by use of "rail to rail" transhipment facilities;
- To the extent possible, standardize the track gauge used on the continent;
- Use rolling stock equipped with changeable gauges; and
- Convert freight wagons to flat beds, suitable for transportation of containers.

Ports

- Replace obsolete and inappropriate equipment at ports with modern container-handling facilities;

- Develop container terminals at ports to facilitate efficient handling and storage of containers;

- Develop more inland terminals ("dry ports") to serve both landlocked countries and the interior areas of coastal countries; and

- Train local staff to run containerized systems that are highly mechanized and computerized.

Transport efficiencies

Several actions need to be taken to improve the efficiency of Africa's transport services. Particular care has to be taken to avoid inefficient monopolies and other rent-seeking behaviour so that essential services support rather than strangle export growth. In this regard, competition in freight forwarding and in the freight transport market should be encouraged. Increasing vehicle utilization through better competition will push older less efficient vehicles out of business.

Other measures to improve the efficiency of transport services include raising the skill level and access to machinery of vehicle mechanics working in the informal sector and placing emphasis on the repair and reconditioning of parts rather than replacements; giving more responsibility to drivers and encouraging them to take closer interest in vehicle mechanics and the business side of running a vehicle; and informing owners and drivers of the advantages of slow vehicle running speeds that include the reduction of fuel consumption, maintenance costs and accidents. Finally vehicle utilization and safety can be increased by the use of two drivers per vehicle.

International transport patterns and practices have been changing rapidly, with the introduction of improved systems for transferring cargo between different transport modes, the rapid development of technologies capable of tracking shipments from door to door, and the growth of containerized transportation. This has resulted in the growth of multi-modal transport operators (MTOs), responsible for the movement of goods through various channels from origin to final destination on one transport document. MTOs represent an integrating factor of international transportation and, thus, for the expansion of trade since they ensure the non-interrupted flow of goods from origin to destination. Apart from ensuring a secure, personal and straightforward transportation of goods, MTOs are a bridge over the gaps created by differences in cultures, languages, and commercial practices. However, the absence of a uniform international convention on multi-modal transport hinders the development of this form of transportation in Africa. The ratification and accession to international treaties and conventions to enhance the use of multi-modal transport on the continent should be encouraged, as well as the establishment of indigenous MTOs.

Removing roadblocks

The challenge of removing roadblocks and preventing the diversion of goods on Africa's roads is enormous, because the problems are extensive, deep-rooted and inherently difficult to come to grips with. Efforts made in some countries and subregions to alleviate these problems should be objectively assessed and good practices disseminated. Overall, improvements have to be based on political agreements and interventions from the highest government levels. This, in fact, is a prerequisite to sustainable solutions. NEPAD, through its Peer Review Mechanism, could play a lead role in this regard.

Air transport

In 2001, Africa accounted for approximately 3.5% of the world's air cargo traffic in terms of tonnage. The total international flows moving into, and out of Africa totalled approximately 961,000 tons, and Europe accounted for 65% of all African foreign air trade. There is a need for a thorough appraisal of the potentials of air transport to enhance both intra-African trade and the continent's trade with other regions of the world. The inadequacy of land transport infrastructure and services in Africa provides an added incentive to improve the efficiency of air transport. This is particularly relevant with regard to the enhancement of intra-African trade. The Yamoussoukro Decision adopted in 1999 was a major breakthrough in the sector, resulting in a speeding up of the liberalization of access to the air transport market in Africa, and the introduction of airport space management reforms. However, efforts still need to be made to ensure that the Decision is fully implemented.

"Improving the efficiency of air transport would enhance intra-African Trade"

Speeding up customs procedures

The problem of slow and cumbersome border procedures needs to be addressed by reducing to the minimum the number of trade documents and copies required and by harmonizing the nature of the information to be contained in these documents. Such documents should be produced in accordance with international accepted standards, practices and guidelines, and they should be adaptable for use in computer systems. In addition, the introduction of one stop-border post operations should be encouraged.

Overall, customs administrations in most African countries require a fundamental shake-up if these countries are to fully benefit from the liberalization process. Customs administrations need to attain high levels of professionalism and integrity and should be technology-based, with the goal of providing a paperless processing system. Closer working relationships need to be established with tax departments. There is a need for clear, transparent procedures and regular joint meetings between customs, importers, brokers, freight forwarders and port authorities.

In policy terms, the following actions are urgently required:

- Redefine comprehensively the customs' operational role and procedures, with new control strategies that allow for minimum interference with trade, yet ensure proper enforcement of fiscal and trade laws;

- Adopt innovative and flexible management systems, with decentralization of responsibilities and decision-taking, and with greater autonomy and accountability for the administrators in the field;
- Privatize functions that can be effectively performed at a lower cost by the private sector, for example, the operation of warehouses;
- Invest in human resources, technology and audit-based systems; and
- Establish firm management control, particularly in connection to integrity, with a clear, well-articulated code of conduct, willingness to take disciplinary action and effective internal control systems.

Customs reforms in recent years have sometimes been undermined by lack of government commitment and poor use of information technology. However, Morocco is one African country that has managed to overcome these obstacles, thanks to the collaboration of public and private actors, who are committed to tackling corruption and to improving customs procedures. The Moroccan experience in customs reforms is therefore a good example for other African countries to study (see box 5.7).

Box 5.7

Best practice in customs reform: lessons from Morocco

The Moroccan reforms have, since their inception in the mid-1990s, offset the decline in revenue from customs duties, increased revenue from value-added tax and boosted imports. Customs services still continue to generate important shares of budget resources. These reforms have addressed four essential areas.

First, customs procedures have been simplified and computerized. Selective customs controls have been introduced for passengers and freight in the form of green (clearance without inspection) and red (inspection required) channels in international airports. Secondly, all routine functions are now performed by the Customs Administration computer system. The system allows information to be exchanged with users so that traders can obtain free estimates of duties and taxes payable when goods are imported.

Thirdly, the management of special customs procedures, particularly for goods admitted temporarily, have been improved thanks to a computer-assisted facility. Finally, the Customs Administration has become more transparent and more responsive to the needs of the private sector, as indicated by the availability of a wide range of information, a website, a newly-created consultative committee and streamlined customs procedures.

Periodic surveys indicate that the outcomes of the reforms are greatly appreciated and that they should continue if Morocco is to eliminate, by 2010, customs duties on imports from the EU, which is Morocco's main trading partner.

Source: World Bank, 2002

New Technology

If properly utilized, recent advances in science and technology, especially in information technology are capable of reducing transport costs and customs delays, thus enhancing trade volumes in Africa. ASYCUDA or systems such as the Tunisia TradeNet can both simplify and speed up customs procedures (as explained in boxes 5.3 and 5.4). There is, however, a need to create training centres that can deliver courses to the principal actors in international trade.

A further example of an important technical aid to trade is provided by the newest shipment tracking systems, which are designed to keep track of vehicles so that customers can find out exactly where a shipment is located at any given time. The Advanced Cargo Information System (ACIS), designed by UNCTAD and currently used in a number of African countries, can track cargoes in port, as well as on roads, railways and inland waterways. Most East African countries already use both port trackers and rail trackers. Other African countries should be encouraged to use such systems.

Trade standards

To reduce the negative impacts of the multiplicity of standards on Africa's trade, the following actions are paramount:

- Establish regional certification centres for diagnosis and analysis, in conjunction with the EU;
- Introduce joint investigations of perceived health hazards; and
- Simplify the multiplicity of standards and ensuring that these standards conform to WTO levels.

Subregional initiatives

For many years, African countries have recognized the importance of a subregional approach to facilitating trade on the continent, but most trade facilitation initiatives have so far had very limited success because of non-compliance and incomplete or poor implementation. One exception is the Northern Corridor from Mombasa, Kenya, to Bujumbura, Burundi, where transport facilitation measures have already halved average transit times. In West Africa, ECOWAS Heads of State have called for member States to monitor the implementation of decisions and protocols on free movement, but the national monitoring committees are not yet reporting regularly to the ECOWAS Secretariat; this is an illustration of the still low political priority being accorded to trade facilitation by Africa's subregional economic communities.

Trade facilitation in the multilateral framework–Africa's position

In Geneva, prior to the Cancun WTO Ministerial Conference in 2003, the Chairman of the WTO Council on Trade in Goods, in which the issues of trade facilitation are discussed, admitted that while many countries had highlighted the benefits of trade facilitation, at the same time, they also appreciated concerns that had been raised with the difficulties of developing binding rules on trade facilitation. Some delegations had suggested working on guidelines, which could serve as target for internal reform and for the identification of technical assistance needs that could then be transformed into binding rules once developing countries had sufficiently developed their internal capacities. Broadly, members were of the view that any evolution of trade facilitation had to reflect the needs and the specific situations of members, and their ability to implement whatever may be agreed upon in the future, to allow for the full enjoyment of the benefits accruing from trade facilitation.

The discussions at Cancun revealed further polarization and divergence of views between advocates (the demanders) on the "Singapore Issues" (including trade facilitation) on one hand and those opposed to their inclusion in the WTO work programme on the other. As is now evident, no agreement was reached at Cancun on any of the Singapore Issues (which also include trade and investment, trade and competition policy, and transparency in government procurement). Negotiations at the WTO have, however, continued after Cancun about a multilateral framework for trade facilitation that should be developed in the framework of the Doha work programme.

Many African countries at the Seattle WTO Ministerial Conference in November 1999, while appreciating the importance of trade facilitation as an "economic phenomenon", expressed reservations at that stage as to the need for a "multilateral framework" on trade facilitation. This was still the position of many of these countries at the Doha WTO Ministerial Conference in November 2001. While acknowledging that African countries were coerced into accepting the wording of the Doha Declaration on "trade facilitation", many would have preferred that this issue, like many of the other Singapore Issues, not be included on the Doha agenda. The Abuja Ministerial Declaration on the WTO's 4th Ministerial Conference, adopted by African Ministers of Trade in Abuja, Nigeria, in September 2001, stated:

> "We recognize that issues such as trade and investment, competition, transparency in government procurement, trade facilitation, trade and environment and e-commerce are important. However, we agree that these issues are not a priority at this stage and on-going processes should continue in order to prepare for possible future work in this area".

Furthermore, in "Africa's Negotiating Objectives for the 4th Ministerial Conference" the Ministers stated that:

> "The general assessment is that trade facilitation measures are necessary and beneficial to all countries. In this context, on-going work within and outside the WTO (e.g. rules of origin, customs valuation) should continue. Improved facilitation will require increased technical and financial assistance to narrow the technology and human resources gaps that exist between developed and developing countries".

Certain positions on the issue of a multilateral framework on trade facilitation emerged in the run-up to the Cancun WTO Ministerial Conference. The position among LDCs may be stated as follows:

> "Some aspects of trade facilitation are vital for LDCs. For instance, the question of understanding of international standards is vital for the promotion of LDC exports. Our standards institutions should be strengthened immediately, so that they can properly advise our exporters. On the other hand, much current thinking on trade facilitation pre-supposes the establishment of common procedures, rules and regulations on the movement of goods. To implement such laws and procedures will be very costly for LDCs, which they cannot afford at this stage. Hence, it is too early for the development of an agreement within the WTO in this area. Outside of the WTO framework, current efforts to assist the LDCs in this area may continue".

African countries will require extensive technical assistance to master the art of doing business in a competitive and highly sophisticated trading environment, with or without a multilateral framework on trade facilitation. There is clearly a need to build on the current efforts by African countries individually and collectively through subregional economic communities to reduce transaction costs, for both domestic and international trade.

After a Trade Facilitation Forum held in 2002, the UN Regional Economic Commissions proceeded to develop a project on trade facilitation. The objective of the joint project of the five Regional Commissions is to strengthen both the international competitiveness as well as the negotiating capacity of developing countries by sharing knowledge on problems and best practices in the various countries and regions on: (a) trade promotion and diversification; (b) greater participation by SMEs in global supply networks; (c) designing and implementing trade facilitation policies at national and regional levels, and (d) greater use of knowledge management and information and communication technologies in supply chain management. Such measures would help to focus and enhance trade facilitation capacities for in Africa.

Conclusions

Much needs to be done, as a matter of priority, to equip African countries with the infrastructure and skills needed for its effective participation in global trade.

Trade facilitation needs to be looked at in the broadest possible context. All sectors that have significant impact on trade facilitation should be tackled in a comprehensive manner. Policy coherency, strategies, finance and institutions should be aligned in order to bring the desired results. Improvements in port facilities should be aligned with customs rules and regulations, transport infrastructure as well as services. Further efforts should be made in the dissemination of information technology especially in countries where telephone and Internet services are inadequate. Most importantly, Africa needs to develop the personnel to cope with the accelerating changes that are taking place in information technology, not only as users but also as contributors.

Given the seriousness of the various problems discussed in this chapter and the resource and capacity constraints faced by African countries in general, and SSA countries in particular, it will be extremely difficult to address all problems simultaneously. While a comprehensive approach is necessary in the long term, actions need to be prioritized in a rational way in the medium term.

Annex

A5.1: Trade Facilitation Measured Worldwide

Transport cost rates				Delays at the customs (days)			
Five lowest rates				**Five best-performing countries**			
Africa		Rest of the World		Rest of the world		Africa	
Lesotho	0.000443	Mexico	0.0002	Estonia	1	Botswana	4
Gambia	0.024187	Slovenia	0.018976	Bulgaria	2	Namibia	4
Rwanda	0.038694	Poland	0.029204	Georgia	2	Ghana	5
Ghana	0.040125	Turkey	0.030721	Croatia	2	South Africa	5
Nigeria	0.043194	Hong Kong	0.031297	Czech Rep.	2	Egypt	5.5
Five highest rates				**Five worst-performing countries**			
Africa		Rest of the World		Rest of the world		Africa	
Guinea-Bissau	0.232934	Moldova	0.173938	Kyrgyzstan	10	Uganda	14
Eq. Guinea	0.243227	Hungary	0.174879	Lithuania	10	Malawi	17
Burundi	0.280751	Estonia	0.179005	Ukraine	10	Nigeria	18
Uganda	0.322751	Vietnam	0.183058	Venezuela	11	Cameroon	20
Mali	0.392903	Peru	0.213639	Ecuador	15	Ethiopia	30
Average cost rates in regions of the world				**Average delay in regions of the world**			
Latin America	0.0743			Africa	11.35294		
Western Europe	0.0418			Sub-Saharan Africa	12.13333		
Transition countries	0.1088			Latin America	7.184211		
Asia	0.0881			Western Europe	3.888889		
Industrial countries	0.0472			Transition countries	4.368421		
Africa	0.1316			Asia	5.5		
Sub-Saharan Africa	0.1364			Industrial countries	3.888889		

Note: *The transport cost rate is the ratio of transport costs as a percentage of the value of imports.*

Source: *ECA, from official sources*

References

ADB (African Development Bank) (2003), *African Development Report 2003: Globalization and Africa's Development*, ADB, Tunis

Amjadi, A. and Yeats, A.J. (1995), "Have transport costs contributed to the relative decline of sub-Saharan African exports?" World Bank Policy Research working paper 1559, Washington DC

Anson, Jose et al (2003), "Tariff Evasion and Customs Corruption: does pre-shipment inspection help?" World Bank working paper, 9 October 2003, World Bank, Washington DC

Biggs, T., Nasir, J., and Fisman, R. (1999), "Structure and Performance of Manufacturing in Mozambique," Regional Programme for Enterprise Development (RPED) paper no 107, August 1999, World Bank, Washington DC

Booth, D., Hanmer, L. et al. (2000), "Poverty and Transport," report prepared for the World Bank in collaboration with DFID, Overseas Development Institute, London

Clark, X., Dollar, D. and Micco, A. (2001), "Maritime Transport Costs and Port Efficiency", mimeo, World Bank, Washington DC

De Castro, C.F. (1996), "Trade and Transport Facilities: review of current issues and operational experience," joint World Bank/UNCTAD publication

Economic Commission for Africa (ECA) (2004), *Assessing Regional Integration in Africa*, Addis Ababa

Ellis, S.D. and Hine, J.L. (1998), "The Provision of Rural Transport Services," Sub-Saharan Africa Transport Policy Programme (SSATP) working paper no 37, World Bank, Washington DC

Heggie, I. and Vickers, P. (1998), "Commercial Management and Financing of Roads," World Bank technical paper no 409, World Bank, Washington DC

Hendeson, V., Shalizi, V. and Venables, A. (2001), "Geography and Development," *Journal of Economic Geography*, 1, pp81-106

Hine, J.L., Ebden, J.H. and Swan, P. (1997), "A Comparison of Freight Transport Operations in Tanzania and Indonesia," TRL Report 267, TRL Ltd, Crowthorne, UK

Lane, M. H. (1998), "Customs and Corruption," Transparency International working paper, available online (www.transparency.org/working_papers/lane/lane_customs.html)

Limão, N. and Venables, A. (2000). "Infrastructure, Geographical Disadvantage and Transport Costs," mimeo, World Bank, Washington, and Columbia University, New York

Lisinge, R.T. (2001), *Transport, Sustainable Livelihoods and Travel Patterns in Rural Cameroon,* TRL Ltd, Crowthorne, UK

Marchat, J.M., Nasir, J. et al. (2002), "Results of the Nigeria Firm Survey," final version November 2002, Regional Programme for Enterprise Development (RPED), World Bank, Washington DC

Nathan Associates (2002), "Mainstreaming Trade: a poverty reduction strategy for Mozambique," supported and funded by the Trade Capacity Building Project, USAID, Maputo, Mozambique, October 2002

Otsuki, T., Wilson, J. and Sewadeh, M. (2001), "Saving Two in a Billion: quantifying the trade effect of European food safety standards on African exports," *Food Policy*, 26 (5), pp495-514

Rizet, C. and Hine. J.L. (1993), "A Comparison of the Costs and Productivity of Road Freight Transport in Africa and Pakistan," *Transport Reviews*, 13 (2), pp151-165

Staples, B. (2002), "Trade Facilitation: improving the invisible infrastructure," in Hoekman, B., Mattoo, A. and English, P. (eds) *Development, Trade and the WTO: A Handbook*, World Bank, Washington DC

Tamirisa, N.T. (1999), "Exchange and Capital Controls as Barriers to Trade," IMF Staff Paper 46, pp 69-88, Washington DC

The Economist (2002), "The Road to Hell is Unpaved," 21 December 2002, pp65-67

United Nations Conference on Trade and Development (UNCTAD) (2001), "Transit System of Land locked and Transit Developing Countries," TD/BILDC/AC.1/17, Geneva

——— (2002), *Review of Maritime Transport 2002*, Geneva

Wilson, J., Mann, C. and Otsuki, T. (2003), "Trade Facilitation and Economic Development: measuring the impact," World Bank Policy Research working paper 2988, Washington DC

World Bank (2002), Poverty Reduction and Economic Management (PREM) Notes, Public Sector, no 67, April 2002, Washington DC

Fiscal Implications of Trade Liberalization

Trade liberalization is a potential source of fiscal instability for African countries because of their high dependence on trade taxes for public revenue. The policy challenge is how to maintain fiscal stability while liberalizing trade. For African governments with inefficient tax administrations, and for those that still rely heavily on trade taxes, the problems can be severe. During the late 1990s many African countries struggled to maintain sustainable fiscal positions even when their government revenues were rising. At the same time, they pushed forward with trade liberalization and their trade tax revenues as a percentage of GDP declined.

How should countries react to falls in revenue as tariffs are cut? This is a critical issue for African countries because many have already carried out considerable liberalization of their trade regimes. Negative fiscal impacts often emerge at later stages of liberalization; the boost to revenues from higher trade volumes, as a result of tariff cuts, will be insufficient to outweigh the revenue-dampening effect of the tax reductions themselves. Nevertheless, in the longer term, well-sequenced trade liberalization, coordinated with a coherent trade and industrial strategy, should lead to substantial growth benefits, so increasing the tax base. But how can the reductions in fiscal revenue be buffered in the short to medium term?

Most of the African countries that made the fastest progress on trade liberalization over the last ten years have seen a significant decrease in their revenues from international trade taxes, but several of these have been able to take appropriate action, as this chapter explains. So although trade liberalization can exacerbate fragile fiscal positions, its negative impacts can be offset or reduced with appropriate policies.

The chapter recommends that trade liberalization be co-ordinated with measures on the revenue and spending side of the budget, including raising domestic indirect and direct taxes, strengthening tax administration and collection, and improving the effectiveness of public spending. It also underlines the fact that the maintenance of a sound macroeconomic environment is critical to preventing fiscal distress during trade liberalization.

> *Negative fiscal impacts emerge at later stages of liberalization*

Africa's deficits persist, despite increasing tax revenues

Many African countries still struggle to achieve fiscal stability, as can be seen in figure 6.1. But between 1995 and 2002 the average annual change in the total tax revenue to GDP ratio was positive for many countries, indicating progress in expanding the tax base (see figure 6.2). Although a few countries experienced both decreasing revenues and increasing deficits, for most of those whose budget balance deteriorated, revenues grew. Some countries even managed to improve the budget balance in the face of falling revenues.

African countries depend heavily on their trade taxes as a source of revenue. On the continent as a whole, international trade taxes generated on average 28.2% of total current revenues over the last decade; for sub-Saharan Africa the share was 30.5%. This contrasts with 0.8% for high-income OECD countries, 18.42% for lower medium-income countries, and 22.5% for all low-income countries. Also, while the data show a decreasing trend worldwide, in Africa the share has stayed flat or even slightly increased.

> *In 10 years, international trade taxes generated 28.2% of total revenues for Africa*

Figure 6.1

African countries' average annual change in fiscal balance to GDP ratio, 1995-2002

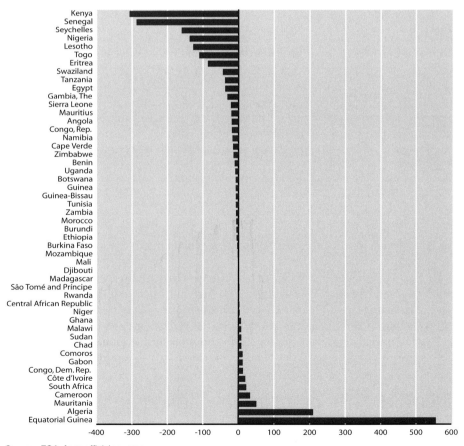

Source: ECA, from official sources

Figure 6.2

African countries' average annual change in tax revenues to GDP ratio, 1995-2002

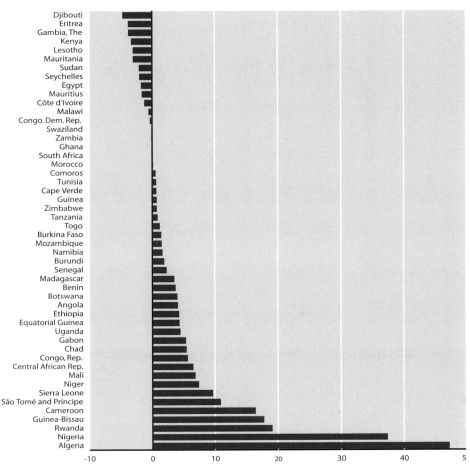

> *The 1990s witnessed moderate progress in trade liberalization*

Source: ECA, from official sources

The 1990s witnessed moderate progress on trade liberalization in Africa as a result of a combination of unilateral trade reforms and various bilateral, regional, and multilateral trade agreements. The average index of trade restrictions, which captures the average level of tariffs (see Annex A6.1), decreased slightly from 9.8% in 1985 to just over 9% in 1990, and then dropped to around 7% in 2002. The reduction in trade tax rates combined with the weak expansion of the tax base drove trade tax revenues down as a percentage both of GDP and of total government revenues. But this was compensated by higher revenues from the taxation of domestic goods and services and from direct taxes on income and profits (see figure 6.3).

Figure 6.3

African countries' deficit and budget items, 1980-2002 (% of GDP)

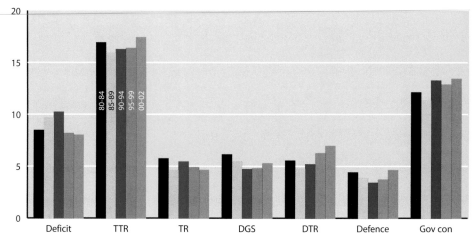

Notes: *Deficit = fiscal deficit excluding grants; TTR = total tax revenues; TR = trade tax revenues; DGS = taxes on domestic goods and services; DTR = direct tax revenues; Gov con = government consumption. See Annex A6.2 for these and other definitions of variables.*

Source: *ECA, from official sources*

Tax collection is often hampered by inadequate administrative capacity

African countries' fiscal problems cannot be blamed solely on the negative fiscal impact of trade liberalization. It is notable that, on average, total tax revenues increased, even as revenues from trade taxes fell. As indicated by the increase in some spending items, such as government consumption and defence expenditure, other factors need to be taken into account in policy formulation and projections of revenue.

The risks and challenges of trade liberalization

Trade is a source of revenue on which many African governments survive. ECA data demonstrate that reliance on revenues from taxes on international trade is inversely related to income levels (see figure 6.4). In poor countries, the lack of administrative capacity reduces the efficiency of tax collection, while the large size of the informal and subsistence sectors means that a large proportion of transactions cannot be taxed. The influence of powerful lobbies makes some sectors off-limits to the tax authorities. As a result, the domestic tax base is narrow and governments try to meet their fiscal needs by charging high rates on easily taxable sectors such as trade (Kubota, 2000). With governments operating under severe resource constraints, revenue-raising concerns are often cited as a reason for some governments' resistance to trade policy reforms in Africa (Khattry, 2002).

The picture is not all negative, however. Positive fiscal effects can arise from the elimination of trade-related subsidies and tariff exemptions. The effect of cutting tariffs is ambiguous. On the one hand, lower tariffs imply lower tax rates and hence smaller revenues.

On the other hand, the volume of imports tends to expand when tariffs are reduced, and hence the tax base will grow. Which of the two effects is larger will depend on the extent to which import demand increases when tariffs are cut. If the increase is sufficiently high, then revenues will rise.

Figure 6.4

African countries' reliance on trade taxes measured against income levels, 1990-2003 averages

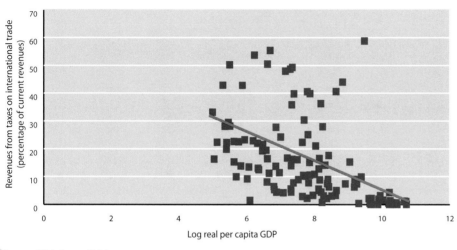

Source: *ECA, from official sources*

The picture may also be complicated by other effects. This is because trade liberalization is often accompanied by a devaluation of nominal and real exchange rates. This raises the domestic value of imports, with a positive impact on revenues, but the domestic cost of government spending programmes will increase. Consumption will switch from tradable to non-tradable goods: revenues from trade taxes will therefore fall and those from domestic indirect taxation will increase. The overall effect of devaluations is, therefore, also ambiguous. Longer-run effects may be driven by enhanced growth performance as a result of trade liberalization. If growth increases, then the increased income levels will translate into a larger base for direct domestic taxation. Table 6.1 summarizes the revenue implications of the different elements of trade liberalization programmes.

When trade restrictions are high, cutting tariffs normally boosts trade volumes and revenues. But as tariffs are cut further the revenue impact will become smaller and then negative. Because many African countries have already liberalized, they cannot expect further substantial increases in trade tax revenue and may see declining revenues. This effect is illustrated by a "Laffer" curve, tracking the relationship between trade restrictions and revenues (see figure 6.5). When the trade regime is very restrictive because of high tariff rates, trade volumes are likely to be severely compressed (to the right of the curve). Reducing the restrictions will result in a strong increase in trade volumes, more than compensating for the lower tax rate, and leading to higher trade tax revenues.

Table 6.1

How trade liberalization is expected to affect revenues

Items in the trade reform package	Impact on revenues
Replace non-tariff barriers with tariffs	Positive
Eliminate tariff exemptions and subsidies	Positive
Reduce tariff dispersions	Neutral/Positive
Eliminate state trading monopolies	Neutral/Positive
Reduce high average tariffs	Ambiguous
Reduce medium or low average tariffs	Negative
Lower maximum tariffs	Ambiguous
Eliminate export taxes	Neutral/Negative
Initial exchange rate depreciation	Neutral/Positive

Sources: *Compiled from analysis reported by Sharer et al., 1998, Ebrill et al., 1999, Adam et al., 2001, and Hoekman et al., 2002*

However, when the trade regime is already fairly liberalized, further reductions in restrictions will not cause a sufficiently large increase in trade volumes to offset the lower tariffs (to the left of the curve). Overall revenues will therefore decrease (Ebrill et al., 1999; Khattry, 2002; Agbeyegbe et al., 2003; Ekpo, 2003).

Figure 6.5

African countries' trade restrictions and revenues from international trade taxes

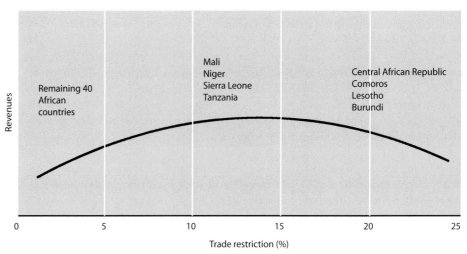

Source: *Calculations by ECA*

Because higher fiscal revenues lead to lower deficits, the inverse-U relation between trade restrictions and revenues translates into a U-shaped relationship between trade restrictions and the deficit. So for countries that have already carried out some trade liberalization, further liberalization is likely to increase the deficit. This is the case for many African countries.

In figure 6.5, the estimated Laffer curve for African countries shows revenue maximization between 10% and 15% of the index of trade restrictions. This index captures average "realized" tariffs, being defined as trade tax revenues divided by total trade value, variables which are available for a relatively large sample of African countries (see Annex A6.1). The Laffer curve can also be constructed using official tariff rates but with a smaller sample size for reasons of data availability, as discussed in the Annexes. Because of liberalization during the 1990s, many economies are now operating on the upward sloping side of the curve. They will therefore face reductions in revenues as a result of further trade liberalization.

What governments can do in response to falling revenues

Fiscal problems will arise when trade restrictions drop below their revenue-maximizing level of around 10% to 15%. In 2002, there were only four African countries with trade restrictions above 15% and thus on the downward sloping side of the Laffer curve. These were the Central African Republic, Comoros, Lesotho and Burundi. Four others – Mali, Niger, Sierra Leone and Tanzania – had restrictions between 10% and 15%. For the remaining countries, the trade restriction index was below 10%. How can these countries buffer the decrease in revenues that further trade liberalization is likely to bring about?

One strategy is to combine tariff cuts with a point-for-point increase in domestic consumption taxes (Keen and Lighthart, 1999). Under certain conditions this can be shown to lead to an increase in social welfare as well as public revenues. The introduction of a value-added tax (VAT) in particular has advantages over other sales and consumption taxes as it discourages tax evasion and does not hamper the competitiveness of domestic producers compared to foreign firms. Budgetary data indicate that revenues from domestic taxation on goods and services (including VAT) have grown as trade tax revenues have fallen. Direct tax revenues can also be increased through strengthening the tax collection system and eliminating tax holidays and other exemptions, although in poor African States with large informal sectors this is difficult.

The option of expenditure reduction is obviously problematic because many spending items are rigid or else are vital for human welfare. Spending on poverty reduction, the social sectors and infrastructure cannot easily be cut. It may also be hard to reduce government consumption and defence spending. Even if cutting expenditure proves impossible, enhancing the efficiency and effectiveness of existing spending will in the long run help to enhance productive capacity of the economy and therefore increase the tax base.

Fiscal stability during trade liberalization requires a stable macroeconomic environment, with low and predictable inflation and steady growth in per capita GDP. Adverse changes in the terms of trade will have a negative impact on the fiscal balance. In the long term, reducing vulnerability to such shocks, through diversification of exports and appropriate exchange rate policies, is essential to achieving fiscal stability. The experiences of some fast-liberalizing African countries illustrate these policy responses and are discussed in the following sections.

How fast liberalizers have performed

The moderate pace of liberalization for the continent as a whole hides significant cross-country differences (see table 6.2). A group of fast-liberalizing countries can be identified. These are the ten countries that saw the greatest reduction in the index of trade restrictions between 1995-2002, namely Mauritania, Seychelles, Ghana, Tunisia, Burkina Faso, Equatorial Guinea, Sudan, Mauritius, Morocco, and Senegal. Their experiences are a useful benchmark to assess the extent of fiscal problems arising from trade liberalization. In this section we distil the main policy responses from these countries, while the following section looks at some of the individual country experiences in more detail.

In 1995, all the "fast liberalizers" had fairly low trade restrictions. Only in Sudan, Burkina Faso and Seychelles was the index above 10%, but even for these it was below 15%. The fast liberalizers were on the left side of the Laffer curve in figure 6.5. Further trade liberalization after 1995 led to decreasing trade tax revenues, but most countries did not suffer an increase in their fiscal deficit. Of the ten fast liberalizers, only Seychelles and Mauritius saw an increase in the deficit, net of grants, between 1995 and 2002. The rest were able to reduce their deficits or move from deficit to surplus (see figure 6.6).

Declines in the trade tax revenues of the fast liberalizers are shown in figure 6.7. Changes in total tax revenues were relatively smooth, with sharp decreases only in Sudan, Seychelles and Mauritania. Fast-liberalizing countries were generally able to offset smaller trade tax revenues with other sources of taxation (see box 6.1). Domestic taxes on goods and services increased in most countries. Several countries also managed to raise revenues from direct taxes on income and profits (see figure 6.8). By contrast, non-tax revenues played a limited role in buffering the effect of lower trade tax revenues. Only in Mauritania and Sudan was the share of non-tax revenue in total revenue significantly higher in 2002 than in 1995, in Sudan's case because of the emergence of the oil sector.

Between 1995 and 2002, the ten fast liberalizers generally showed good macroeconomic performances with decreasing inflation and positive growth rates in per capita GDP. The exchange rate black market premium was generally on a downward trend, indicating reduced distortions in the economy. However, the terms of trade fluctuated or declined in most countries as a result of volatile or falling international prices for most exportable goods (see table 6.3). Seychelles had the weakest macroeconomic environment and was the country with the largest deterioration in the fiscal position (see figure 6.6). In Mauritius, despite an otherwise sound macroeconomic environment, the deficit increased because of the public investment programme undertaken by the Government in the early 2000s.

Table 6.2

Average rate of change in African countries' trade restrictions, 1980-2002 (%)

Country	80-89	90-02	95-02
Mauritania	0.355	-5.947	-14.595
Seychelles	not available.	-9.942	-12.904
Ghana	1.477	-9.26	-12.78
Tunisia	5.72	-6.487	-11.496
Burkina Faso	2.471	-4.286	-11.024
Equatorial Guinea	-18.927	4.346	-10.967
Sudan	not available.	not available.	-10.473
Mauritius	0.282	-6.062	-7.551
Morocco	-4.672	-4.011	-5.932
Senegal	not available.	-7.94	-4.903
Côte d'Ivoire	-9.667	-3.072	-3.937
Mozambique	0.97	-3.598	-3.148
Uganda	-15.891	6.107	-2.967
Lesotho	-3.557	2.888	-2.786
Malawi	28.006	-9.319	-2.613
Kenya	not available.	13.606	-2.155
South Africa	14.105	-6.659	-2.116
Cape Verde	3.558	0.577	-1.978
Ethiopia	-3.184	1.543	-1.099
Cameroon	8.435	-2.24	-0.719
Algeria	5.464	3.459	-0.244
Togo	-2.127	-0.714	-0.208
Eritrea	not available.	-5.377	0.63
Congo	not available.	-4.2	1.202
Egypt	-15.067	0.896	1.286
Guinea	5.985	8.569	1.391
Guinea-Bissau	-39.659	19.145	1.597
Madagascar	0.373	-1.808	2.568
Gambia	-20.382	-0.948	3.005
SãoTomé et Principe	n.a	0.054	3.271
Africa	-0.239	1.518	3.587
Sub-Sahran Africa	-0.279	1.853	3.671
Djibouti	not available.	n.a	4.498
Zambia	12.256	1.784	4.709
Sierra Leone	26.307	2.543	5.529
Mali	-7.726	4.308	6.262
Gabon	n.a	3.213	7.077
Burundi	not available.	4.83	7.29
Benin	v	5.977	8.683
Niger	4.969	3.574	10.442
Angola	not available.	not available.	11.987
Chad	10.078	3.796	13.04
Nigeria	n.a	not available.	13.378
Comoros	not available.	6.365	16.462
Tanzania	-3.378	9.382	20.368
Central African Republic	-1.456	10.307	22.345
Zimbabwe	not available.	not available.	30.668
Rwanda	4.072	17.065	46.5
Botswana	-8.187	not available.	not available.

n.a. denotes not available

Note: *No data are available for Democratic Republic of Congo, Liberia, Libya, Namibia, Swaziland or Somalia.*

Source: *Calculations by ECA*

Figure 6.6

Fiscal deficit (DEF) in fast-liberalizing countries, in 1995 and 2002 (% of GDP)

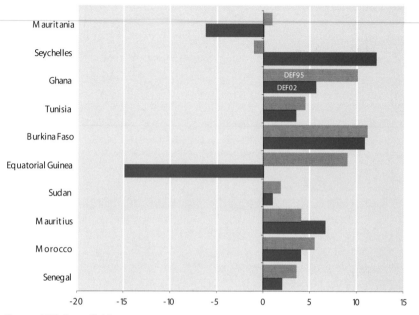

Source: ECA, from official sources

Figure 6.7

Cumulative change in trade tax revenues (TR) and total tax revenues (TTR) in fast-liberalizing countries, 1995-2002 (%)

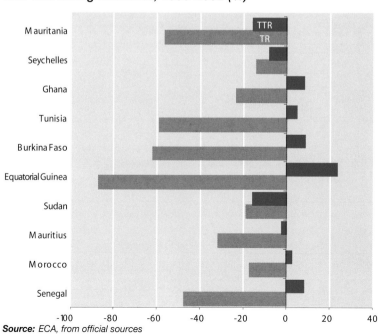

Source: ECA, from official sources

Figure 6.8

Cumulative change in domestic direct (DTR) and indirect (DGS) tax revenues in fast-liberalizing countries, 1995-2002 (%)

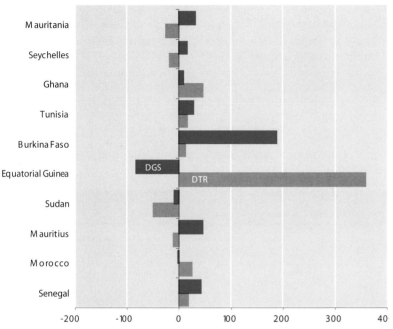

Source: ECA, from official sources

Table 6.3

Macroeconomic trends in fast-liberalizing countries, 1995-2002

	Black market premium	Terms of trade	Inflation	GPD per capita growth
Mauritania	Decreasing	Deteriorating	Decreasing	Low
Seychelles	Decreasing	Fluctuations	Increasing	Negative
Ghana	Decreasing	Fluctuations	Decreasing[a]	Low
Tunisia	Increasing	Fluctuations	Decreasing	High
Burkina Faso	n.a.	Deteriorating	Decreasing	Low
Equatorial. Guinea	Decreasing	Fluctuations	Decreasing	High
Sudan	Decreasing	n.a.	Decreasing	High
Mauritius	Decreasing	Improving	Fluctuations	High
Morocco	Fluctuations	Improving	Decreasing	Low
Senegal	Decreasing	Deteriorating	Decreasing	High

Notes: *Black market premium data end in 2000/01. n.a. denotes non-availability*
[a] *while decreasing, inflation in Ghana remains above 15%. GDP per capita growth is classified "high" if the average annual rate of growth is above 2.5%. Note that Senegal is practically at the threshold (2.59%).*

Sources: *Africa Database (World Bank, 2003); International Financial Statistics (IMF, 2003); Economist Intelligence Unit*

To sum up, some countries were able to counter the negative fiscal effects of trade liberalization with a mix of tax and non-tax policies (see table 6.4). Tax-policy responses mostly involved heavier reliance on indirect domestic taxes. The main non-tax policy response was strengthening macroeconomic performance; non-tax revenues played a limited role. As we see in the next section, responses on the spending side varied. In addition, several countries in the group improved the institutional environment. Better governance, especially in the form of a more efficient bureaucracy, can play a role in achieving fiscal stability. This is because it directly affects the ability of the tax agency to maintain the fiscal base for domestic taxation and to administer the tax system efficiently (see box 6.2).

> "Tax and non-tax policies counteract negative fiscal effects of trade liberalization"

Table 6.4

Summary of fiscal developments and policy responses in fast-liberalizing countries, 1995-2002

Country	Deficit	Trade tax revenue	Total tax revenue	Domestic direct tax revenue	Domestic indirect tax revenue	GC	Macro[a]	GOV
Mauritania[b]	+/-	-	-	-	+	-	Moderate	=
Seychelles	+	-	-	-	+	+	Weak	n.a.
Ghana	-	-	+	+	+	-	Moderate /weak	+
Tunisia	-	-	+	+	+	+	Moderate	+
Burkina Faso	=	-	+	+	+	=	Moderate/ Weak	+
Eq. Guinea	-	-	+	+	-		Sound	n.a.
Sudan	-	-	-	-	=	+	Sound	+
Mauritius	+	-	=	-	+	-	Sound	+
Morocco	-	-	=	+	=	+	Moderate	-
Senegal	-	-	+	+	+	-	Sound	+

Notes: *GC = government consumption; GOV = government effectiveness (see Annex A6.2 for these and other definitions of variables).*

[+] denotes increase between 1995 and 2002; = denotes no significant change between 1995 and 2002; - denotes decrease between 1995 and 2002.

[a] *summarizes trends displayed in table 6.3.*

[b] *in Mauritania, the cumulative deficit change between 1995 and 2002 was positive. However, over most of the period, the overall balance was actually worsening. The sharp improvement that drove most of the cumulative change was realized between 2001 and 2002. In that period, also government revenues peaked (IMF, 2003). Estimates for 2003 suggested a further deterioration of the deficit. However, disaggregated data on TTR, DTR and DGS are not yet available for 2002/2003. They thus refer to end 2001.*

Sources: *Africa Database (World Bank, 2003), International Financial Statistics (IMF, 2003), Economist Intelligence Unit; data on government effectiveness from Kaufmann et al, 2001*

Box 6.1

Is VAT an equitable and efficient source of revenue for the state?

Value-added tax has been introduced in some African countries, with varying degrees of success. In several African countries, VAT was introduced as part of overall tax reform during trade liberalization. In some of these countries — Algeria, Morocco, and Tunisia — VAT was administrated quite effectively and helped to boost fiscal revenue.

VAT is widely accepted as having non-distortionary effects on the economy. However, taxing consumption may be more regressive than taxing income, and this is a particular concern in poor countries, especially as in many of their economies commodity taxes have traditionally accounted for a higher proportion of government revenues than income taxes. In addition, VAT tends to be less effective in developing countries that have large informal sectors.

In practice, the revenue performance of VAT and its distributional effects will depend on the tax's specific design and on the quality of its administration. For equity reasons, multiple rates and exemptions can be used, although these complicate the administration of the tax and can lead to efficiency losses. In Ethiopia, studies have shown that VAT is in fact progressive, with the richest 10% of the population facing the highest effective VAT rate. The introduction of VAT has also unlocked new sources of revenue which have supported spending on health, education and poverty alleviation programmes.

Currently, VAT compliance is low in many African countries. In Zambia, for example, non-compliance is estimated at 50% because of the failure by businesses to register as taxpayers or to file tax returns and as a result of under-reporting of sales for tax purposes. The introduction of VAT should therefore be accompanied by the strengthening of tax administration to maximize efficiency. There should be a reduction of bottlenecks, such as delays on VAT refunds to companies, which can negatively affect business liquidity. VAT exemptions should be minimized, to simplify administration, and registration thresholds need to be set at an appropriate level.

Sources: *Abed, 1998; Mackenzie, 1991; Munoz and Sang-Wook Cho, 2003; Pellechio and Hill, 1996*

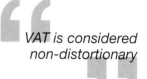

VAT is considered non-distortionary

Box 6.2

Improving tax administration is the key to higher revenue

Tax evasion lowers fiscal revenue in Africa. Most African countries suffer from a "tax gap" — the difference between the tax payable and that collected — of more than 40%. This is caused by inefficient administration within the taxation system. Improving tax administration could reduce the gap and enhance fiscal revenue. Key problems that need to be addressed in tax administration reform include the lack of financial and material resources, poorly trained staff, ineffective procedures, the absence of effective taxpayer services and corruption.

Tax evasion has a negative externality: businesses may feel that they are facing unfair competition from those evading taxes, reducing their own motivation to pay. Strengthening tax administration therefore has the potential to improve voluntary compliance. Establishing monitoring units

Box 6.2 (continued)

Improving tax administration is the key to higher revenue

for different groups of taxpayers such as small- and medium-sized enterprises has been effective in some cases. Frequent auditing can also improve compliance, as in Uganda, where 60% of firms are audited.

In 1985, Ghana restructured its tax system. Before the reform, morale among staff was low, corruption was rife and qualified personnel were difficult to attract and retain. Under the reform, institutions were restructured, human resource issues, such as pay and incentives, were reviewed and training programmes were put into place. Audit practices were improved and in 1989 the tax system was computerized allowing the introduction of unique taxpayer identification numbers. Following the reform, fiscal revenue increased despite reductions in trade tariffs.

Sources: *Abed, 1998; AERC, 1998; Chen and Reinikka, 1999; Tanzi and Casanegra de Jantscher, 1987*

Country experiences and lessons

The experiences of the fast-liberalizing countries have several common features, but also some important differences. The effects of trade liberalization in four of these countries illustrate the importance of tax policy responses and macroeconomic stability in containing the negative fiscal impacts of liberalization. In Senegal, early liberalization efforts combined with a poor macroeconomic environment pushed up the fiscal deficit but, in the second half of the 1990s, improving macroeconomic conditions and good tax-policy responses led to improvements in the fiscal situation. Ghana applied a set of policy responses similar to those in Senegal, but against an unstable macroeconomic background. Seychelles and Mauritius suffered from increasing deficits during liberalization over the second half of the 1990s. However, most of the deterioration in the fiscal stance was as a result of external shocks and changes on the spending-side of the budget, rather than from the negative revenue impact of trade policy reforms. In addition to examining the experience of fast liberalizers, it is worth looking at what happened at the other end of the spectrum. The Central African Republic, for instance, experienced fiscal difficulties.

Senegal – higher domestic taxes and an improved macroeconomic environment

The first attempts at trade liberalization in Senegal took place in the second half of the 1980s with a phased reduction in quantitative restrictions along with tariff cuts. This failed to stimulate trade (see figure 6.9) and led to a fall in international trade tax revenues from 4.45% of GDP in 1985/1986 to 3.78% in 1989/1990. As a result, the fiscal deficit (excluding grants) grew from 3.8% in 1985/1986 to 4.4% in 1989/1990. The rising deficit was also exacerbated by a decrease in revenues from domestic taxes on goods and services.

A more recent phase of trade liberalization began in 1994. In that year, following a prolonged economic and financial crisis, the CFA franc (the common currency in the subregion) was devalued, heralding a phase of economic recovery. A further decisive push to liberalization came with the adoption of a common external tariff by the West African Economic and Monetary Union (UEMOA) in 1997, with full implementation in January 2000. The index of trade restriction decreased from 7.06% in 1997 to 6.15% in 1999 and 4.12% in 2000. A similar downward trend is seen in the IMF index of trade restrictiveness, which fell from 8 in 1997 to 6 in 1998 and 1999 and then to 5 in 2000.

The impact on trade tax revenues of the second wave of liberalization was sharp: these fell from 5% of GDP to 2.5% between 1995 and 2002. The policy response was to increase revenues from domestic taxes (see figure 6.10). In particular, the reliance on taxes on goods and services increased through VAT reform (rates were unified in September 2001). On the expenditure side, government consumption decreased and the public sector wage bill was cut from 48% of the total budget to 34%.

VAT reform increased the reliance on taxes on goods and services

Improved macroeconomic performance also helped to buffer the impact of the decline in revenues. Per capita GDP returned to positive growth of 2.5% between 1995 and 2002, after several years of contraction. Aggregate GDP growth was above 5% after 1994 and averaged just under 5% between 1995 and 2002, following six years of low and negative growth. The inflationary consequences of devaluation were quickly stabilized. Inflation jumped to 32% in 1994, but was reduced to 7.85% in 1995 and 2.75% in 1996. It has remained fairly low since then, despite moderate increases in the early 2000s. The black market premium also fell from 6% to 1%.

The overall fiscal outcome from such responses was positive. Total tax revenues increased from 15.7% of GDP in 1995 to slightly more than 17% in 2002. The deficit fell from 3.5% of GDP in 1995 to 1.8% in 2002 although it reached 3.2% in 2001. The 2002 outturn and estimates for 2003 show continuous progress towards balance.

Ghana – macroeconomic instability hampers fiscal performance

Ghana has a long history of monetary and fiscal instability. There were large swings in inflation during the 1990s, with the rate never falling below 10% and a peak of 60% in 1995. Inflation declined during the second half of the 1990s, reaching 15% in 2002. The fiscal deficit fluctuated above 10% of GDP for much of the 1990s and only in 2000 returned to the single-digit level. High and unpredictable inflation and large deficits hampered overall economic performance and forced Ghana into low-growth equilibrium (ECA, 2003). After wide fluctuations during the 1970s and early 1980s, the real GDP per capita growth rate has stabilized since 1985 at below 3%.

Given this fragile macroeconomic environment, the risk that trade liberalization would push the country back into a situation of growing deficits and fast growth of monetary aggregates was, and still is, high. Between 1995 and 2002, the index of trade restriction declined from 8% to around 2.5%. Helped by favourable trends in international prices and the terms of trade, trade as a percentage of GDP doubled between 1995 and 2002 (see figure 6.9).

Figure 6.9

International trade in four fast-liberalizing countries, 1970-2003 (% of GDP)

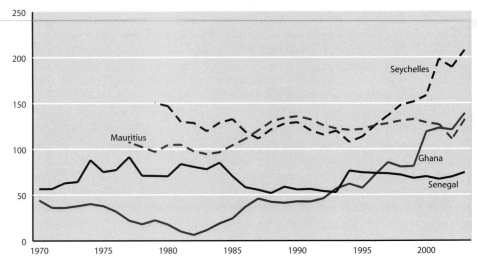

Source: ECA, from official sources

Figure 6.10

Cumulative change in tax and non-tax revenue reliance in four fast-liberalizing countries, 1995-2002 (%)

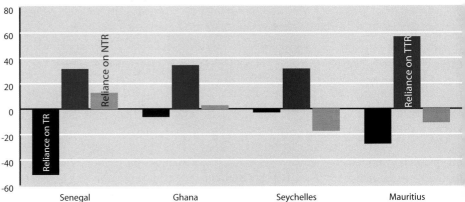

Notes: TR = trade tax revenues; TTR = total tax revenues; NTR = non-tax revenues (see Annex A6.2 for definitions of variables).

Source: ECA, from official sources

International trade tax revenues went up between 1995 and 1998 as trade volumes, clearly compressed in the pre-liberalization regime, began to grow. Thus, the expansion of the tax base was initially sufficiently strong to more than offset the effect of lower tax rates. During the period, total tax revenues as a percentage of both GDP and government revenues also increased, while the reliance on non-tax revenues fell from 28% to about 14%. Despite this, the deficit increased.

In the late 1990s, trade liberalization began to have a negative impact on trade tax revenues, which fell by 45% between 1998 and 2002. Appropriate responses had to be put in place to prevent further deterioration of the fiscal stance. As in Senegal, domestic taxation increased as reliance on trade tax revenues went down. After an initial fall between 1998 and 1999, total tax revenue was kept stable through increases in taxes on domestic goods and services and higher direct taxation. The reliance on non-tax revenues also increased (see figure 6.10). Government consumption remained fairly stable between 1995 and 1999 at around 8% of GDP. The level of consumption later declined, as attempts were made to cut overall expenditure in response to lower trade tax revenues. The share of the budget allocated to public sector wages fell slightly between 1995 and 2001, although in 2002 expenditures again increased because of grade adjustments in the Ghana Education Service and the payment of duty allowances to public health system operators.

Liberalization can produce higher tax revenues

The case of Ghana illustrates how the fiscal effects of trade liberalization interact with broader macroeconomic factors. When liberalization produced higher tax revenues between 1995 and 1998, the deficit increased because a lax fiscal policy pre-dated liberalization. Eventual progress on fiscal stabilization was made thanks to tax reforms introduced in 1999, even as trade liberalization began to have a negative impact on revenues.

Seychelles and Mauritius – policy responses blunted by low growth and high spending

Seychelles and Mauritius are the two fast-liberalizing countries that saw significant deteriorations in their fiscal positions between 1995 and 2002. In both, revenues from trade taxes fell as trade restrictions were reduced.

In Seychelles, trade liberalization led to a modest fall in trade tax revenues (see figure 6.10). Trade tax revenues fell from 12.5% of GDP in 1995 to 9.8% in 1996 and then stabilized at above 10% of GDP. With the exceptions of 1994 and 1995, the deficit was high throughout the 1990s. However, the peaks seen between 1998 and 2000 when the deficit ranged between 15% and 24% of GDP occurred when revenues from trade taxes were fairly constant and total tax revenues were even increasing.

Fiscal problems in the Seychelles were heavily influenced by broader macroeconomic factors. The economy is driven by the tourism and tuna-fishing sectors, which were both sluggish between 1998 and 2002. Tourism suffered again following the 11 September attacks in 2001, but it was equally damaged by cost factors, reflecting the overvaluation of the currency, and these pushed tourists towards competing destinations such as Madagascar, Mauritius and Comoros. Falling income levels reduced the tax base; revenues from direct taxation fell by around 2% of GDP between 1999 and 2001/2002. At the same time, there were increases in government consumption, social welfare expenditure and the public sector wage bill, forcing total spending upwards.

In Mauritius, trade tax revenues fell between 1995 and 2002 while reliance on domestic taxes increased (see figure 6.10). A small decrease in revenues from direct taxes on profits and incomes was more than compensated for by higher indirect taxes, especially by the increase in the VAT rate from 10% to 12% in 2001. Non-tax revenues fell from 15.3% of total revenues in 1995 to 5.4% in 1996, and then peaked at over 14% in 1997 and 1998 before returning to around 10%.

The fiscal deficit rose in 1996 and 1997 as tax and non-tax revenues fell before returning to around 4% of GDP. In 2001 and 2002, the deficit rose to over 6% of GDP. With total revenues almost unchanged, the upsurge in the deficit resulted from higher capital spending.

In both countries, the fiscal impact of trade liberalization was exacerbated by poor growth performance (in Seychelles) and by higher public spending (in Mauritius). Despite attempts to buffer the impact of trade liberalization by increasing domestic taxation, these other factors hampered fiscal stabilization and led to larger imbalances.

Central African Republic – a non-liberalizing example

In several African countries the index of trade restrictions increased over 1995-2002. Some non-liberalizers experienced fiscal difficulties. In cases such as the Central African Republic, this stemmed from the fact that countries were operating on the downward sloping side of the Laffer curve (see figure 6.5). Increased restrictions compressed trade and led to a contraction in revenues. The index of trade restriction in the Central African Republic increased from 8.1% in 1996 to 14.3% in 2001. Trade dropped from 44% of GDP in 1997 to only 27% in 2001. The cumulative change in trade tax revenues was close to zero, with 2001 revenues being slightly below their value in 1995, and much below their 1998 value (see table 6.5). Among the group of countries that also saw increases in trade restrictions, Burundi experienced similar outcomes.

Table 6.5

Central African Republic: trade restrictions and fiscal developments, 1995-2002

	TR	TTR	DGS	DTR	TR reliance	TTR reliance	NTR reliance	
Cumulative change (%)	-1.10	6.90	8.52	20.80	-15.70	-7.56	197.10	
	1995	**1996**	**1997**	**1998**	**1999**	**2000**	**2001**	**2002**
GDP growth	4.90	-8.10	7.50	3.90	3.60	1.80	1.00	0.80
GDP per capita growth	3.84	-6.67	2.74	2.53	1.82	0.91	0.05	-1.15
Inflation	19.19	3.72	1.61	-1.89	-1.41	3.20	3.83	2.30
Deficit	-11.40	-4.96	-6.30	-8.61	-8.68	-9.27	-7.94	n.a.

Estimates for 2003: Aggregate GDP growth -0.7%, Inflation 3.2%, per capita GDP -2.61%

Notes: TR = trade tax revenue; TTR = total tax revenue; DGS = taxes on domestic goods and services; DTR = direct tax revenues; NTR = non-tax revenues.

Source: ECA, from official sources

The revenue structure of the Central African Republic changed in response to its decreasing international trade tax revenues. The fall in trade taxes was compensated for by greater reliance on non-tax revenues. Total tax revenues as a percentage of GDP went up as a result of increasing revenues from indirect and direct taxation. These fiscal developments took place against a difficult macroeconomic background. Real GDP growth fell before stagnating in the early 2000s and real per capita GDP started to decline in 2002. Although inflation fell from 19.2% in 1995 to 2.3% in 2002, this was the result of the economic slowdown. The fiscal deficit fell, but it remained well above 6% of GDP throughout the period. The policy response was successful in preventing further deterioration of the fiscal stance.

Improving the tax administration increases the leverage of the economic base

Conclusions

Because African countries rely on international trade taxes for a large share of their total revenues, the policy challenge is how to maintain fiscal stability when liberalizing trade. The experience of industrial economies shows that at advanced stages of economic development the revenue side of the budget can be structured in such a way to achieve a stable fiscal position even with negligible revenues from trade taxes. However, it is clear that for developing and low-income economies the problem is more complicated: bottlenecks and structural constraints exist, which limit the domestic economic base and the ability to tax it. This explains both the high reliance on trade taxes and the resistance to trade liberalization by some governments.

Trade liberalization is most likely to pose serious fiscal problems at later stages. Early liberalization can actually result in increasing revenues, as the trade-increasing effects of lower tariffs may be sufficiently strong to compensate for reduced tax rates. Countries operating at a level of trade restriction above a given threshold will see increases in revenues as a result of trade liberalization, but most African countries are now below this threshold. Further trade liberalization will therefore lead to smaller trade tax revenues. Without appropriate responses, this will push down total tax revenues, with adverse effects on the fiscal deficit. The experience of fast-liberalizing countries provides some lessons on the type of responses that can be implemented:

- The decrease in trade tax revenues can be matched by an increase in revenues from domestic indirect taxation. In particular, most countries have increased reliance on VAT, which reduces the possibility of evasion and does not hurt the external competitiveness of domestic producers.

- Tax administration should also be strengthened in order to increase both the leverage on the existing economic base and the economic base itself. This will involve reducing inefficiencies in tax administration and collection, eliminating tax holidays and reinforcing co-operation with tax agencies in other countries.

- The macroeconomic environment heavily affects the fiscal deficit. By achieving a sound macroeconomic stance (e.g. low and predictable inflation, high GDP growth), countries can progress toward fiscal stability even during fast liberalization. Careful management of the spending side of the budget is required, to avoid sharp rises in government consumption.

- The fiscal stance is also affected by the quality of governance, especially the efficiency of the bureaucracy and the stability and predictability of the political environment. Effective institutional reform is likely to help fiscal consolidation.

This mix of tax and non-tax policy interventions can buffer the negative fiscal effects of liberalization, without the need to cut crucial spending items related to infrastructure development, poverty reduction, social security and welfare.

Annexes

A6.1 Tax Revenues and Trade Restrictions

Trade restriction index

A problem widely debated in the literature is how to measure trade liberalization (Rodriguez and Rodrik, 1999; Dollar and Kraay, 2001). Trade volumes are likely to reflect factors in addition to trade policy measures. At the same time, information on statutory tariffs is often fragmented for African countries. A feasible alternative is to look at the effective rate of taxation on international trade, which is a measure of average "realized" tariffs (Khattry, 2002). Trade tax revenues are a function of the tariff rate and the tariff base:

Trade tax revenues = tariff rate × tariff base

Here, the tariff base is trade values, so:

Trade tax revenues = tariff rate × trade values

Re-arranging gives the index of trade restriction:

Tariff rate = trade tax revenues / trade values

This gives an idea of "realized" tariffs: the measure is based on how much tariff revenue is actually collected. The measure will differ from official tariffs because of imperfect collection and measurement errors.

Data are available to construct the index for fairly long time periods for most African countries. There are limited data on official tariffs and tariff revenue. But for overlapping periods and countries, the index correlates strongly with the tariff rates reported in Dollar and Kraay (2001).

Estimation

Much of the analysis of the fiscal implications of trade liberalization has focused on the estimation of correlations between trade restrictions (and/or volumes of trade) and revenues from trade tax revenues (and/or total tax revenues). The regression model for this type of analysis usually includes a large number of control variables. From a comparative survey of the existing literature, the following are identified as the most widely-used regressors:

(a) the terms of trade index, (b) the real effective exchange rate index, the initial level of per capita GDP, (c) sector shares of GDP, (d) the level of revenues from other forms of taxation, (e) the level of major spending items (typically government consumption in percent of GDP), and (f) indicators of trade restrictions and trade volumes in both linear and non-linear form.

The trade tax revenues regression equation will therefore include all of the above, plus an indicator of institutional quality to proxy for the administrative capabilities of the tax agency. The results of the panel estimation are reported below in the table A6.1. Dynamic models, estimated by the Generalized Method of Moments estimator of Arellano and Bond (1991), produce results that are not qualitatively different from those retrieved from static equations. Because several of the control variables in the basic model happen to display non-significant coefficients, estimates obtained from a more parsimonious specification of the model are also reported. It can be seen that the non-linear effect of trade restrictions and volumes does persist.

The last column of the table displays the estimated coefficient from a regression of total tax revenues. When estimating such a model, the inclusion of trade tax revenues among the set of regressors raises a problem of multi-collinearity. This is obvious since several variables (especially those related to external shocks and competitiveness) affect total tax revenues mostly through their impact on trade tax revenues. To overcome the problem, the total tax revenues regression includes a small set of controls in addition to trade tax revenues. The estimated coefficients confirm that holding revenues from indirect taxation constant, the correlation between trade tax revenues and total tax revenues is positive.

The regression was repeated using average official tariff rates. This reduced the sample size because of limited official tariff data, reducing statistical significance. The results are qualitatively unchanged, indicating a non-linear relationship as before. Experimenting with the set of controls (for instance, dropping one of the controls that do not pass a zero restriction test) reveals that the coefficient on squared official tariffs is in fact different from zero in most specifications. This is unsurprising since the two measures are conceptually identical, although will differ empirically because of measurement errors.

A6.1 Econometric results

	TR	TR	TR	TR	TTR
TOT	0.369786^c	-0.19952	0.505052*	-0.35654	
REER	-0.5941^c	-0.39826	-0.51747*	-0.42944	
GDP p.c.	0.089759^c	0.143462^b	0.451289^b	-0.73926	
Institution	0.074514	0.214104	0.361056*	0.573442^c	-2.05217^b
Agriculture	-0.04326	0.060569			
DGS	-0.04936	-0.00618			
GC	0.048376	0.04221			
Urban					0.084466^c
ITR	0.804888^b		0.901305^b		
(ITR)^2	-0.02476^c		-0.03057^a		
TRADE		0.08677^b		-5.36E-05^b	
(TRADE)^2		-0.00033^b		0.054565^b	
TR					1.00995^a

Notes: *See A6.2 table for definitions of variables. The dependent variable is total revenues from trade taxes in per cent of GDP (TR) for the first four columns and total tax revenues in per cent of GDP (TTR) for the last column. Constant term is not reported.*

^{a} *denotes significance at 1% level.*

^{b} *denotes significance at 5% level.* ^{c} *denotes significance at 10% level.*

Source: *Calculations by ECA*

A6.1: Econometric results

The data set used for this chapter is a panel of annual observations taken over the period 1980-2002/03. All African countries are included with the exception of Democratic Republic of Congo, Eritrea, Liberia, Libya and Somalia, for which no data are available on several of the variables of interest. Variable definitions and abbreviations are given in the table below.

The panel has been assembled from a variety of sources. The World Bank's Africa Database provides time-series for most of the variables over the period 1980-2001. Strings for each country have been updated using the IMF *International Financial Statistics 2003* and *Government Financial Statistics 2003*, the IMF *World Economic Outlook 2003*, the IMF Country Reports produced in 2002 and 2003, and the Economist Intelligence Unit. Clearly, when combining data from different sources, a preliminary check of consistency of the series was undertaken. This check also involved, for sufficiently long strings, a test of structural breaks. Data on political and institutional variables are from Kaufman et al. (2001) and the Polity IV Database. Finally, the data on non-African countries are obtained from various issues of the *World Development Indicators* of the World Bank.

For 2003, most of the data are still projections or estimates. For this reason, the analysis generally focuses on the period up to 2002. Moreover, in a limited number of cases (i.e. Central African Republic) data on some of the fiscal variables are produced with a one- or two-year lag (i.e. none of the sources in 2003 reports data after 2001). However, 2002 is the reference year for the large majority of countries and variables, and hence in the text it is commonly indicated as the end of the sample period

A6.2 Description of the data set and variables

Variable	Abbreviation	Definition
Deficit	DEF	Fiscal deficit excluding grants (% of GDP)
Lagged deficit	LDEF	One period lagged value of deficit
Age dependency ratio	DEP	.....
Inflation	DCPI	Annual rate of change of consumer price index
Total tax revenues	TTR	Total revenues from taxation (% of GDP)
Trade tax revenues	TR	Revenues from taxes on international trade (% of GDP)
Taxes on domestic goods and services	DGS	Revenues from domestic taxation of goods and services, including revenues from VAT and other indirect taxes on consumption (% of GDP)
Direct tax revenues	DTR	Revenues from direct taxes on domestic profits and incomes (% of GDP)
Non-tax revenues	NTR	Revenues from sources other than domestic and international taxes, including revenues from entrepreneurial activities of the public sector, administrative fees, and fines (% of total government revenues)
Government consumption	GC	Consumption expenditure of central government (% of GDP)
Grants	GRANTS	Total grants received by the country (% of GDP)
Population	POP	(Log) of total population
Agriculture share	AGR	Contribution of the agricultural sector to value added GDP (%)
Urbanization	URB	Total population share of population living in urban areas (%)
Terms of trade	TOT	(Log) index of terms of trade. An increase in the index denotes improvements in the terms of trade
Shocks to terms of trade	DTOT	First difference of TOT
Real effective exchange rate index	REER	.....
International trade	TRADE	Total trade (exports plus imports) of goods and services, excluding financial services (% of GDP)
Trade restriction index	ITR	Effective tax rate on international trade, measured by revenues from trade taxes as a percentage of trade volumes
Major political changes	POLCH	Dummy variable taking value 1 in year t if in that year a major political change was observed. Major political changes include: (a) change in the institutional system, (b) change in the ideological orientation of the government, (c) change in the degree of democracy of institutions
Government effectiveness	GOV	Indicator of the effectiveness of government, broadly defined to include the efficiency of the bureaucracy, the credibility of government statements and policies, the reliability of the public administration, all obtained from survey data

References

Abed, G. (1998), "Trade Liberalization and Tax Reform in the Southern Mediterranean Region," International Monetary Fund (IMF) working paper 98/49, IMF, Washington DC

Adam, C., Bevan, L. and Chambas, G. (2001), "Exchange Rate Regimes and Revenue Performance in Sub-Saharan Africa," *Journal of Development Economics*, 64, pp173-213

AERC (African Economic Research Consortium) (1998), "Tax Reform and Revenue Productivity in Ghana," AERC, Nairobi

Agbeyegbe, T., Stotsky, J. and Wolde Mariam, A. (2003), "Trade Liberalization and Tax Revenue Relationship in Sub-Saharan Africa," paper presented at the Ad-Hoc Expert Group Meeting on Maintaining the Government Fiscal Base in the Context of Trade Liberalization, ECA, Addis Ababa, October 2003

Arellano, M. and Bond, S.R. (1991), "Some Tests of Specification for Panel Data: Monte Carlo evidence and an application to employment equations," *Review of Economic Studies*, 58, pp277-297

Chen, D. and Reinikka, R. (1999), "Business Taxation in a Low-revenue Economy: a study of Uganda in comparison with neighbouring countries," Africa Region working paper 3, World Bank, Washington DC

Dollar, D. and Kraay, A. (2001), "Trade, Growth and Poverty" World Bank working paper 2615, World Bank, Washington DC

Ebrill L., Stotsky, J. and Gropp, R. (1999), "Revenue Implications of Trade Liberalization," International Monetary Fund (IMF) occasional paper 180, IMF, Washington DC

Economic Commission for Africa (ECA) (2003), *Economic Report on Africa 2003*, Addis Ababa

Ekpo, A. (2003), "Government Revenue Implications of Trade Liberalization in Africa," paper presented at ECA Expert Group Meeting on Maintaining the Government Fiscal Base in the Context of Trade Liberalization, ECA, Addis Ababa, October 2003

Hoekman, B., Michalopoulos, C., Schiff, M. and Tarr, D. (2002) "Trade Policy Reform and Poverty Alleviation," World Bank Report, Washington DC

International Monetary Fund (IMF) (2003), "Islamic Republic of Mauritania: 2003 Article IV Consultation," IMF country report 03/314, Washington DC

Kaufmann, D., Kraay, A. and Zoido-Lobaton, P. (2001), "Governance Matters II: updated indicators for 2000/2001," mimeo, World Bank, Washington DC (econ.worldbank.org/files/11783_wps2772.pdf)

Keen, M. and Lighthart, J. (1999), "Coordinating Tariff Reduction and Domestic Tax Reform," International Monetary Fund (IMF) working paper 99/93, IMF, Washington DC

Khattry, B. (2002), "Fiscal *Faux Pas* ?: an analysis of the revenue implications of trade liberalization," Mimeo, Department of Economics, University of Massachusetts, Amherst

Kubota, K. (2000), "Fiscal Constraints, Collection Costs and Trade Policies," mimeo, World Bank, Washington DC

Mackenzie, G. A. (1991), "Estimating the Base of VAT in Developing Countries: the problem of exemptions," International Monetary Fund (IMF) working paper 91/21, IMF, Washington DC

Munoz, S. and Sang-Wook Cho, S. (2003), "Social Impact of a Tax Reform: the case of Ethiopia," International Monetary Fund (IMF) working paper 03/232, IMF, Washington DC

Pellechio, A. and Hill, C. (1996), "Equivalence of the Production and Consumption Methods of Calculating the VAT Base: application in Zambia," International Monetary Fund (IMF) working paper 96/67, IMF, Washington DC

Rodriguez, F. and Rodrik, D. (1999), "Trade Policy and Economic Growth: a skeptic's guide to the cross-national evidence," National Bureau of Economic Research (NBER) working paper 7081, New York

Sharer, R. et al. (1998), "Trade Liberalization in IMF-supported Programs," International Monetary Fund (IMF), World Economic and Financial Surveys, Washington DC

Tanzi, V. and Casanegra de Jantscher, M. (1987), "Presumptive Income Taxation: administrative efficiency and equity aspects," International Monetary Fund (IMF) working paper 87/54, IMF, Washington DC